Twilight in America

The Untold Story of Islamic Terrorist Training Camps Inside America

Published by PRB Publishing.

5046 6332   2/13

ISBN 978-0-9850267-0-7
Printed in the United States of America.

Cover design created by Ron Bell of AdVision Design Group (www.advisiondesigngroup.com).

CONTENTS

Introduction

More than nine years have passed since I first learned about the kidnapping, torture and beheading of journalist Daniel Pearl by Muslim terrorists, yet I remember the impact it had on me as if it were yesterday.

Pearl, a celebrated Wall Street Journal reporter, was first reported kidnapped in Karachi, Pakistan, on January 23, 2002. It made only a mild ripple in the news because all of America was in the grip of "shock and awe"—President George W. Bush's explosive response to the September 11, 2001, attacks on America.

It wasn't until photos began to surface of Pearl being held captive with a gun to his head, looking battered and obviously tortured, that I began to take notice. Then, on February 22, 2002, the horrifying video was released showing his beheading. Like every American citizen, I was riveted to the news on a daily basis.

I had more than the average citizen's interest in the news. Mine was a personal interest in the war on terror and acts of violence against our cities and institutions. I was in New York City on September 11, 2001, on a business trip when the airplanes slammed into the World Trade Center towers and the whole world changed forever. From the safety of my hotel room I watched in horror with members of my staff as the gigantic clouds of dust, like nuclear explosion fallout, roared through the streets of Manhattan. Panicked New Yorkers filled the streets. Had I booked a hotel room closer to Ground Zero, we would all have been swallowed up in the fallout.

Like most Americans, my first reaction was shock. I was seeing it with my own eyes, but I could not believe it. For the next several days I was trapped in New York City, so I helped distribute food and water to the stricken survivors. When I returned home, I was deeply affected by what I had experienced, and I began to pay closer attention to the news and all things involving Islamic terrorism.

So when Daniel Pearl was first reported kidnapped a little more than four months later, the obvious work of terrorists, my interest was keen. A few weeks later, when the story was being relegated to the back pages, the gruesome video was released showing Pearl's execution. It was first delivered to the FBI by Islamic sources in Pakistan. When the FBI confirmed its authenticity, the TV media showed an edited version, which also became viral on the Internet.

If you have seen the video, you have probably seen the edited version, which shows Daniel Pearl "confessing" to being a Jew and making other statements under duress. Reports from those who have seen the unedited version are chilling. Pearl's throat was first cut, then he was stabbed repeatedly and finally beheaded with a blunt sword. It was later learned that he had also been shot in the leg during a previous attempt to escape. His killers bragged that the sword they used to saw off his head was so dull they had to use two swords to finish the job.

The unedited video also demonstrated that the killers enjoyed the torture, mutilation and murder of Daniel Pearl. A New York Times article that week described an earlier kidnapping and beheading that occurred in October 1994. "A gleeful young kidnapper... told three British tourists chained to the floor that ... 'We've just told the press we're going to behead you,'" the article states. The kidnapper was Ahmed Omar Sheikh, 21 years old at the time, and he was laughing at the fun he'd had at this earlier kidnapping. Later, Omar would become one of Daniel Pearl's kidnappers and torturers.

Much later, Khalid Sheikh Mohammed, the so-called mastermind of the September 11 attacks, would boast: "I decapitated with my blessed right hand the head of the American Jew Daniel Pearl, in the City of Karachi, Pakistan." Some debate whether or not Mohammed's confession is true, but it doesn't matter. What matters most is that the gory crime and method of assassination was the first in a series of beheadings by Islamic terrorists following the September 11 attacks which horrified and riveted the nation. It seemed no one was safe.

It wasn't until April of 2002 that Pearl's body was found buried in Karachi. He had been dismembered, cut into 10 pieces, with his body parts buried in plastic bags in a shallow grave on the compound where he had been held captive.

After the Daniel Pearl execution I began to learn of other events, seemingly unconnected, which later would prove to point right back to the events and people who conspired to kidnap and murder Pearl.

First, there was the revelation that Daniel Pearl was in Pakistan to investigate Richard Reid, the shoe bomber, and the radical connections Reid may have had in Pakistan. At the time he disappeared, Pearl was tracking down reports that Richard Reid had visited a radical Pakistani cleric at his walled compound in Lahore.[1] Reid, who had attempted to blow up an American Airlines flight in December 2001, about one month before Pearl was kidnapped, had been radicalized while serving time in a British prison. A native of Great Britain, he was on his way to becoming a career criminal, with 10 convictions already behind him at the age of 20. In 1995 he entered prison again for petty theft, and there he converted to Islam. When he got out in 1996 at the age of 22, he joined a mosque and began his journey toward extremist Islam. Soon he was visiting jihadist Muslims in Afghanistan and Pakistan for indoctrination and terror training.

The jihadi cleric who Reid visited in Pakistan, and who may have hosted him just prior to the attempted shoe bombing, was Sheikh Mubarik Ali Shah Gilani, whose radical teachings impressed Reid. The FBI has confirmed that Richard Reid considered Sheikh ("teacher") Gilani to be his spiritual leader.

On December 22, 2001, just a few months after the September 11 attacks, Reid boarded a flight from Paris to Miami and, midway, attempted to ignite a bomb hidden in his shoe. Reid was eventually subdued by passengers, who used plastic handcuffs, seatbelt extensions and headphone cords to tie him up. The flight was diverted to Boston and Reid was immediately turned over to authorities.

Just a few weeks later in Pakistan, following the Richard Reid trail, journalist Daniel Pearl was kidnapped. The trail he was on led to the door of the same radical, reclusive sheikh who had mentored Richard Reid: Sheikh Gilani.

I remember hearing the name of Gilani after Pearl was executed, but paying little attention at the time. It was only after more details came out identifying Richard Reid as a follower of Gilani that I began to take more notice of the name.

Was this the man who was responsible for Daniel Pearl's death? I wondered. Was Sheikh Gilani's organization, known as Jamaat Al Fuqra, responsible for Pearl's death? I was not the only one to raise the question. Although the media continued to report that Al Qaeda was responsible for Pearl's kidnapping and death, Sheikh Gilani was quietly arrested and questioned in Pakistan, but no involvement in the kidnapping or beheading of Daniel Pearl was determined. He denied knowing anything about Pearl, and he was released. The conclusion investigators reached was that the kidnappers tricked Pearl into believing they were taking him to interview Gilani, but instead they brought him to their torture compound where he was brutalized for a month and then beheaded.

One inconsistency went unnoticed by many in Gilani's statements to investigators. He denied knowing anything about Daniel Pearl, who Pearl was, what he did for a living, or even that Pearl wanted to interview him. But in a later, wildly rambling essay which Gilani called his autobiography and which he entitled "Pillar of Lies," he stated that he knew Pearl was a U.S. intelligence operative who wanted to find him and have him assassinated. "Obviously, Daniel Pearl was to target me and then an assassination team would be sent to kill me," Gilani stated.[2]

As the president and founder of a conservative watchdog group based in southwestern Virginia, I was busy during the months following the September 11 attacks advocating for other issues of importance to our members. But I kept a watchful eye on the news, the memories of the attacks that I had witnessed in New York City still so vivid in my mind that they haunted me at night. Like all Americans, I wanted the guilty to pay. The name of Sheikh Gilani and his terrorist organization, Jamaat Al Fuqra, which in Arabic translates to "community of the impoverished," stayed with me. But his was just one of hundreds of names of extremist Muslims and organizations I heard on the news almost daily during that time.

More news began to surface that would continue to show the interconnectedness of Islamic terrorism in America. In October 2002, the Beltway snipers made news. After a 23-day killing spree in the Washington, D.C., area during which 10 people were murdered, two Muslim men were arrested as the snipers.

John Allen Muhammad, 41 at the time, and John Lee Malvo, then just 17, began their killing spree in the Washington, D.C., region on October 2, 2002, when they shot and killed James Martin, a 55-year-old program analyst, in the parking lot of a grocery store. The next day, October 3, five more people were shot, four of them in the span of two hours. One was killed mowing the grass, another man was killed while pumping gas. Another woman was killed sitting on a bench waiting for a bus, while another young woman was killed while she was vacuuming her car at a gas station. All of them were murdered with a single shot fired from a rifle—fired, it was later learned, through a hole drilled in the back of the killers' car trunk.

It came out only later that the two had killed a man in Alabama and shot two others in sniper attacks in Louisiana. Much later it was revealed that Muhammad, the mastermind and elder of the two, had a plan to wage jihad (Islamic holy war) against America by kidnapping young American boys and brainwashing them into turning against their country. His intent was to train them, as he had trained Malvo, to kill in the name of Allah.

One minor report surfaced that the Beltway snipers had links to the terrorist group Jamaat Al Fuqra. But what really got my attention was when the FBI descended on an obscure Virginia location known as Red House, in Charlotte County, close to where I lived and operated my company headquarters. Without my knowing it, an Islamic compound of more than 200 people had been quietly established over the years in Red House. The Beltway snipers were believed to have hidden out there during their killing spree, and may also have received shelter at another Islamic compound in Commerce, Georgia.

When I learned this news about the Red House compound and possible links to the Beltway snipers, I was alarmed. I did a simple search of "Al Fuqra" on the Internet and was shocked to see the name of Mubarik Ali Gilani pop up everywhere in connection to Al Fuqra. Gilani, in fact, was the founder of Al Fuqra, a terrorist organization that advocates jihad against America, but Gilani was also the leader of a group known as Muslims of the Americas (MOA), which owns the Red House compound. What's more, MOA has, at one time, operated by some accounts 35 other similar Muslim compounds across the United States. Gilani is the leader of both groups—Jamaat Al Fuqra and Muslims of the Americas—which are really one in the same. I would soon learn that these interlinked groups have even more front names.

In plain view, as if declaring to the world they have nothing to hide, the Muslim residents of the Red House compound have erected a sign along the rural road that leads into their camp, the same green-colored sign placed on every street corner in the state, obtained from the Virginia Department of Transportation. It reads: "Sheikh Gilani Ln."

It was not difficult to research Al Fuqra. As soon as I began to dig a little deeper, I learned that the group was responsible for dozens of terrorist attacks, assassinations, fire bombings, pipe bombings, sniper murders and other acts of Islamic violence and conspiracy across the country, dating back to 1979. The common thread in all the reports was Sheikh Gilani, the so-called peaceful teacher and spiritual leader who led a reclusive life in Pakistan, the same Sheikh Gilani whom the investigators had failed to prosecute for the Daniel Pearl kidnapping and murder, or for inciting shoe bomber Richard Reid to violence. The same Sheikh Gilani who was arrested but then released in Pakistan.

Why, I wondered, was this obvious connection not being reported widely in the media? Why were dozens of Islamic compounds—all of them tax exempt—founded by a known terrorist living in Pakistan, allowed to exist on American soil? Why were criminals able to hide in these camps, and why are the camp leaders even now teaching their residents how to become snipers, how to sneak up behind the "enemy" and slit a throat, knife-fighting skills, hand-to-hand combat, bomb-making instruction and more.

This book will explain how all these activities are happening right now in dozens of Muslim compounds under the guise of constitutionally protected "religious freedom" ... how the poor, black, criminally susceptible element in America is being hijacked by Al Fuqra to turn against their fellow citizens and commit Islamic holy war ... how Al Fuqra is planning future attacks against America ... and how local and federal authorities are turning a blind eye to the coming danger.

This book will connect all the dots for you, from the first World Trade Center bombing in 1993, to Daniel Pearl, to multiple terrorist attacks across the nation and the world, to links to Al Qaeda, to money-laundering schemes that rob American tax dollars to fund terrorism, to Islamic terror training camps through the United States ...

... to the shocking revelations of abuse, corruption, terrorism and murder by an undercover agent who lived in an MOA compound for eight years ...

... and finally to the insulated, reclusive, aging Sheikh Gilani in Pakistan, who serves as the inspiration for it all.

The plan and ultimate goal of radical Islam is not just to inflict terror by attacking our nation, but to inspire homegrown terrorism from within, committed by Americans against Americans. The plan is working, and the goal is being achieved.

In the 1990s, Gilani's American recruits were required to sign an oath, stating: "I shall always hear and obey, and whenever given the command, I shall readily fight for Allah's sake."[3] This makes one thing clear about the Daniel Pearl case: He was on the trail of a very big story.

In recent months these Muslim compounds have appeared to be sleeping, with no obvious terrorist activity occurring to the outside world. The far-off sound of rapid gunfire every now and then in the backwoods of rural Virginia, Georgia and South Carolina does not raise many eyebrows. But it is just a matter of time before the homegrown jihadists awake from their sleeper cells and sound the battle cry.

Twilight In America

"One of the (federal) investigators recalled carrying a three-year-old boy down a steep mountain to a trailer that was being used to contain the occupants of the (Islamic) compound during the search. As the investigator was putting the child down, a resident woman warned the child, 'Don't look at them; they're the devil!' Although the child had shown no fear or discomfort around the investigator up to that point, he and the other children quickly responded by moving away from the investigator and looking at him with distrust. The investigator noted that all of the children in the compound were home-schooled and received early training to prepare them for terrorist activity in later years."

"The current whereabouts of these children, now young adults, is unknown."

From a 2005 U.S. Department of Justice report describing a 1992 search of a Muslim compound in Buena Vista, Colorado, following a tip that Islamic terrorists and their families were hiding there and stockpiling weapons.

CHAPTER 1

White Collar Terrorists

THERE IS A HOUSE IN TUCSON, ARIZONA, AT THE NORTHWEST CORNER OF Euclid Avenue and Sixth Street that "draws the attention of almost everyone who passes by," states *The Tucson Weekly* newspaper. On one of the walls, in large blue lettering, is spelled out, "Happiness Is Submission to God."[1]

In mid-January of 1990, several members of the Tucson Police Department visited a Muslim cleric who lived in this building. His name was Rashad Khalifa, and he had turned his home into a Muslim mosque; its adherents celebrated a controversial brand of Islam called United Submitters International, a non-violent branch of Islam.

In many ways Khalifa was living out the American dream. He emigrated from Egypt to the United States as a teenager in 1959. As an adult, he earned a Ph.D. in biochemistry and became a naturalized American citizen. For one year, Khalifa worked as a science adviser for the Libyan government, then he worked as a chemist for the United Nations. Following those positions, he became a senior chemist in Arizona's State Office of Chemistry in 1980. Khalifa's son, Sam Khalifa, was also living the American dream: Sam was the first major league player of Egyptian descent in major league baseball, playing for the Pittsburgh Pirates.

Khalifa's background in science and mathematics spurred him to study the Quran in a new way, and soon he had developed a controversial theory. Khalifa initially began his intense study of the Quran to teach Islam to his American wife and his children. He determined, through a computerized numerological analysis, that the number 19 provided a key to the contents of the Quran.[2] Many American Muslims received his conclusions with enthusiasm, and together they formed the religious group United Submitters International, with Khalifa as the "imam," or mosque leader. The group considered itself to be the true voice of Islam. They preferred not to use the words "Muslim" or "Islam," instead choosing to use the English word "submitter," which is the equivalent in Arabic.

The Submitters believed Khalifa was a messenger of Allah, and referred to him as Allah's "messenger of the covenant,"[3] as prophesied in the Quran. They believed other "corrupted" religions, including Judaism, Christianity, Hinduism, Buddhism and mainstream Islam, would eventually die out and "submission" would prevail.

Ultimately, Khalifa would expand his theory of 19 by calculating the exact date of the Day of Judgment. Mainstream Muslims denounced his efforts as a hoax, but Khalifa continued his studies, and announced that his chart of 19s proved that the final two verses of Sura number nine in the Quran were not written by the prophet Mohammed and must be eliminated. Then he published a Quran without those verses and declared himself a prophet, inflaming the Islamic world. In 1989, about a year before the death plot against him was revealed, the 11th Islamic Council of Religious Scholars met in Mecca and branded Khalifa an infidel, an unbeliever.

Anyone who has witnessed the worldwide explosion of Islamic radicalism in recent years knows what such a brand means: It is a death sentence for the "infidel."

Khalifa, 55, knew that his teachings on Islam were stirring up a hornet's nest with some Muslims around the world, but he was not prepared for what police officers told him when they arrived at his house that afternoon in 1990. Khalifa was told he had been targeted for assassination by a group known as Jamaat Al Fuqra, the "community of the impoverished" in Arabic, which intended to kill him because he had blasphemed the religion of Islam.

Khalifa was told that an unrelated investigation in Colorado had revealed written plans to murder him. One packet of information taken from a Colorado storage locker owned by Jamaat Al Fuqra outlined the murder plot in chilling detail. The packet included intricate interior and exterior surveillance photographs of Khalifa's mosque and a four-page handwritten murder plan that called for Khalifa to be attacked at night and stabbed to death in his home mosque. Colorado Springs investigators immediately notified authorities in Tucson about the death plot, and a team of policemen was dispatched to Khalifa's home to warn him that he was a marked man.

At the time the murder plot was revealed, Khalifa appeared every inch the scholar. He had bushy, graying hair, a round serious face, and wore heavy, dark-rimmed glasses. When the Tucson police came to his home to warn him of the murder plot, he admitted that some of his writings had not been well received. He also told police he had recently received death threats from someone in Colorado. Less than two weeks later, on January 31, 1990, he was murdered. He was stabbed 19 times—some accounts say up to 29 times—and his body was drenched in the accelerant xylol, but was never set on fire. The murder was "a carbon copy of the handwritten plan," according to Doug Wamsley, Colorado's then assistant attorney general. The written plan called for attacking Khalifa in the mosque's kitchen at night, proceeding by "the quietest method feasible: (aka) knife" ... and eliminating any witnesses, if necessary.[4] The plan warned that the assassins should expect that Khalifa "may not be there" at the time they anticipated, and therefore, "as we wait, everyone who comes must be eliminated until he shows up."[5]

> *"Colorado Springs police investigators checked with the Tucson, Arizona, police department and found that no attack on the mosque or any of its members had at that point taken place. Tucson police did visit the mosque and interview the Imam (the leader of the Tucson congregation), a man by the name of Rashad Khalifa. Mr. Khalifa acknowledged that he had written several documents concerning the Quran, and that the views he expressed in these articles were not very popular with many other Muslims. Mr. Khalifa said that as a result of his research and publication, he felt that he had enemies from Saudi Arabia to Arizona, but that he had never heard of an organization called Fuqra. He did say that he had received threatening telephone calls 'from Colorado.' Approximately two weeks after his interview by the Tucson police, Mr. Khalifa was murdered at the mosque by an as yet unidentified intruder who stabbed him to death. The use of a knife to accomplish the murder was one of the methods discussed in the targeting package found in Colorado Springs."[6]*

Seven arrests were made in connection with conspiracy to assassinate Khalifa. But the big break in the case came in 2009, almost two decades after the murder took place, when Glen Cusford Francis, 52, was arrested in Calgary, Canada, after DNA linked him to the murder. A citizen of Trinidad and Tobago, where other Al Fuqra compounds are located, Francis was extradited to the Unites States in October 2009 to face first-degree murder charges in the death of Khalifa.

In those two decades, the group known as Jamaat Al Fuqra—also known as Soldiers of Allah, Muslims of the Americas, Muhammadin Soldiers, Muhammad Commandos of Sector Five, and possibly more names—was being carefully watched by federal and state investigators.

A New Breed of White Collar Criminals

By the time the media and public learn about acts of terrorism, they have already been displayed through violence, or planned acts of violence thwarted in the nick of time, like the underwear and shoe bombers. Yet in order to arrive at that point of violence, when knives are drawn and plunged into victims, when bombs are detonated, when coordinated attacks are carried out and dozens, or hundreds, of people lie dead, there is a lengthy planning stage where the seeds of destruction are planted. This planting and nourishing period requires a source of continual funding, which in the case of domestic terrorism usually comes from a time-tested, reliable source: white collar crime.

The National White Collar Crime Center within the U.S. Department of Justice monitors crimes commonly referred to as "white collar." Typically, white collar crimes have included money laundering, identity theft, credit card fraud, insurance fraud, immigration fraud, illegal use of intellectual property, tax evasion and other similar crimes. In the past, white collar crimes have rarely been associated with acts of Islamic terrorism, but now the two go hand in hand.

"Terrorist activities require funding, not only for weaponry, but also for training, travel and living expenses," states a Department of Justice report.[7] "In addition, the need for anonymity during the planning stages of terrorist activities requires various acts of deception, such as the creation and use of false identifications."

In 2005, the Department of Justice released a report entitled, "Identifying the Links between White Collar Crime and Terrorism." In shocking detail it described the numerous activities of Jamaat Al Fuqra, aka Soldiers of Allah, Muhammadin Soldiers, Muhammad Commandos of Sector Five and Muslims of the Americas, to fund its many terror cells through white collar crime. The FBI has estimated losses to American businesses from terrorist-related white collar crimes to be billions of dollars every year.

On The Radar

Although the earliest verified attack by Al Fuqra members was documented in 1979, when there were two separate attacks against a Hare Krishna temple in San Diego, California, and an attack on an Iranian Shiite mosque in Queens, New York, Al Fuqra did not really register on federal authorities' radar until 1983. That was when it began a series of terrorist attacks that it called its "Jihad Council for North America," which ultimately led to the arrest and conviction of Stephen Paul Paster, a leading Al Fuqra member.

Paster was one of the few white members of Jamaat Al Fuqra in the United States, which usually recruits its terrorist members from the poor black communities of America and often from America's prison population. Paster, one of the principle bomb makers for Al Fuqra in the 1980s, blew off most of one hand while planting a pipe bomb at a Portland, Oregon, hotel owned by followers of the late Indian guru Bhagwan Shree Rajneesh. Paster was taken to a hospital for treatment following the explosion, but he escaped custody and remained on the run for two years until police caught up with him at a Fuqra house in Colorado.

It was in 1983, after a killing and double firebombing in Detroit, Michigan, that the FBI connected Paster to Al Fuqra. The bombings had targeted the Ahmadiyya Islamic movement, led by guru Rajneesh, whose adherents are considered infidels, or heretics, by mainstream Islam chiefly because they do not believe Muhammad was the last prophet. Many of the followers of the Ahmadiyya movement are of Indian origin, an ethnicity virulently despised by Jamaat Al Fuqra and its founder, Sheikh Mubarik Ali Gilani.

Although investigators connected Paster to the bombings in 1983, they were not able to catch up with him until 1985 when they stopped a vehicle in Englewood, Colorado. Police had been staking out a house in the Englewood neighborhood, suspecting it was being used by Al Fuqra members, when late one day they stopped a car leaving the residence and saw "in plain view" a homemade weapon near the driver's side door.[8] The driver was Stephen Paster, who was wanted for the bombing in Detroit two years earlier.

Immediately, the Arapahoe County Bomb Squad and Bureau of Alcohol, Tobacco and Firearms were called to the scene to search Paster's car for illegal weapons and explosives. The weapon sitting "in plain view" on the seat was a handmade, eight-inch pipe bomb. Investigators noted that the firing mechanism had two springs attached to one end, and the bomb had a glue-like substance along one side. Inside the car was also found a shopping list that even a novice could interpret as a recipe for making a bomb: a CB mobile antenna, a car cigarette lighter plug, microphone plug, toy radio-controlled car or walkie-talkie and various electronic parts.

Paster served four years of a 20-year prison sentence for the bombing in Portland. Although he was suspected in several other bombings, he was never charged. He served just four years, and immediately after his release in 1989 he moved to Lahore, Pakistan, where U.S. intelligence sources say he currently provides explosives training to visiting Fuqra members.[9]

Inside the Storage Locker

During the years between Paster's arrest and the discovery of the storage locker in Buena Vista, Colorado, federal and state investigators continued to monitor the activities of Al Fuqra. What they were learning was frightening: Al Fuqra, under another tax-exempt organization name, Muslims of the Americas, was purchasing large tracts of land and creating compounds across the United States for the purpose of training American citizens, most of them poor blacks who were converted to Islam and radicalized in the art of jihad, or holy war.

The discovery of the storage locker in Colorado was one of the most thoroughly investigated and well-documented cases in the Al Fuqra investigation. But it was discovered almost by accident, in the course of an inquiry into robberies in the area. Investigators were led to the locker in hopes of finding some of the stolen items. What they did discover was of much more importance: The locker contained evidence of dozens of terrorist-related crimes, including numerous white collar schemes, plus bomb-making materials and terrorist weapons. This was the same storage locker in which was also found the packet of information detailing the soon-to-be-executed assassination of Tucson imam Rashad Khalifa.

Also seized at the storage locker were target-practice silhouettes labeled "FBI Anti-Terrorist Team" and "Zionist Pig."

The name Jamaat Al Fuqra was becoming more understood by federal investigators, but it was still a constantly shifting group of terrorists that had a chameleon-like ability to assimilate into its surroundings. The name Jamaat Al Fuqra was used interchangeably with Soldiers of Allah, Muhammadin Soldiers and Muslims of the Americas. In later years, more aliases would be added.

In a 2005 report issued by the U.S. State Department, Jamaat Al Fuqra is described as "an Islamic sect that seeks to purify Islam through violence." In 2005 it was listed as one of dozens of groups operating within the United States with the intent to wage war against America through terrorist acts. The report also acknowledged that "members have purchased isolated rural compounds in North America to live communally, practice their faith, and insulate themselves."[10]

The report also notes that there is no evidence that Jamaat Al Fuqra has any external sources of funding. This finding made perfect sense at the time, because Al Fuqra had mastered the crime of white collar deception carried out for decades beneath investigators' radar. This white collar criminal activity has netted individual Fuqra cells millions of dollars to fund their terrorist schemes.

In 2005, an internal Department of Homeland Security report, which was not released to the public, warned that Jamaat Al Fuqra was linked to Muslims of the Americas and had the capacity to attack the United States.[11] This finding was more than two decades late in warning that Al Fuqra was able to attack the homeland, because its terrorist operatives had been killing and bombing American citizens and sites since 1979. Yet it did confirm what was yet unknown: Al Fuqra was one and the same with Muslims of the Americas, the seemingly docile Islamic group that was purchasing land and establishing what they said were "peaceful" Muslim compounds across America, led by Pakistani Sheikh Mubarik Gilani.

Unfortunately, with the flimsiest of excuses, the State Department has refused to classify Al Fuqra as an officially recognized terrorist organization since its 2005 document was released, stating that "because of the group's inactivity (in recent years), it was not included in the most recent terrorism report."

The Evidence

What investigators found inside the locker was shocking on two fronts. First, they found weapons and evidence of violent terrorist attacks already carried out, and some planned for the future, such as the murder of Rashad Khalifa in Tucson, and planned attacks against American landmarks, business sites and religious groups. Second, the storage locker revealed how the terrorists were making their money to pay for their weapons and other terrorist activities. They found boxes of fraudulent claims for worker's compensation which, investigators soon realized, were the central source of the terrorists' funding in many regions across the United States. To accomplish their goals, Fuqra members created aliases and fraudulent companies that were used to scam the system and extract money from the American worker's compensation system—in other words, from American taxpayers.

Investigators also learned that Al Fuqra, like other Islamic terrorist groups, "are in many ways similar to traditional organized crime groups" in that they maintain detailed documents of planned and ongoing activities, including murders, bombings and schemes to fraudulently obtain financing. "Members also frequently maintain written contractual agreements among themselves, such as those found in Colorado documenting agreements concerning the allocation of any income a member receives to the organization or leader, duties that a member is responsible for executing, and crimes a member has agreed to carry out."[12] (Appendix A)

In a detailed Justice Department report, investigators proved that Jamaat Al Fuqra had created a fraudulent security company, known as Professional Security International (PSI). PSI would become the key to Al Fuqra's money laundering and money transfers, as well as a clearinghouse for planned terrorist activities.

In the report, investigators concluded: "By maintaining a company such as PSI, Fuqra members have been able to establish the appearance of legitimacy and negotiate security contracts with federal government centers and international airports that house sensitive information."

Colorado law enforcement determined that wherever Al Fuqra members are active, PSI and similar security businesses are usually in operation.

In the mid-1990s, the Colorado Attorney General's Office successfully prosecuted members of Al Fuqra. In addition to acts of domestic terrorism, Fuqra members were also found guilty of perpetrating numerous white collar crimes, including insurance fraud stemming from the worker's compensation scheme that spanned more than seven years.

Found in the storage locker of Jamaat Al Fuqra in Colorado Springs were the following items, originally discovered by agents with the Colorado Department of Revenue, Liquor and Tobacco Enforcement Unit:

1. Thirty pounds of explosives.
2. Three large pipe bombs (completely wired and ready to detonate).
3. Two shape charges.
4. Bomb-making instructions.
5. Ten handguns (some with obliterated serial numbers).
6. Silencers (in various stages of manufacture).
7. A number of improvised explosive devices (IEDs), including CO_2 canisters configured into explosive devices.
8. Numerous "Talibeen Fuqra Jamaat" membership applications.
9. Instructional materials detailing methods of guerilla warfare, bombings, sniping, target selection and surveillance.
10. Documents indicating potential "targets" in the Los Angeles, Tucson and Denver areas (including photographs, map, and notes).
11. An envelope containing several newspaper clippings of a triple homicide of three East Indians in Washington State.
12. Military training manuals.
13. A business card of Professional Security International (PSI) showing James D. Williams as president and director.
14. Documents with details of dates and activities indicating that Fuqra members "knowingly and with malice aforethought conspired to commit" the crimes of worker's compensation fraud.
15. Fifty-four blank, embossed birth certificates from North Carolina and Louisiana.

16. A packet of information with a detailed description of the methods that should be used to murder Rashad Khalifa at his mosque in Tucson, Arizona.[13]

Since 1979, Al Fuqra has been implicated by federal and state authorities in dozens of acts of terrorism and terrorist-related activities, ranging from assassination to firebombings, financial fraud totaling millions, conspiracy, torture and more. (Appendix B)

More Discoveries Ahead

Within two years of the shocking discovery of the storage locker in Colorado, investigators would also uncover the first of possibly three dozen Muslim compounds located on American soil, possibly more, founded by Al Fuqra as secret bases for the psychological and physical training of Islamic terrorists, to be trained from infancy in the art of jihad. These compounds, housing radical Islamic terrorists, are as dangerous as any in the world, existing in the backyards of rural Americans from California to Virginia, and from New York to Florida. (Appendix C)

In a 2006 interview, Susan Fenger, chief criminal examiner for the Colorado State Department of Labor and Employment and head of the Colorado Al Fuqra investigation, said the terrorist training camps in the United States owned by Al Fuqra are also used as collection centers for funds sent to their leader, Sheikh Gilani, in Pakistan. Authorities estimate that, to date, less than $20,000 of the $335,000 funds stolen in the white collar terrorist scams in Colorado have been accounted for, leading them to believe the money was sent to Sheikh Gilani in Pakistan.[14]

When asked if Gilani himself is a terrorist, Fenger responds: "I have no doubt whatsoever. In fact, I have concrete evidence that he is."[15]

The revelation of the Colorado storage locker was also a turning point for federal and state investigators who had been on the trail of Al Fuqra for a decade. As they would soon discover, the trail would continue to lead them to larger and larger terrorist targets, to the slaughter of innocent people around the nation in the name of purifying Islam, all the way to Niagara Falls in Canada, to the World Trade Center, to the Beltway region of our nation's capital and beyond.

The father of all these terrorist activities, the man who masterminded the fraudulent white collar criminal empire for his jihadist followers, is an obscure Muslim cleric named Sheikh Mubarik Ali Gilani, who, from his seclusion in Lahore, Pakistan, called to his people in America—with a persistent rhythm like that of a sub-machine gun—to wage holy war.

Identifying the Links

between

White-collar Crime and Terrorism

for the Enhancement of Local and State Law Enforcement

Investigation and Prosecution

NATIONAL WHITE COLLAR CRIME CENTER

September 2004

This project was supported by Grant No. 2003-LJ-CX-1018 awarded by the National Institute of Justice, Office of Justice Programs, U.S. Department of Justice. Points of view in this document are those of the author and do not necessarily represent the official positions or policies of the U.S. Department of Justice.

This document is a research report submitted to the U.S. Department of Justice. This report has not been published by the Department. Opinions or points of view expressed are those of the author(s) and do not necessarily reflect the official position or policies of the U.S. Department of Justice.

This report, issued in 2005 by the Department of Justice, concluded that losses to American businesses from terrorist-related white collar crimes to be billions of dollars every year.

"Come join my troops and army, says our Sheikh Gilani. Prepare to sacrifice your head. A true believer is never dead. Say 'Victory is in the air,' The infidel's blood will not be spared."

From Sheikh Gilani's writings, seized by U.S. investigators in 1991[1].

CHAPTER 2

Pillar of Lies

LORETTA AND MIKE ALLEN[2] CHERISH THE COUNTRY LIFE. THEIR home in rural York County, South Carolina, is modest, but well loved. Their three children run barefoot in the summertime with neighborhood friends. Their dog, Pete, loves to roam the nearby woods chasing squirrels and rabbits, sometimes bringing home a furry trophy of his exploits—which, more often than not, he proudly deposits on the Allens' front stoop.

"That's why we moved to the country," says Loretta, "because you can live your country life without being crammed up against each other in the city. When we moved here we loved the openness."

Not long after moving to their neighborhood in York County, Pete broke away from his chain in the back yard and wandered off into the woods, his nose to the ground in search of a good hunt. The wooded property behind the Allens' land was unfamiliar to the dog, and soon Loretta and Mike feared Pete was lost. Mike's brother, Sam, who lived nearby, decided to hike into the woods a short distance, hoping he would locate Pete quickly before the dog was hopelessly lost in the vast acreage.

As Sam walked through the woods he called to the dog. Suddenly, an African-American man emerged from a small tent that had previously blended invisibly into the wooded surroundings. Dressed entirely in Islamic garb, wearing a turban and long robe, the man stood before him brandishing an AK-47. Sam froze in his tracks.

"Stop," said the man. "You're not allowed past this point."

Stunned, Sam explained that his brother's dog had wandered away and he was going to look for him in the woods.

"No you're not," said the guard emphatically. "This isn't your property."

This was when the Allens first learned that the Muslim community known as Holy Islamville, founded by Sheikh Mubarik Ali Gilani of Pakistan, and encompassing more than 75 acres of countryside in York County, South Carolina, existed in their back yard. Sam left the woods that day feeling more than uneasy. Who were these people living in the woods behind their homes? Why were they carrying guns and stationing guards along the perimeter? How was he supposed to help his brother retrieve Pete on this heavily armed and guarded property?

Sam spoke with his brother, Mike, and the two men decided to enter Islamville to find the dog. Neighbors told them that a dirt road which disappeared into the woods was the way in. Mike and Sam got into Mike's truck and headed down the road. After traveling a short distance, they arrived at a small guardhouse, more like a shack, as Mike describes it. Just as before, a black man emerged in Muslim garb carrying an assault weapon; he stopped Mike and Sam.

"Your dog is not here," said the guard after they described their mission, but Mike and Sam insisted Pete was on the property. Several other men, carrying AK-47s and M-16s, came over and finally agreed to allow Mike and Sam to look for the dog. Four armed, Islamic men piled into a truck and escorted Mike's truck into the compound.

Within a few minutes they spotted Pete, sniffing around the edge of the woods. Before they left, again escorted by the armed Muslims, Mike and Sam got a good look at some of the homes on the compound. About 50 people, they would later learn, lived in about a dozen old, run-down mobile homes and a few newer brick structures. They saw women and children on the compound, all of them black. The women wore traditional Islamic head coverings and long robes.

The Allens would later learn that Holy Islamville is run by the group Muslims of the Americas, and that it contains an important mosque that has attracted some well-known Muslim leaders since it was "consecrated" by Sheikh Gilani as the first Muslim shrine in North America. This honored status was bestowed after a series of alleged "miracles" occurred there centered around a fax machine at the site—including visions of rainbows and the name of Mohammed shimmering on the wall as Islamic prayers were coming through the fax.

Inside the mosque at Islamville are two large tapestries which hang on the wall, one bearing the 99 names of Allah in Arabic and the other displaying Quranic verses known as the "four Quls" (Islamic sayings). Both were gifts from Sheikh Gilani, the aging founder of Muslims of America, the founder of the International Quranic Open University which originated in Saudi Arabia, the leader of the radical terrorist groups Jamaat Al Fuqra, Soldiers of Allah, Muhammadin Soldiers and Muhammad Commandos of Sector Five, and the man whom journalist Daniel Pearl was scheduled to interview when he was kidnapped, beheaded and dismembered. [3]

Mission to America

In the late 1970s Sheikh Mubarik Gilani was a middle-aged man, probably in his early 40s, when he visited the United States from his native Pakistan. The details of Gilani's upbringing and formative years are closely guarded, with the only published narrative of his young life told in a rambling essay he penned himself, filled with contradictions and fanciful tales of miracles, physical transportations and reincarnations, meetings with the ancient Islamic prophets, and other odd tales of mysticism.

In an excerpt from Gilani's autobiography, which he has aptly titled *Pillar of Lies* and which is posted online at the Muslims of the Americas web site, he describes his mission as "the story of a person sent by the Holy Last Messenger (Mohammed) to guide, educate and reform people fully supported with signs, miracles and divine knowledge unveiling the mysteries behind the man dubbed 'most mysterious' by western media and refuting the lies media terrorists have produced."[4]

Gilani's family, he claims, descends from the prophet Mohammed, coming from Baghdad to Pakistan several centuries ago. From birth, Gilani continues, he was imbued with a special quality that set him apart.

"Many people would come to me and ask me to pray for them, or ask for spiritual advice, and for some kind of help they needed," he writes. "By the grace of Allah, our family was one of the wealthiest in this country (Pakistan) and had no financial problems ... When I was the age of 10, my grandmother use to say it was very common for her to behold with open eyes Hazrat Ali. He would appear from nowhere and would pick me up, and take me away with him ... He would take me away for some time and then he would bring me back. I was being prepared to play my future role. One could say this was my first unsolved mystery; only those who understand know well that Hazrat Ali is the king of Walis and Sufis."[5]

It's not clear to whom Gilani is referring when he says he was spirited away by Hazrat Ali, but it is most likely a reference to the ancient Islamic warrior who fought Muslims and non-Muslims during the early part of the seventh century. Gilani's reference to the Sufis is a description of his preferred brand of Islam, sometimes referred to as "mystical Islam," which encourages the practitioner to seek the type of out-of-body experiences Gilani professes to have achieved many times. Sufis also claim to be in contact with non-human entities. The so-called "Whirling Dervishes" of Turkey, who spin around as a form of Islamic worship, are Sufi Muslims.

"While growing up I had many experiences that at the time I did not understand," Gilani writes in *Pillar of Lies*. "I use to receive visits from many non-human beings. They became my followers. They would serve me and served me well."

Gilani created this mythical aura around himself as a means of convincing his followers that he was divinely appointed to lead them, and that he has the ability to transport himself through time to conspire with Islamic notables of the past. Finally, he writes, he received his calling to begin a ministry in America:

"Once I remember I was high up in the Himalayan Mountains and being served by my non-human followers," he writes. "From there I was guided to go to America."

What is known for certain about Gilani is that he visited the United States in the late 1970s and early 1980s, and lived in the Brooklyn, New York, area for some time, preaching anti-Semitic sermons to Muslims and advocating violence as a method of purifying Islam.[6] One of Gilani's first filmed appearances circulated among his American followers shows him wearing a military camouflage jacket, an ammunition belt across his chest, a turban and traditional Islamic robe, sporting a thick beard above a rotund belly. In this recruitment video

Gilani is heard declaring: "We give (recruits) highly specialized training in guerrilla warfare ... We are at present establishing training camps ... You can easily reach us at Quranic Open University offices in upstate New York or in Canada or in Michigan or in South Carolina (York County) or in Pakistan. Wherever we are, you can reach us."[7]

His preaching in the early 1980s was infected with anti-Israeli vitriol and encouraged an Islamic holy war against the Soviets for their involvement in Afghanistan. The Soviet war in Afghanistan was a 10-year conflict than began in 1979 when the Soviets invaded Afghanistan in support of the Marxist government already in power, and unsuccessfully fought the Islamist Resistance. Gilani's influence, along with other radical Islamic groups, including Osama Bin Laden's Al Qaeda, helped fund the Afghan resistance with money from American Muslims, along with other sources. Gilani also helped the war effort by training American Islamic guerilla fighters and sending them to the Afghan battlefield.

During his early days preaching in New York, Sheikh Gilani became revered by the loose-knit Islamic community centered at the Brooklyn mosque where he did most of his proselytizing. To cement his leadership, Gilani orchestrated a coup of the existing Dar ul Islam organization that already had the loyalty of the Brooklyn Muslims. Dar ul Islam literally translates as "house of Islam" in Arabic, implying that it is the legitimate abode of Islamic thought and action. Stemming from the 1960s social upheaval which spawned a large black Muslim movement in the United States, Dar ul Islam was, at one time, "the largest indigenous Muslim group" in the nation.[8]

Under the tutelage of Dar ul Islam leaders, an active prison outreach was undertaken beginning in the 1960s and lasting through the 1980s, during which black Muslims became a prominent force in New York state prisons.[9] Dar ul Islam established a powerful lobby which helped Muslim prisoners win the right to create prison mosques. When Gilani began preaching in New York, and also in New Jersey mosques, he developed a loyal following among several high-ranking Dar ul Islam members.

"The brothers fell in love with (Gilani)," said Al-Amin Abdul Latif, president of the Islamic Leadership Council of New York City at the time, and a former high-ranking Dar ul Islam member. "The leadership accepted him ... For many of us, loyalties were very strong. That caused a split in the Dar." In 1980, the leader of Dar ul Islam in the United States, Abdul Karim, abdicated his leadership to follow Sheikh Gilani.[10]

Gilani himself described the coup in his autobiography *Pillar of Lies*, but painted a different picture of how it played out. "There were two sheikhs, the old sheikh and I, the new sheikh. Therefore, they plotted to kill one of us and they decided it would be me. I was told about this plot of assassination and I could have left the U.S. to protect myself. Nevertheless, I told my faithful friends ... 'I cannot leave my post. I have been sent and I will keep doing my duty until I meet my Allah.'

"The following day I saw four to five members of Dar ul Islam and I was told that these were the ones with the task to assassinate me. I said, let them come ... They came, and to our surprise, a few of them fell at my feet weeping. This shocked even me. I was later told that the Holy Last Messenger (the prophet Mohammed) appeared to them the previous night. He ordered and warned them that it is he who has sent me as his khalifa (leader) to guide the American Muslims, and with that they realized their mistake and sought forgiveness. Of course, I forgave them and they became my loyal and dedicated followers and instruments in propagating Islam in America."[11]

This was when Gilani first named his new brand of Islam "Jamaat Al Fuqra," meaning "community of the impoverished." Learning from his predecessors in New York, Gilani continued recruitment among the black prison population, many of whom would join Gilani after they finished serving their sentences.

Around this time, Gilani preached to his followers in clear, precise terms that jihad, holy war, against America was the only path to Islamic purification. "We are fighting to destroy the enemy," he said. "We are dealing with evil at its roots, and its roots are America."[12]

Almost immediately, Gilani's disciples began their American crime spree. A campaign of ethnic and religious cleansing was launched against those who opposed the teachings of Gilani. Indian and Hindu sects were targeted, bombings were carried out against rival Islamic factions and, as described in Chapter One, assassinations were conducted, one of them against the Muslim mosque leader in Tucson, Arizona.

Gilani and his followers have always denied any involvement in terrorist activity, but the documentation is irrefutable. Over the years, at least a dozen Al Fuqra members have been convicted of crimes including murder, conspiracy to commit murder, firebombing, gun smuggling, workers' compensation fraud in the United States and Canada, drug crimes and others. Furthermore, al Fuqra members are suspects in at least 10 unsolved assassinations and 17 firebombings between 1979 and 1990. (Appendix D)

The Early Years of Al Fuqra

A significant link between Muslims of the Americas and Al Fuqra was established by the Colorado State Attorney General's Office, whose lead investigator, Susan Fenger, stated that "Muslims of the Americas is, in reality, only a front organization. It's just a cover for the fact that they carry out terrorist activities."[13]

While prosecuted criminal activity committed by Gilani's followers has waned in recent years, due to the intense scrutiny by law enforcement of Gilani's American compounds, some terrorist activity and jihad training continues. In 2002, a resident of a California compound owned by Gilani's Muslims of the Americas was charged with first-degree murder in the shooting of a sheriff's deputy. Another member was charged with gun smuggling. Furthermore, the state of California launched an investigation into the whereabouts of more than a million dollars in public funds given to a charter school run by Fuqra leaders, eventually prosecuting an Al Fuqra/MOA member in 2006 in connection with the scam. Members of a Gilani compound in Red House, Virginia, were also convicted of firearms' violations in recent years. In 2006, Canada deported three men after they completed their prison sentences for a 1994 conviction of conspiring to bomb a Hindu temple and East Indian movie theater in Toronto, Ontario. All the men, members of Jamaat Al Fuqra, were arrested in 1991 while crossing the border from the United States into Canada.[14]

Also noted by investigators and intelligence sources are the group's continuing links with guerrilla training in Pakistan, although all this terrorist and criminal activity is denied by Gilani, and Gilani and his followers even deny the existence of Jamaat Al Fuqra.[15] (Appendix D)

But these lesser-known terrorist attacks and financial scams pale in comparison to the other attacks linked to Jamaat Al Fuqra, including the first World Trade Center bombing in 1993, and the Beltway Snipers' reign of terror in 2002 (these terror attacks are detailed in later chapters).

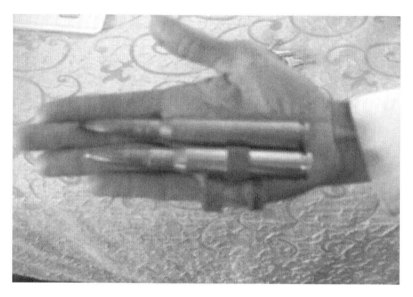

50 cal. Shells, known as "armor piercing" rounds, retrieved by a private investigator at the York, SC, MOA/Al Fuqra compound.

A Cost Effective Strike

According to one report issued by the Center for Policing Terrorism, "Fuqra's core of trained operatives in the United States ... have been directed to lie dormant until needed to support a cost-effective strike."[16] Jamaat Al Fuqra is "capable of committing violence toward any proponent of a belief set that does not match their own," according to the Center's Zachary Crowley.[17]

This frightening warning was corroborated when, in 2010, a former undercover agent with the New York Police Department, who lived among Al Fuqra/MOA for eight years in their Hancock, New York, compound, confirmed that the group has a secret army of trained guerillas ready to strike "when the time is right."[18]

As always, terrorist activity requires funding. In Brooklyn in the early 1980s, once Gilani had firmly established his grip on the Dar ul Islam converts, his recruits signed papers officially transferring the majority of their income to help foreign Islamic organizations, including groups in Gilani's native Pakistan. Recruits who demonstrated exceptional physical prowess and cunning were trained as guerilla warriors, and many were sent to fight against the Soviets in Afghanistan.[19]

Beginning in the 1980s, Gilani's group and his followers began purchasing vast amounts of acreage across the United States, continuing over the next 10 years, for the creation of Muslim compounds. Gilani's communes were billing themselves as havens where Muslim converts, most of them inner-city blacks and many of them recruited in prison, could build new lives. Law enforcement identified at least 35 known compounds—some accounts say 36, with many of them now inactive or greatly reduced in population as members have moved into surrounding neighborhoods at the command of Gilani and their leaders. These camps include the 72-acre camp located in York County, South Carolina, near the home of Mike and Loretta Allen. Several others are believed to exist under the radar. One compound is the first camp founded, a 70-acre tract in Hancock, New York, known as Islamberg, which serves as headquarters for Muslims of the Americas and for Gilani's Open Quranic University. There are also compounds in Red House, Virginia; Commerce, Georgia; Dover, Tennessee; and dozens more. Several camps are reported to exist in Canada, including one outside of Ontario in Combermere, and there are more "jamaats" in the Caribbean, including a large presence in Trinidad and Venezuela.[20](Appendix E)

What Does Sheikh Gilani Believe?

While it may be obvious what Gilani believes, given the openly ji-hadist activities of his followers, and based on Gilani's own statements, the U.S. State Department has taken Jamaat Al Fuqra and all its associated groups (Muslims of the Americas, Soldiers of Allah, Muhammadin Soldiers, Muhammad Commandos of Sector Five) off its official list of terrorist groups.

What does Sheikh Gilani really believe, based on his activities and own writings?

Gilani always preached a strict Sunni, Sufi-style anti-western dogma that calls for violence as a means of purifying Islam. Al Fuqra's documents and Gilani's own speeches are peppered with references to Zionist conspiracies and a call to arms. Adherents believe they must put into practice every commandment from the prophet Mohammed, including the edict in Surah 48:29 to kill unbelievers, which states: "Muhammad is the Apostle of Allah. Those who follow him are merciful to one another, but ruthless to unbelievers." Surah 9:5 in the Quran must also be followed; it states: "Kill the Mushrikun (unbelievers) wherever you find them, and capture them and besiege them, and lie in wait for them in each and every ambush."

Yet Gilani hypocritically denies his own statements and the activities of the terrorist groups he formed. On the Muslims of the Americas web site, Gilani states: "For the past 25 years I, and the members of MOA, and the staff ... at Islamberg (the New York headquarters for MOA) have adamantly denied knowledge of any such organization (as Jamaat Al Fuqra) in the U.S., Pakistan or elsewhere." Gilani has made this statement even after making public pronouncements as head of Jamaat Al Fuqra ordering his adherents to train for jihad and to "purify Islam through violence."

"The U.S.," Gilani continues, "has become a pawn of hidden hands that use America's wealth and the innocent blood of their sons and daughters to wage their wars against Muslims."[21]

The "hidden hands" he refers to are no doubt the chief enemies identified by Gilani, the Jews and all unbelievers, including Americans who oppose Gilani's belief system.

Yet even while denying the very existence of the terrorist groups he has formed, and claiming to have only peaceful intentions, Gilani also states that "he who fights with the sole objective that the word of Allah should become supreme is a Mujahid (a holy warrior) in the cause of the Lord. A Mujahid is thus a noble person who offers his life for the achievement of lofty ends."[22]

A University Education

In the late 1970s Gilani founded the International Open Quranic University, which is networked with Islamic schools throughout the United States. The IOQU is also used as a curriculum in the dozens of known Islamic camps throughout the United States owned by Muslims of the Americas. The curriculum relies heavily on Al Fuqra texts and Islamic educational materials.

"Schooling in the system is profoundly slanted to the Al Fuqra world view," says Zachary Taylor of the Center for Policing Terrorism. "One woman, a spokeswoman for the York, South Carolina, compound, attended the International Open Quranic Universities. Her thesis topic, for which she received her advanced degree, detailed every facet of the 'Satanist-Zionist conspiracy' to blame Muslims for the World Trade Center bombings."[23]

In the late 1970s Sheikh Gilani decided to take up medicine, but not just any kind of medicine. His specialty became "quranic psychiatry." In 1977 Gilani says he was named vice chancellor of the International Quranic Open University, where he says he was performing miraculous healings. Yet it is unclear whether the university actually has, or ever had, a physical building in the Middle East, or if Gilani was even officially made its leader, or if he proclaimed himself vice chancellor.

Gilani says he was named imam (leader) of quranic sciences "in a meeting of physicians and researchers" in Taif, Saudi Arabia. In his writings, Gilani states that in the late 1970s he was asked to serve as honorary professor of psychiatry at the "specially established Institute of Quranic Psychiatry in the Psychiatry Hospital" in Saudi Arabia.[24] Gilani admits in his memoirs, *Pillar of Lies,* that he did not take well to college studies, and that he ultimately earned his F.A. degree, the Pakistani two-year equivalent to the 11th and 12th grades of high school.

A quick look at the Quranic Open University's web site (www.iqou-moa.org) lists only two contacts, both in New York and

Virginia, not coincidentally where two Islamic camps purchased by Gilani's front organization, Muslims of the Americas, are located.

Gilani has held his thousands of devoted followers in thrall with fanciful tales like the following, taken from his Quranic Open University web site:

"His Eminence Sultan Mohyuddin Syed Mubarik Ali Shah Gilani invented a methodology that scientifically proved the healing power of Divine Words in the Holy Quran and prayers of the earlier messengers. For more than 30 years, thousands have benefited physically, spiritually and mentally from the El-Gilani Methodology (EGM) of quranic therapy.

"By the permission of the Almighty Creator, Dr. Gilani and his dedicated staff of quranic therapists have successfully treated patients with cancer, AIDS, paranoid delusions, infertility and a wide range of other ailments. In fact, for the first time in medical history a brain-dead patient was revived using quranic therapy in a Germantown, Pennsylvania, hospital."

The web site describes many "miracle" cures, including one of a patient, Ismail, who was "diagnosed with a physiological mental disorder," where doctors wanted to "drug him and give him electric shock therapy." According to Gilani's posted writings, the patient was mentally deranged because he listened to Michael Jackson music.

The patient was ill "for over 10 years due to breaches of Sharia (strict Islamic law), whereupon he listened to shaitanic (satanic) western music. The music of Michael Jackson causes people to go crazy because the devil actually comes wherever the music is played or listened to." One of Gilani's followers confronted the patient Ismail and exorcised an angry, evil "entity" from him. "This entity came out atop (Ismail's) physical body and confronted (Gilani's follower) face to face with its red eyes and smoky figure. I heard him say 'I will destroy you, I will kill you!' (The entity) became very, very angry ... I called upon my beloved Murshid (Gilani) to come and assist me. In the next moment His Eminence Sultan Mohyuddin Syed Mubarik Ali Shah Gilani came to my aid. He ... came in full form and in full garments. He stood between me and the entity facing me. He was telling me to follow him in doing intense thikr (remembrance) ... He (Gilani) projected Ism Allah on the entity, whereupon the entity became weaker and weaker until it was destroyed."[25]

Gilani's miraculous appearance in the above narrative is an example of his claim that he is able to transport himself through time and space to meet the needs of his followers and convene with ancient Islamic prophets.

What's more, Gilani has convinced his American followers that he can change into animals, and that he miraculously transports himself from Pakistan to the United States by channeling the forest creatures that live in the woods surrounding the Muslim camps. Gilani's followers not only fervently believe that he actually has these shape-changing abilities, but they fear they are constantly being watched by their leader. It is the Islamic version of Big Brother.

"The sheikh (has the) unique ability to transform himself into animals such as a wolf, a bird, a duck, a bear and several other animals," writes one of his followers in an online blog. "Once in a while the (compound) members may stop in front of one of those animals claiming that it's the sheikh who has come to visit them. So they'll admire a certain bird or duck with a specific symbol thinking it's their sheikh."[26]

Human Satans

Gilani often targets Jews as the prime enemy when it comes to quranic healing. "Jews are an example of human Satans," he states. "The Satan has followers among human and non-human beings. The human followers are human Satans while the non-human followers are jinn (genie, or spirit) Satans. According to holy Quran, human Satans are tougher and more dangerous than jinn Satans. Jews are an example of human satans. This is why Jews are the founders of Satan worship and Masonic lodges and are now trying to take over the entire globe in which the global religion is to be Satanism."[27]

Gilani writes further: "Under the influence of a jinn, a person can sing and dance for hours without tiring and can demonstrate a great amount of paranormal activities like Uri Geller.[28] In a quranic psychiatry clinic, a therapist carries out certain tests to determine the main cause of mental disorders. He or she is trained to use a thread of a particular length. This is given to the patient who holds it for some time. It is then measured very carefully. The quranic therapist reads certain prayers, blows on the thread, and measures the thread again. The thread will either increase, decrease, or stay the same in length. If no change is registered, of course this means the disorder has a physical cause. If it has increased by a good length, this is due to the influence of a non-human agent. If it has decreased in length, this is due to sorcery. If it has increased length but not very much, this is the effect of the evil eye. For each change, a special prescription is applied. One may also use the footprint test in the same manner as above."[29]

These bizarre theories on psychiatric treatment may sound like the ramblings of a benign madman, but Sheikh Gilani is not the fool his writings would indicate. He holds the lives of thousands of devoted followers in his hands. On his word, they will kill, and have killed, on many occasions. At his command, the thousands of American Muslim families living in his compounds across the United States will forego sound medical treatment and instead employ the deranged quranic psychiatry methods which Gilani has developed. And at Gilani's command, his thousands of poor, mostly black devoted followers in the United States will send the majority of their earnings—by some accounts up to 70 percent—back to their sheikh who lives in comfort and seclusion in Pakistan, potentially orchestrating future attacks against Americans by controlling the minds, bodies and finances of his brain-washed followers.

Pillar of Lies

In his autobiography, *Pillar of Lies*, Gilani describes his uniqueness this way: "I live in a different plane of existence. I am not like other people. I am a mystery and riddle even to my own self. What all I know, I cannot reveal, and what all I reveal is very little."

Gilani boasts that he "saved hundreds of Americans' lives by curing them of various diseases" and "saved thousands of Muslim youth from leading lives of crime," this, despite the evidence that he ordered his followers to commit assassinations, firebombings, theft, white collar fraud and more during a reign of terrorism that began in the late 1970s.[30]

In another absurd distortion of reality, Gilani asserts that "the young American Muslims among my followers are not on the streets. They are home with their parents and elders. This is a phenomenon unknown this day and age."

The reality is quite different, however. Several generations of children have been raised in poverty in MOA camps, trained in the art of jihad beginning when they are just toddlers. Unable to easily assimilate into normal American life, they often leave the camps for a life of crime or violent terrorist activity. The women suffer an equally dismal fate, enslaved to their men, forced into polygamous marriages, forced to have as many children as possible, sometimes beaten and raped, all under the banner of religious submission to Islam and the stifling rules of MOA that women must endure.

"Why," pleads Gilani, "do not the American authorities express some gratitude for the help I have given to their fellow countrymen?"[31] These outrageous statements are the true pillar of lies upon which Gilani's terrorist empire rests. His claim that he has helped the poor, black Muslim population of America, whom he often recruits from prisons, is a dangerous and false assertion. On the contrary, Gilani has committed the worst type of crime against America's African-American population by luring them into a life of abject poverty, obeisance to a man most have never seen, devotion to the point of death for many, and lives filled with hatred for their home country. And in the process, he has created an independent army of jihadists who have been killing their own countrymen for decades.

Typically, Gilani's response is another contradiction. "These people (Al Fuqra members who committed crimes) had their own secret cells and they were committing these crimes before I came to America."

The truth, of course, is that the crimes began when Gilani began giving the orders.

Today, Gilani is an elderly man in his seventies, living in seclusion in Lahore, Pakistan, and little is heard from him save for the odd online posting of disjointed essays detailing more quaranic healings or the even odder video postings that occasionally surface in which he rambles incoherently about his accomplishments. Yet investigators have noted that Gilani has many underlings who run his vast empire smoothly. And he has ordered his followers to lay low, blend in with their surroundings and await further instructions.

Terrorists Working Together

"I do not know Osama Bin Laden nor have I ever met him or any member of Al Qaeda," states Gilani in *Pillar of Lies*. "There is no end to the lies."

But, like many of Gilani's statements, his assertion is once again false. Al Fuqra and Al Qaeda were linked in a Royal Canadian Mounted Police Report issued in April, 2003. Furthermore, Gilani was present at a terrorist conference also attended by Osama bin Laden in 1993. That was when the Popular Arab Islamic Conference (PAIC) was convened to bring together Sunni, Shiite and secular Marxist terrorist groups in Khartoum, Sudan. According to *Wall Street Journal* reporter Mira Bolen, it was a "who's who of Islamist terror."[32] Islamic leaders from Iran and Afghanistan were in attendance at the PAIC meeting, along with delegates from Hamas, Hezbollah, Palestinian Islamic Jihad, the Popular Front for the Liberation of Palestine and the Democratic Front for the Liberation of Palestine.[33]

"Osama Bin Laden, not yet a kingpin but living in Sudan while developing the organization and funding for his nascent network, was there," writes Bolen. "So was Sheikh Gilani."[34]

Terrorist groups around the world are more and more cooperating with each other in order to accomplish their common goal of eradicating the infidel and imposing Islam on the conquered people. Former CIA Director George Tenet has said that "the mixing and matching of capabilities, the swapping of training, and the use of common facilities among terrorist organizations is common in the modern world."[35]

In a report released by the Center for Policing Terrorism, evidence is revealed that Al Fuqra has shown "willingness to work with" a domestic group known as the El Rukn, a gang of drug dealers and pimps that operated in the Chicago area into the 1990s, members of which dabbled in international terrorism by offering their services as domestic terrorists to ousted Libyan leader Muammar Gaddafi. Gaddafi is widely rumored to have funneled money to Gilani's Muslims of the Americas. Al Fuqra has also been implicated in smuggling weapons with Hamas and working with members of the Egyptian Islamic Jihad, among many other jihadist groups.[36]

"With ever closer associations developing between international terrorist networks," says the Center's Zachary Taylor, "it is only a matter of time before Al Fuqra assists an organization in an assault on United States soil."[37]

Sixth Sultan

In 2009 Gilani announced that he had met with the long-awaited Mahdi, the Islamic messiah. The Mahdi supposedly appeared to Gilani in 2009 because Gilani claims to be the sixth Islamic sultan and predecessor to the Islamic messiah. The meeting is the supposed signal for the end times, in which the Mahdi will unite with Jesus to usher in Armageddon and the final phase of world history.

"He (Gilani) ascended along with the Khalifahs and Talibs in the higher realms of the non-physical world and there, as directed, he introduced once again, Hazrat Imam Mahdi and told his Khalifahs and others to inform the world about the expected arrival of the promised Mahdi," writes one of Gilani's followers. "Imam Mahdi was neither tall nor short. He was average height. He had a bright complexion. His beard was neatly shaped. He was handsome and had a mature disposition. He looked to be in his mid to late thirties."

"Muslims the world over should prepare themselves to receive him," Gilani's web site continues. "Sheikh Gilani confirms that it is not a matter of decades for physical appearance, rather just a matter of years ... The tide is about to turn. The world will change forever and for good. The end time has started."[38]

Gunfire at Night

Back in South Carolina, Mike and Loretta Allen, who live adjacent to the Holy Islamville compound in York County, are worried about the nocturnal activities carried out by their Muslim neighbors. Sometimes they hear rapid gunfire, loud explosions, the sound of many guns being fired simultaneously and high-powered assault weapons being shot with thundering booms. Some of these explosive sounds have been recorded; they are proof that the residents of Islamville conduct weapons training on a regular basis, often in the dead of night.

Shortly after midnight on September 11, 2003, the second anniversary of the September 11 attacks, they heard something over a loudspeaker coming from the camp. The language spoken was Arabic, but it was coming through the rolling woods that separate their home from the compound so loudly that the Allens became concerned. Although they did not understand the words, they feared that the Muslims in Holy Islamville were celebrating the September 11 attacks.

They called the York County Sheriff's Department, which quickly dispatched an officer to the Allens' home. When the officer arrived, the Arabic chanting stopped. The Allens, standing in their back yard with several other neighbors, had long suspected that the residents of Islamville had a police scanner, and that they knew the comings and goings of all the Sheriff's personnel. So they asked the officer to create a ruse and radio back to headquarters that she had left the neighborhood. As soon as the message was radioed in, the loudspeaker resumed. But this time the message was in English, and it was unmistakable:

"KILL ALL AMERICANS!"

"Did you hear that?' Loretta asked the officer. She answered, "Yes, I heard it."

Then another proclamation was heard:

"IT NEVER WOULD HAVE HAPPENED IN AMERICA SAVE FOR THE IGNORANCE OF ALL AMERICANS!"

The "it" referred to was the attack on the World Trade Center, the Pentagon, United Airlines Flight 93 that went down in Shanksville, Pennsylvania and the deaths of thousands of Americans at the hands of Islamic terrorists on September 11, 2001.

"Did you hear that, too?" Loretta asked the officer. "Yes," she replied. "I heard it."

"Well," said Loretta, "what are you going to do about it? That sounds like a threat."

The officer replied that she would file a report, then left. The next day Loretta called the regional office of the FBI and asked if she could have access to the report, but the Sheriff's Department had never filed one.

The peace and quiet the Allens sought in the countryside of South Carolina have been shattered. They are reminded when they hear random gunfire and gaze into the woods behind their home—the woods that contain guard tents manned by armed Muslims—that the founder of Islamville, Sheikh Mubarik Ali Gilani, has vowed to "purify Islam through violence."[39]

"We are not fighting so that the enemy recognizes us and offers something," Gilani says in a recruitment video. "We are fighting to destroy the enemy. We are dealing with evil at its roots ...

... and its roots are America."

Sign from entrance to Holy Islamville compound run by Muslims of the Americas in York County, SC, where sounds of rapid-fire shooting has been heard.

"There are thousands of people in America who, if they are asked to cut off one limb so that they can stay with (Gilani), they are ready to do that. If you push him to that stage, he has no option but to declare jihad on America; it will blow like a volcano."

Khalid Khawaja, Pakistani jihadist and follower of Sheikh Mubarik Ali Gilani[1].

CHAPTER 3

The Beheading of Daniel Pearl

WHEN *WALL STREET JOURNAL* REPORTER DANIEL PEARL arrived in Karachi, Pakistan, in 2002 the city was a little safer for Americans than it had been in recent months. Usually killed just for the sport of it, an American had not been murdered there in weeks. A local magazine even stopped publishing a foldout, color-coded guide to the likeliest spots in the city to be murdered.

Still, one international journalist commented that "compared with Cambodia, Karachi seemed a walk in the park."[2]

Violence in Karachi was so pervasive before and after the September 11, 2001, terrorist attacks that killings averaged eight per day, not counting "the shootings, bombings, garrotings and throat slittings between ethnic and religious groups, much less the toll racked up in quotidian armed robberies, home invasions, and just-for-the-hell-of-it sniper slayings."[3]

But Daniel Pearl was a crack reporter. He was on the trail of an exploding story, and he made contact with people who could lead him to interviews with high-level jihadists. In Pakistan to track down a spider's web of terrorist links, Pearl and his five-months pregnant wife Mariane traveled to Karachi to meet with a radical Islamic cleric named Sheikh Gilani who might have the information Pearl was seeking.

When reporters come to Karachi, they are given certain guidelines to follow. Daniel Pearl, upon arriving on January 22, 2002, received the same list:

1. Do not take a taxi from the airport; arrange for the hotel to send a car and confirm the driver's identity before getting in.
2. Do not stay in a room that faces the street.
3. Do not interview sources over the phone.
4. Do not discuss subjects such as Islam or the Pakistani nuclear program in the presence of hotel staff.
5. Do not leave notes or tape recordings in your room.
6. Do not discard work papers in the wastebasket; flush them down the toilet.
7. Do not use public transportation or accept rides from strangers.
8. Do not go into markets, movie theaters, parks or crowds.
9. Do not go anywhere without telling a trustworthy someone the destination and expected time of return.
10. And, above all, do not go out alone. Ever.[4]

By now everyone knows that Pearl did, indeed, go out alone on his first night in Karachi. The official story says he foolishly got into a car with people he did not know and was kidnapped by terrorists who trapped him into the meeting, who then took photographs of him with a gun to his head and his hands in chains. The photos were sent to the media and immediately broadcast on all major news outlets. After making bizarre ransom demands and accusing Pearl alternately of being a CIA agent, then a member of Mossad, the Israeli national intelligence agency, he was beheaded about a week later, possibly after he was shot or stabbed to death, his body cut into pieces, stuffed in a plastic bag, and dumped in a remote area of Karachi. The horrifying video of his execution was sent by the terrorists to the media, and it went viral within hours.

Several men were ultimately arrested and found guilty. Khalid Sheikh Mohammed, following his arrest in 2003 for masterminding the 9/11 attacks, admitted: "I decapitated with my blessed right hand the head of the American Jew Daniel Pearl." Mohammed wasn't even a suspect in the beheading of Pearl until this surprising confession was made. To this day there is no proof, other than his word, that he is the killer.

Another "sheikh" admittedly involved in Pearl's death was Ahmed Omar Saeed Sheikh, who orchestrated the details of the kidnapping and lured Pearl to his death. Omar Sheikh was sentenced to death in July,

2002, for his role, but at this writing he is still awaiting appeal. He claims he only planned the kidnapping, not the murder, and should not be executed for a crime to which Khalid Sheikh Mohammed confessed.

A Vast Network

But this summary description of the kidnapping and execution of Daniel Pearl makes the story sound simple when it is exceeding complex. The kidnapping, torture and murder of Daniel Pearl is a vast labyrinth of competing and interconnected jihadi groups, egotistical terrorist leaders and their radicalized followers, false , surprising twists and turns and corruption at the highest levels.

At the center of the mystery is Sheikh Mubarik Ali Gilani. What many do not recall is Pearl's mission in Karachi, Pakistan. He was scheduled to interview Sheikh Gilani, founder of the radical terror group Jamaat Al Fuqra and its American cover group, Muslims of the Americas, when he was kidnapped. Pearl was investigating a report from federal sources that the so-called "shoe bomber," Richard Reid, was a disciple of Gilani and that, in fact, Reid was known to have visited Gilani's training compound in Lahore, Pakistan, prior to the attempted shoe bombing.

Yet the investigating authorities in Pakistan, who were aided by the FBI during the kidnapping phase of the ordeal, located Gilani, detained him, questioned him and, after he protested his innocence, let him go. Even though Pearl was on his way to visit Gilani when he was kidnapped and subsequently beheaded, authorities decided Gilani had no involvement in Pearl's ordeal, and they deemed it a dead-end street.

It is down this street, however, that we will travel right now—to the very end where Sheikh Gilani resides in luxury and seclusion, the founder of a vast empire of jihadi activity and accumulated wealth that has at its epicenter the United States. Much of this empire is in slumber, yet Americans have been warned not to awaken it.

"There are thousands of people in America, who, if they are asked to cut off one limb so that they can stay with (Gilani), they are ready to do that," said Gilani follower Khalid Khawaja, who also described himself as a close friend of Osama Bin Laden. "If you push him to that stage, that he has no option but to declare jihad on America, it will blow like a volcano."[5]

The Shoe Bomber

The sad saga of Daniel Pearl could trail back in any number of directions: to his Jewish heritage, which was a source of supreme inflammation to the kidnappers and killers (despite Pearl's lack of religious conviction and his marriage to an ardent Buddhist) ... to his drive and ambition as a reporter for the *Wall Street Journal*, which led him to Karachi in pursuit of the elusive Sheikh Gilani ... to the 1970s, when Islamic terrorist activity began to make a name for itself around the world, including in the United States. But we will begin the story with Richard Reid, the shoe bomber, whom Daniel Pearl was investigating when he went down the wrong road in Karachi.

When the world got their first look at Richard Reid, he looked more like a slightly goofy, disheveled panhandler than an angry jihadist. The mug shot of Reid after his arrest on December 22, 2001, shows a slightly confused young man with long, frizzy hair sloppily tied back in a ponytail, a dirty, unkempt beard, wide eyes that make him seem almost surprised to be standing before a police photographer, and a hint of a crooked smile that suggests Reid didn't have a care in the world. He like a bungling loser.

Yet this dirty, confused-looking young man had a past, and it wasn't pretty. Richard Colvin Reid was born in 1973 in London. Reid's father was a Jamaican immigrant of African descent and his mother was a white Englishwoman. His father, Colvin, was a career criminal. At the age of 16, Richard Reid left school and joined the family business, becoming a petty crook who landed in and out of jail. Reid became depressed, living most of his life behind bars; but instead of going straight, he blamed racism for all his woes. His father advised him to convert to Islam because Islam, his father believed, wasn't as racist as other religions. Plus, his father said, "they get better food in prison."[6]

So that's exactly what the young Reid did upon his release in 1996: he joined a mosque in London that fomented anti-American views. The mosque was described as "the heart of the extremist Islamic culture" in Great Britain.

Reid was becoming radicalized. He spent 1999 and 2000 in Pakistan and received jihadist training at a terrorist camp in Afghanistan. He also attended an anti-American religious training center in Lahore, Pakistan, led by Sheikh Gilani. During the Pearl investigation, Sheikh Gilani and his followers vehemently protested that they had never heard of Richard Reid, but "he was there," confirmed one Pakistani government official.[7]

Investigators believe it was in Pakistan—whether under the tutelage of Gilani or other jihadists—where Reid was told to blow up an airplane and given instructions on making a shoe bomb. He traveled extensively, back to London, to Israel and Amsterdam, among other locales, and lived in Amsterdam through November, 2001. All the time he was communicating to associates via an address in Peshawar, Pakistan, which was known for its Al Qaeda connections.

Reid and an associate returned to Pakistan in November, 2001, possibly picking up more training, and reportedly traveled overland to Afghanistan. They were given shoe bombs, then Reid traveled to Paris, where, on December 21, 2001, he attempted to board a flight to Miami, Florida. His boarding was delayed, though, because his disheveled appearance aroused the suspicions of airline screeners, and because Reid could not answer all of their questions sufficiently. Screeners also became concerned when he failed to check in any luggage for the transatlantic flight. After additional screening by the French National Police, Reid was cleared and reissued a ticket for a flight on the following day.

Reid e-mailed someone in Pakistan the day of the missed flight and asked, "I missed my plane, what should I do?" The anonymous reply was: "Try to take another one as soon as possible."

On December 22, 2001, he boarded American Airlines Flight 63 from Paris to Miami, wearing his special shoes packed with plastic explosives in their hollowed-out bottoms. In the air, screaming was heard shortly after lunch was served onboard. "When someone screams [that way], you know something bad is happening," remembered one passenger.[8]

Reid was attempting to light a fuse protruding from his shoe, witnesses later said. Packed in the sole were enough high explosives to blow a hole in the fuselage of the plane and bring it down. But thanks to the quick thinking and heroic actions of the flight crew and passengers, Reid's shoe bomb never went off. Two flight attendants struggled with Reid while passengers passed cups of water like it was a country barn burning to help douse the smoking shoe bomb. During the scuffle, Reid bit one of the crew members' thumb; in turn, she threw a bottle of water in his face, while passengers tied him up with their belts and headphone cords. Finally subdued, Reid was sedated with drugs from the onboard medical kit. The rest of the flight was tense, with fears that Reid had a secret accomplice on board. One passenger kept a tight grip on Reid's ponytail during the rest of the flight, while others stood guard. The flight was diverted to Boston, where Reid was taken into custody. Today Reid is in a super maximum security prison serving a life sentence.

The FBI later concluded that the shoe bomb failed to detonate due to the one-day delay in the take-off of Reid's flight. Because Reid wore the shoes for the entire day, his sweaty feet dampened the fuse and it failed to ignite.

Enter Daniel Pearl

Fast forward one month to January 23, 2002. Reporter Daniel Pearl had a busy schedule that day. Reports that Richard Reid had received terror training in Pakistan from an obscure cleric, of whom few had heard, Sheikh Gilani, focused the reporter's attention like a laser beam. The report first surfaced in a story in the January 6, 2002, edition of *The Boston Globe*, written by reporter Farah Stockman. It reported that U.S. investigators had learned that Reid was a follower of Sheikh Gilani, and that he had received terror training in Pakistan under Gilani's tutelage. Pearl was fascinated by the unknown sheikh, so he arranged to meet with Gilani later that day, a day stacked up with appointments like rungs on a ladder. First, he was to meet with an agent at the U.S. Consulate for a security briefing, then a representative of the Pakistani Federal Investigation agency, the director of the Pakistan Civil Aviation Authority, then Sheikh Gilani at the end of the day. There was also a dinner planned in his honor by some friends and colleagues around 8 p.m. His wife, Mariane, was expecting him.

How did Pearl arrange the meeting with Gilani? This would ultimately become the critical question as investigators rushed to save his life after the kidnapping. First, prior to arriving in Karachi, Pearl contacted a former Pakistani intelligence pilot (formerly connected to Pakistan's Inter-Services Intelligence, the ISI) and known terrorist and friend to Osama Bin Laden by the name of Khalid Khawaja. Khawaja was also a follower of Gilani—an important point to remember—and he gave the sheikh high praise:

"I am telling you, Osama doesn't have many people in America" as Sheikh Gilani does, Khawaja said in a 2002 interview. "I am sure of one thing, Osama does not have even one of his followers as committed as Sheik Mubarik Gilani. Osama does not have even one as committed as the least of his people."[9]

Khawaja was a favorite among journalists, known for his inflammatory quotes. "America is a very vulnerable country," he told CBS in a 2001 interview. "Your White House is the most vulnerable target. It's very simple to just get it ... No American is safe now ... This is a lifelong war."

Khawaja later testified that he told Pearl he could not arrange an interview with Gilani. Sheikh Gilani, he said, did not grant interviews. This, however, was not true at the time. Gilani had allowed an interview in 2001 with CBS, and again in March, 2002, following the Pearl murder.

Whatever Khawaja did or did not promise regarding an interview, it was now openly known by a Gilani devotee that reporter Daniel Pearl was snooping around about shoe bomber Richard Reid. It is hard to imagine that Khawaja did not report this information to Gilani, even if Khawaja was unable to arrange an interview.

After seeking help from Khawaja, Pearl then went to a "fixer" named Asif Faruqi to make contact with Gilani. A "fixer" is someone who offers assistance to foreign journalists, like Pearl, who are trying to get a story, using their local experience and contacts to pave the way. Mariane Pearl, Daniel's wife, called them the "lifeblood" of the foreign journalist, because without a "fixer" it can be very difficult to get a story or to connect with the right people. Faruqi was a Pakistani reporter based in Islamabad, and his contacts in the world of the jihadist were numerous.[10]

Here's how investigators say the initial connection was made: Faruqi the fixer asked around, and a journalist friend of his named Zafar told him about a man named Arif who knew another man named Bashir, who could lead them to Gilani. Arif (a.k.a. Hashim Qadeer), was an Islamic terrorist wanted by the police. Dealing with shady characters who employ multiple pseudonyms could not have been surprising for Pearl, since journalists know you have to wade through lower-level jihadists to get to the jihadist at the top.

Bashir also had another name, Ahmed Omar Saeed Sheikh, the infamous "Omar Sheikh" who ultimately arranged the kidnapping.

However, Omar Sheikh wasn't exactly a lower-level jihadist; he was internationally known to have connections to Osama Bin Laden and Al Qaeda, and he had served prison time for other kidnappings. It was Omar Sheikh who was the Donald Trump of the kidnapping world. He earned good money arranging kidnappings of foreigners and is known to have sent money from his kidnappings to 9/11 hijacker Mohammed Atta. Omar Sheikh admits to murder, as well, with poison being his preferred method—although an occasional throat slitting was not outside his repertoire. The ruthless Omar Sheikh frequently talked with kidnap victims about their pending beheadings, telling them about the pleasures of martyrdom. Holy warriors, he would tell them as they nervously awaited execution, ejaculated at the moment of death knowing that they had entered heaven.[11]

Thus, the chain of connections went something like this:

Khawaja
$\rightarrow$ Zafar $\rightarrow$ Arif $\rightarrow$ Bashir Omar Sheikh
Faruqi Fixer

A Conversation With Sheikh Gilani

At some point prior to the abduction, Pearl was reported to have actually had a ten-minute conversation with Sheikh Gilani himself.[12] Although this detail was reported by a Pakistani reporter, it was not considered important enough by U.S. investigators to bear much mention or further scrutiny. This crucial tidbit of information, if, in fact, true, proves that when he was interrogated during the kidnap phase, Gilani lied about not knowing who Pearl was.

At this point, then, the chain may have looked like this:

Khawaja
Sheikh Gilani(?)$\rightarrow$ Zafar $\rightarrow$ Arif $\rightarrow$ Bashir Omar Sheikh
Faruqi the Fixer

By the time Pearl was abducted, his main contact had become Omar Sheikh, whom he knew as Bashir. There is no doubt at this point that Omar Sheikh was pretending to be a friend in order to lure Pearl into the hands of the kidnappers. Omar Sheikh admitted this later during interrogation. Not only is such a tactic common among terrorists, but the commandment to kill the non-Muslim is written in the Quran: "Fight and slay the pagans (or infidels, unbelievers) wherever you find them." (Surah 9:5). It is also the credo by which Sheikh Gilani's radical followers live: "Act like you are his friend, then kill him, just like from the book."[13]

Prior to Daniel Pearl's arrival in Karachi, he and Omar Sheikh, a.k.a. Bashir, corresponded frequently. In an attempt to establish a meeting with Gilani, Pearl even met with Omar Sheikh at the Akbar International Hotel in Rawalpindi, Pakistan, on January 11, 2002, just 12 days before he arrived in Karachi for his anticipated meeting with Gilani.

"It was a great meeting," Omar Sheikh later told investigators. He had shaved his beard and worn sunglasses for the meeting with Pearl. "We ordered cold coffee and club sandwiches and had great chitchat."[14]

On January 16, 2002, Pearl and his wife, Mariane, were in Peshawar when an e-mail arrived from "Bashir" Omar Sheikh. Using the e-mail address "Nobadmashi@yahoo.com," which is Urdu for "no rascality," Omar Sheikh apologized to Daniel Pearl for not contacting him sooner.

"I was preoccupied with looking after my wife, who has been ill," Omar Sheikh wrote, an apparent ploy to tug at Pearl's heartstrings. She "is back from the hospital and the whole experience was a real eye-opener. Poor people who fall ill here and have to go to hospital have a really miserable and harassing time. Please pray for her health."[15]

Three days later, on January 19, Omar Sheikh sent another e-mail saying that Sheikh Gilani was in the city of Karachi and wouldn't be returning to his home in Lahore, Pakistan, for "a number of days." Bashir told Pearl he could wait for Gilani's return, send e-mail questions to Gilani, or, "If Karachi is your program, you are welcome to meet him there."

Danny chose the latter.

'We Knew Nothing'

The day of the scheduled meeting with Sheikh Gilani, January 23, 2002, Pearl raced around the city keeping his appointments. One of them was with Randall Bennett, the U.S. Consulate's regional security officer who was stationed in Karachi at the time. Bennett had been in Karachi for more than three years and knew most of Pakistan's Islamic militants. Pearl met with Bennett for a security briefing and asked him pointedly what he knew about the shoe bomber's mentor, Sheikh Gilani, and his organization, Jamaat Al Fuqra. "Is it safe to meet Gilani?" Pearl asked.

"I told him we knew nothing about them," Bennett later stated in a videotaped interview. Gilani's "name had not come up and his organization hadn't come across my desk."

Watching this interview, which was conducted in 2007 and posted online, it is inconceivable that Bennett could not have known about Gilani and Al Fuqra. The U.S. Justice Department, State Department, FBI and numerous state and regional investigatory units most certainly knew about Al Fuqra and its leader. As early as 1980, Al Fuqra was beginning to register on their radar. In 1989 the FBI stumbled across the now-infamous storage locker in Colorado that contained boxes of detailed information about terrorist activity and related white-collar crime, as well as weapons and explosive parts belonging to Jamaat Al Fuqra members. They also found the written plan to murder the mosque leader in Tucson, Arizona, which was carried out just a few weeks later.

By 1993, Jamaat Al Fuqra and Sheik Gilani were implicated in the first World Trade Center bombing after investigators learned that one of the planners of the attack, Rodney Hampton-El, was a Fuqra member. By 1995, Jamaat Al Fuqra was on the State Department's list of known terrorist organizations. By 2002, the year Daniel Pearl was killed, the Justice Department was knee-deep in an investigation into Jamaat Al Fuqra and was preparing to release an important report on the group.[16]

In 2005, two years before Randall Bennett's online interview, a Department of Homeland Security report titled "Integrated Planning Guidance Report" warned that "other predicted possible sponsors of attacks (against the United States) include Jamaat Al Fuqra that has been linked to Muslims of America."[17]

How then, could the U.S. Consulate's representative in Karachi not know about this terrorist group? Furthermore, in an apparent contradiction, Bennett says earlier in the same recorded interview that "Gilani was the head of a less-known terrorist organization," implying some prior knowledge of the sheikh and his group, then denying he knew anything about them a few minutes later.

Yet, if Randall Bennett is telling the truth that he knew nothing about Gilani and Al Fuqra when Daniel Pearl met with him on that fateful day, then Bennett was the victim of a massive cover-up himself, a cover-up in which scores of government investigators and law enforcement officials purposely did not reveal to their consulate representative in Pakistan the existence of a terrorist group with links to jihadists around the world, including the granddaddy of them all: Osama Bin Laden.

It is more likely, however, that Bennett could not, or would not, admit what the U.S. government already knew, possibly because he had given tacit approval to Pearl to meet Sheikh Gilani.

What is certain is that the U.S. government knew about Gilani and Al Fuqra at least 13 years before Daniel Pearl was killed.

Whatever Bennett knew, or didn't know, he still gave Pearl sound advice that day. He told him that if he met Gilani, he must do so in a public place. Pearl then asked if it would be safe to visit Gilani at his madrasa (religious school).

"No go," Bennett says he told Pearl. "Madaris are typically affiliated with radical groups. Danny seemed to understand this and accept it." Pearl left the briefing, and Bennett had the impression "that he did not intend to do that" (meet Gilani at his madrasa).

Later in the day—the day of his kidnapping—Pearl received a phone call from a man who called himself Siddiqi, a follower of Gilani's. Omar Sheik, whom Pearl knew as Bashir, had passed along Pearl's cell phone number to Siddiqi, the next person in the kidnapping chain. Siddiqi called Pearl and told him to meet Sheikh Gilani at the Village Restaurant in Karachi, located next to the busy Metropole Hotel, at seven o'clock. It was as public a place as you can get in Pakistan, so Pearl agreed to the meeting.

In their scramble to understand the kidnap plot, investigators would later learn that Siddiqi's real name was Mansur Hasnain, a known highjacker and comrade of Omar Sheikh. The two terrorists had a couple of things in common. In 1999 they both took part in the hijacking of an Indian airliner with 155 passengers and crew aboard. In the process, they slit the throat of a honeymooning Indian businessman and demanded the release of another Islamic jihadist. After a six-day standoff in Kandahar, the ransom demands were met and the two terrorists got away with their fellow hijackers.

They also shared a corrupt connection to the Pakistani ISI, the Inter-Services Intelligence Agency. The ISI operated much like the CIA, but has been linked for decades to terrorists and terrorist organizations. Hasnain, along with members of the ISI, was implicated in an attempted assassination attempt against then-President Pervez Musharraf. Furthermore, Omar Sheikh had the legal and financial backing of the ISI to conduct acts of terror. The ISI even hired a lawyer to defend him following a 1994 kidnapping.

The chain of complicity now looked like this:

Khawaja
Sheikh Gilani(?) → Zafar → Arif → Bashir Omar Sheikh → Hasnain
Faruqi Fixer

Jaish-e-Mohammed

Omar Sheikh and Hasnain shared yet another critical link: They both had connections to the radical, violent jihadist group known as Jaish-e-Mohammed, a terrorist group which is considered the parent group in Pakistan of Sheikh Gilani's Jamaat Al Fuqra. Although Jaish-e-Mohammed has been officially banned in Pakistan, its violent tentacles stretch throughout the world. The New York City Times Square bomber, nabbed in May, 2010, among other prominent jihadists, was a member of Jaish-e-Mohammed.

The U.S. Treasury froze Jaish-e-Mohammed's assets in October, 2001, before it was designated a Foreign Terrorist Organization by the U.S. State Department the same year. Jaish was re-designated a Foreign Terrorist Organization in 2008.[18]

Forgotten in all the detail surrounding Daniel Pearl's kidnapping and beheading is this: In December, 2001, while the world was still reeling from the 9-11 attacks, Pearl wrote a story that received minor attention in the *Wall Street Journal*. It was about the Pakistan ISI's support of the jihadi organization Jaish-e-Mohammed. Pearl learned that the group still had its office running and bank accounts working at the time, even though President Musharraf claimed to have banned the group. Pearl's article stated that the Jaish-e-Mohammed group was also connected to the Al Rashid Trust, one of the first financial entities whose assets were frozen by the United States after the 9-11 attacks, and through which funding may have been funneled on its way to the hijackers. Pearl had stumbled upon this information while researching the shoe bomber's connection to Al Fuqra, which, in turn, Pearl learned, was an offshoot of Jaish-e-Mohammed in Pakistan.

Further proof of this connection between the two terrorist groups is evidenced by a published report that the leader of Jaish-e-Mohammed, Maulana Azhar, had been seen at Sheikh Gilani's house.[19]

Jaish-e-Mohammed, among other groups, is a member of the International Islamic Front (IIF) in Pakistan, founded by the late Osama Bin Laden, and also known as Al Qaeda.

Another fact worth mentioning about Jaish-e-Mohammed is that, according to the Anti-Defamation League, it also goes by the name of Jamaat Al Furqan.[20] The similarity of the name to Gilani's Jamaat Al Fuqra is obvious. The word "furqan" in Arabic roughly translates to "truth," implying a discernment between right and wrong.

There is a constantly shifting nature to terrorist groups and the terrorists themselves. They adopt new names and identities as the situation warrants; they merge themselves into new groups, splinter off into others, cooperate to accomplish greater jihadist impact, and they war among themselves for dominance. Above all else, however, is the overriding theme of hatred toward Jews, Americans and, in the case of Gilani, Hindus—and the stated goal to propel Islam to supremacy in every country on earth.

Into A Waiting Car

Late in the day on January 23, 2002, Daniel Pearl briefly called his wife, Mariane, to let her know where he was. "I think I've found the shoe bomber's e-mail address," he told her excitedly. Pearl had met with representatives from Cybernet, an internet service provider that was helping him track the e-mails of the shoe bomber which were made from an internet café in Karachi. Pearl told his wife he was heading to the seven o'clock meeting with Sheikh Gilani at the Village Restaurant and would be a little late to dinner; he would be home by nine. "I love you a lot," he told her.

From there, his footsteps are hard to follow, but investigators believe he never interviewed Gilani or even met with him. Instead, according to the taxi driver, who dropped him off in front of the Village Restaurant, he met a waiting car that contained the kidnappers. Omar Sheikh was with the men, according to the taxi driver who later identified him from a photo. Seeing Omar Sheikh, whom Pearl had grown to trust as "Bashir," probably gave him some peace of mind about getting into the car with the strangers.

At this point, three new players entered the drama—known as Saquib, Naseem and Adil. These were the kidnappers who took over at the restaurant. Omar Sheikh states that he turned Pearl over to the three and never saw Pearl again. Investigators believe they were recruited at the last minute by Omar Sheikh to hold Daniel Pearl captive, but it will never be known for certain how involved they were in the plot.

The three shared something in common with Omar Sheikh, the leader of the kidnapping ring, and all the other jihadists involved. They were members of Jaish-e-Mohammed, the terrorist group known as a sister group to Sheikh Gilani's Jamaat Al Fuqra.

Khawaja   Saquib
Sheikh Gilani(?) → Zafar → Arif → Bashir Omar Sheikh → Hasnain → Naseem
Faruqi Fixer   Adil

The kidnappers released a bizarre and shifting set of ransom demands. They wanted 2 million dollars, the release of all Pakistanis being detained by the United States at Guantanamo Bay and a shipment of F-16 fighter jets Pakistan had bought from the United States in the 1980s—a purchase which was stopped when Congress cut off military sales to the country. Pearl's wife, Mariane, and a team of Karachi and U.S. investigators worked night and day to bring Daniel home alive, but to no avail. Except for the money, the ransom demands were considered time-wasting diversions.

The kidnappers also accused Pearl of being an agent for the CIA. This charge, along with other absurd ransom demands and claims, was denied by the CIA and by the *Wall Street Journal*, Pearl's employer. Subsequently, when Pearl's killers released a videotape of his execution, it was titled "The Slaughter of the Spy-Journalist, the Jew Daniel Pearl."

The rest of the Daniel Pearl story is a tragic one. The three kidnappers took him to a desolate house on the outskirts of Karachi, where he was tortured and held for another week, maybe longer, until Khalid Sheikh Mohammed, the 9-11 mastermind, showed up and slit his throat. The gruesome video of Pearl's beheading was released on

February 21, 2002, nearly a month after his abduction and three weeks after he was killed. On May 17, 2002, his dismembered body was found.

Investigators believe there were many more people involved in the plot, but Khalid Sheikh Mohammed was probably the biggest name to emerge from the Daniel Pearl kidnapping and execution. However, Mohammed did not confess to his role until he was interrogated years later for masterminding the 9-11 attacks. Like all the other players in the drama, Mohammed had connections to Jaish-e-Muhammed, which had connections to Gilani's Jamaat Al Fuqra, all of which had connections to Al Qaeda.

The Search for Gilani

Prior to Pearl's execution during the kidnapping phase, investigators learned through Pearl's e-mail record that he was on his way to visit Sheikh Gilani. When they did a simple Google search of Gilani's name, they found thousands of references to his terrorist background and leadership of Jamaat Al Fuqra. Randall Bennett, the U.S. Consulate agent who claims to have told Pearl he knew nothing about Gilani, must have felt like a fool when page after page of googled information began to light up the computer screen.

During this phase, prior to Pearl's death, the investigators assembled around the computer, including Pearl's wife, laughed at some of Gilani's wackier statements—that he believes in invisible forces, genies ("jinn"), and that he claims to have the power to transport himself through time and space and transform himself into an animal. He's either crazy, or an idiot, or both, they concluded. In his online photos he looks "dull."[21]

A few days after Pearl was kidnapped, Sheikh Gilani disappeared from his compound in Lahore. Searching everywhere investigators followed up on a rumor that he was in the Punjab province near Kashmir, a favorite hideout for jihadists, and the location of another residence Gilani is rumored to have. They went to his second home, but he had fled again. Finally, he was located in the city of Rawalpindi and arrested. Some accounts state that Gilani turned himself in, but Pearl's widow, Mariane, writes in her memoir that it took a team of police to track Gilani down and put him in custody.[22] Gilani was transported by plane to Karachi and interrogated.

Perhaps it is no coincidence that Jaish-e-Mohammed, the sister group to Gilani's Jamaat Al Fuqra, has walled off a 4.5-acre compound in Pakistan's Punjab province, near the sheikh's second home.[23]

Detained in Karachi, Sheikh Gilani denied knowing anything about Daniel Pearl. He denied knowing anything about Richard Reid, the shoe bomber. He denied any involvement in any terrorist activity, ever. Amazingly, he was let go by Pakistani investigators.

Much later, Gilani would contradict himself with several outrageous statements. In an online essay, Sheikh Gilani writes that prior to Daniel Pearl's abduction, Farah Stockman, the *Boston Globe* reporter, requested an interview with him to discuss the shoe bomber. He says she soon confessed to him that she was an agent for the United States. Gilani writes that Stockman also told him another U.S. agent "would be coming to stretch the lie even further, and that that person turned out to be an 'alleged' reporter from the *Wall Street Journal* (Pearl)."[24]

Gilani writes that his father was so shocked by what the reporter Stockman was saying about Richard Reid being connected to Gilani that he "started weeping, and before evening he passed away." Gilani continues, "After my father's demise, I moved to the mountains. There is a village there in which I was building a school for girls. After 15 days up in the mountains, I learned through a local newspaper that one reporter (Pearl) had been abducted."[25]

But Pakistani police found Gilani's father alive at the time of his arrest on January 30, 2002, after Pearl's kidnapping.[26]

Gilani and the ISI

The Pakistani Inter-Services Intelligence Agency has always been known for its corruption and sponsorship of terrorism. The links are so well known and widespread that they need not be detailed here. The important facts to note, however, are how this corruption is linked to the Daniel Pearl case.

The first, most obvious, connection is the release of Gilani, a terrorist with known ties to the ISI, following a cursory interview with the sheikh in connection with Pearl's kidnapping. It appears that all Gilani had to do was deny any involvement and he was released. Another rumor floating about is that when Gilani was arrested and briefly detained in connection with the Pearl case, he had actually turned himself in to the ISI to ensure he was in friendly hands. This has never been confirmed, but it raises an intriguing question.

Then there's this: A month before his kidnapping, Pearl wrote a story linking the ISI with another terrorist organization, Ummah Tameer-e-Nau, which was reported to be providing Osama Bin Laden with nuclear secrets prior to the 9-11 attacks.[27]

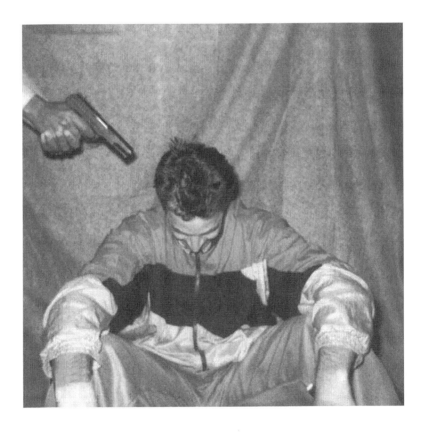

Daniel Pearl prior to his beheading. This photo was widely circulated on the internet prior to his execution.

Also in December 2001, Pearl reported in the *Wall Street Journal* that the terrorist group Jaish-e-Mohammed, which is interconnected with Sheikh Gilani's Jamaat Al Fuqra and ultimately his own kidnapping, was still operating bank accounts with the tacit approval of the ISI. They are known, Pearl wrote, to collect their terrorist-related funds openly in Pakistan with the assistance of the ISI. Jaish-e-Mohammed was also known to have funneled money to the 9-11 hijackers.

"If (Daniel Pearl) hadn't been on the ISI's radarscope before," stated one colleague, "he was now."[28]

The ISI is also suspected of supporting, through various terrorist groups, the 9-11 attacks, not to mention the Taliban resistance in Afghanistan. Even worse, Pakistan's ISI had links to agencies of the U.S. government—and Daniel Pearl may have been investigating these links, as well, when he was kidnapped. In other words, Pearl may have stumbled onto the rumor that key individuals within the U.S. military-intelligence establishment knew about the ISI contacts with 9/11 terrorist Mohammed Atta but failed to act in time to prevent the attacks.[29]

Was Sheikh Gilani more involved than investigators have revealed? Did the Pakistani ISI shield him? Did Pearl speak to Gilani the day of his kidnapping, as some reports indicate? Was the CIA nervous about Pearl's snooping into their involvement with the ISI? All these years later these questions have still not been sufficiently answered.

Perhaps none of these conspiracy theories matter. The final question of why Daniel Pearl was killed may never be answered. He was Jewish ... he was American ... he was snooping into ISI corruption ... he was in the wrong place at the wrong time; any and all of these reasons are likely.

It could all come down to the age-old motive of all kidnappers: money.

The more probing question—who killed Daniel Pearl?—is the one that leads to a vast network of jihadi activity, deceit, violence and, once again, profit. Prior to Bin Laden's death it was estimated that Al Qaeda required a minimum of 300 million dollars a year to fund its terrorist activities. The money has come from simple theft, drug and arms dealing, white-collar crime, government corruption and kidnappings, among other sources.

A cousin of Sheikh Gilani, contacted in Pakistan following Pearl's beheading, confirmed that Gilani is, above all else, a businessman, driven by profit. While Gilani lives in comfort in Pakistan, surrounded by the trappings of his wealth, his thousands of American followers are required to send anywhere from 30 to 70 percent or more of their income to him in Pakistan. That includes American taxpayer money obtained through welfare fraud.

His followers live in rural camps surrounded by poverty and filth, often without running water or any modern conveniences, sometimes while raw sewage bubbles up around their dilapidated trailer homes. They lead lives of fear—fear that their demanding leader in Pakistan may be watching them from the bushes in the form of a fox or a deer. Most of all, the women and children of these camps are treated as slaves, beaten into submission, whipped when they are disobedient, forced to bear children by more than one husband beginning in their teens, and worked nearly to death amidst their unforgiving surroundings.

"He has been doing certain (jihadi) things," said Gilani's cousin, "but he has been in this only for money."[30]

"As you know ... we have already established a fabric, an organization under the auspices of Muslims of the Americas Incorporated. Our organization is called Soldiers of Allah ... We will train you to be like tigers and lions."

Sheikh Mubarik Ali Gilani, speaking in his Soldiers of Allah terrorist combat training video, filmed in the early 1990s.

CHAPTER 4

Soldiers of Allah

THE BAKHARWAL SHEPHERDS OF KASHMIR, INDIA, ARE ALMOST entirely nomadic. Living in the Pir Panjal and Himalayan mountains of the disputed Kashmir Valley, they are mainly goatherds and shepherds, practitioners of the Hindu religion for generations. Every year they take their sheep high into the mountains, above the tree line, to graze in the fertile meadows, sometimes taking a full two months to reach the grazing territories. Moving from one meadow to another, they spend their summers traveling in pairs or large family groups. Their dogs, the famous bhotia, always accompany them.

In the late 1990s, the families of the Bakharwal shepherds had had enough harassment from Muslims living in the region. Many of their women were being repeatedly raped by Muslim terrorists, who cornered them when they were alone. The terrorists harassed, taxed and brutalized the shepherds until they could stand it no longer. The Bakharwal shepherds decided to form a village defense committee to protect their vulnerable, makeshift homes and family members.

They would pay the ultimate price.

On February 8, 2001, the villagers were slaughtered by Islamic terrorists as part of a decades-old campaign of ethnic cleansing against Kashmiri Hindus. When the embers of the burnt-down shacks of the villagers had cooled, the charred bodies of 15 victims were discovered. The burned body of a woman, wrapped around the infant she had been trying to protect, was one of the first located. By the next day, 15 bodies were discovered, seven of them children as young as age four.[1]

Kashmir has been disputed territory by India and Pakistan for decades. Even China has laid claim to portions of the region. In recent years, Muslim radicals have focused more of their energy on annexing this region onto the country of Pakistan, causing the genocide of the Kashmiris to mushroom. Since 1989, nearly half a million Kashmiri Pandits, the ethnic Hindu villagers who are scattered throughout the mountainous region, have been killed or forced into exile.

- The brutality of the Islamists against the Kashmiri Hindus is staggering, including:
- Subjecting Hindus to brutal torture to instill fear among them in order to force them into submission.
- Forced mass exodus of Hindus from the land of their ancestors through kidnappings and torture.
- Attacks, molestations, kidnappings and gang rapes of the Hindu women.
- Destruction and burning of Hindu homes and properties.
- Looting of Hindu properties and theft of their businesses to ensure they do not return.
- Desecration and destruction of their Hindu temples and theft of property from Hindu shrines.

With thousands of Kashmiri Hindus murdered through strangulation, hanging, impaling, branding, burning alive, lynching, bleeding to death, dismemberment, drowning and other barbaric methods, it is no wonder the region has become dominated by Muslims. The Kashmir Valley has a population of around four million, with 97 percent now calling themselves Muslim.[2]

The question of Kashmir is, simply put, who will rule it? Although the region of the Kashmir Valley has been under Indian rule since the 1940s, neither Pakistan nor China respects its official boundaries, and Pakistan believes that not just Kashmir should be annexed to it, but all of India.

Radical Islamists, as in other parts of the world, have steadily waged a war of brutality and aggression against the Kashmiris, with tremendous progress made in the last few decades toward subjugating the people through torture, terrorism and genocide.

Kashmir's future as an Islamic enclave attached to Pakistan has been a motivating force behind Sheikh Mubarik Ali Gilani's war against the "infidel"—the unbeliever. To help motivate people around the world, most notably Americans, to join the fight against the Kashmiri Hindus and to help subjugate the people, Gilani produced a film in the early 1990s introducing himself to the jihad movement. In the process, he has created the most damning evidence there exists today of his role as a terrorist leader.

The film begins with Gilani himself, wearing an Islamic cleric's headgear, white clerical robes covered by a bulky camouflage jacket. He is flanked by two other men, both wearing headgear and camouflage. Gilani himself is heavyset, with a thick black beard streaked with gray. He speaks in Hindi directly into the camera and later switches to English. He hints that he is speaking from a location in Kashmir, and later a translator is able to confirm that much, if not all, of the video was filmed among the mountainous terrain of Kashmir, India.

"On behalf of the Muslims of the Americas, and in the West Indies, in the United States, Canada, and in Pakistan ... I present before you a documentary film showing before in helping and training oppressed Muslims," he begins. "I am proud to say I have to sit with colleagues who have been successful in founding an international organization which is called Soldiers of Allah ... And this documentary is one of the two at present which you will be seeing in which we have reached out (to) Muslims of the Kashmir. And we have prepared them to defend themselves and given them highly specialized, you know, training in guerilla warfare. And not only that, we have enabled them to reach a level where they could instruct others, as well.

"We had to take a lot of risks and undergo a lot of (treacherous) trials and hardships in order to reach them inside Kashmir," Gilani continues. "Life is becoming more hard for Muslims ... therefore, every Muslim, man or woman, should learn to defend himself or herself."

For Gilani, the question of Kashmir was, and is, an important one. A decade before he made his Soldiers of Allah recruitment film, he and other jihadists were intently focused on Afghanistan. During his earliest days in Brooklyn, New York, when he took over a mosque and began preaching jihad, Gilani was in the business of recruiting soldiers to fight the infidel around the world. Back then, the front line was in Afghanistan.

Following Soviet withdrawal from Afghanistan in 1989, many factors converged and Islamic terrorists, most of them based in Pakistan, began to strategize on their next battleground. Having installed a subservient Taliban regime in Afghanistan, they began to install Taliban-like apparatuses in other Central Asian countries, including India.[3] The terrorist leaders, which included Sheikh Mubarik Gilani, decided they needed to settle the score with India on the issue of Kashmir and "avenge" the humiliation of 1971.

The Indo-Pakistani War

The Indo-Pakistani War of 1971 was a 13-day military conflict between India and Pakistan that began on December 3 after Pakistan attacked Indian airbases. The aim was to cripple India and thereby prevent it from supporting Bangladesh in its war for independence.

During the course of the war, Indian and Pakistani forces clashed on the eastern and western fronts, with the conflict coming to an end after the Pakistan military surrendered on December 16. In a humiliating defeat, Pakistan agreed to the secession of East Pakistan as the independent state of Bangladesh. Around 97,368 West Pakistanis who were in East Pakistan at the time of its independence, including some 79,700 Pakistan Army soldiers and paramilitary personnel, were taken prisoner. For Pakistan it was a complete and utter loss, a terrible psychological defeat at the hands of intense rival India. Pakistan lost half its territory, a significant portion of its economy and its political role in South Asia in just 13 days.[4]

The war also stripped Pakistan of more than half of its population and placed nearly one-third of its army in captivity, establishing India's military dominance of the region. The United States, led by Richard Nixon, backed the Pakistani effort politically and financially against Kashmir. Pakistan was an ally of China at the time, and Nixon was engrossed in opening up the doors of communication with the eastern superpower.

Author Steve Coll, in his book *Ghost Wars*, argued that the Pakistan military's devastating experience with India influenced the Pakistani government to support jihadist groups like Gilani's Jamaat Al Fuqra, which also went by the name of Soldiers of Allah, in Afghanistan and then in Kashmir. Jihadists of all stripes, Coll concluded, were a tool to use against India; they could keep the Indian Army in Kashmir bogged down indefinitely.[5]

This was the political and radical Islamic atmosphere that bred Sheikh Gilani. As a young jihadist, he helped train (soldiers) to fight the

Soviets in Afghanistan. A decade later, his skills as a combat trainer were refined, and he created an underground training video, filmed in the very heart of Kashmir—the next intense focus of his jihadist activities—to recruit and equip Islamic terrorists for battlefield action.

The questions of Kashmir and Afghanistan are of great importance to Sheikh Gilani. Despite his denials to the contrary, he wants to create Islamic states throughout the world and impose strict Sharia law on its citizens. But in many ways even that goal is a smokescreen for the ultimate conquest: America. Gilani's followers would not have purchased dozens of tracts of land in the United States over the past several decades, and he would not have filmed his training video partially in English, unless vulnerable Americans were the ultimate target.

"You can easily reach us, you know, and we are establishing training camps, at present, in other countries," Gilani states in his Soldiers of Allah training film. "You can reach us at Quranic Open University offices in upstate New York, or in Canada, or in Michigan, or in South Carolina, or in Pakistan ... wherever we are, you can reach us. Or the best would be to meet one of our reps who will be glad to give information ... So, brothers and sisters, this is a remarkable achievement which you are going to see. How ... ordinary youth is turned into, you know, very like tigers and they have gone back with their people, and they are training them in the very same ... self defense and guerilla warfare.

"The best course would be to get in touch with the founders of the Muslims of the Americas," Gilani adds.[6]

America Calls

As detailed in Chapter Two, Sheikh Gilani created an aura of mysticism around himself, claiming to be in contact with "non-human beings" he calls jinn, or genies. "I use to receive visits from many non-human beings. They became my followers. They would serve me and served me well," he writes in his autobiography, appropriately titled *Pillar of Lies*.[7]

Gilani needed to convince his followers that he was divinely appointed to lead them and that he has the ability to transport himself through time and space. It was apparently during one of these transportation events that he received his calling to America.

"Once I remember I was high up in the Himalayan Mountains and being served by my non-human followers," he writes. "From there I was guided to go to America."[8]

He lived in Brooklyn, New York, for a while, where he radicalized the local Muslims and began to train them for jihad in Afghanistan. At the same time he preached against all Indians. His group, known at that time as Jamaat Al Fuqra, began its reign of terror against Hindus, Jews, Christians and even Muslims who did not agree with him in Canada and the United States.

At some point in the 1990s, Gilani was in Kashmir filming his extraordinary guerilla training film, "Soldiers of Allah." Portions may also have been filmed right here in the United States, because Gilani introduces his two camouflaged attendants, the black men sitting beside him, as members of the Muslims of the Americas—Gilani's U.S.-based front group headquartered in Hancock, New York.

"The best course would be to get in touch with the founders of the Muslims of Americas," he says in his "Soldiers of Allah" tape. Those leaders can be "easily reached if you wish to train. So the best course would be personal contact and this film, which is being made available to you."[9]

How To Kill The Infidel

Sheikh Gilani's "Soldiers of Allah" training tape is a cold, militaristic educational video for jihadists in training. Yet it contains more subtle and implied drama than a Hollywood film. For beneath the superficial instructions on how to make a bomb, slit a throat, ambush a car, or fire an assault weapon is the constant reminder that Americans are being trained to kill in the name of Islam.

Gilani's constant protestations that he is not a terrorist and does not advocate terrorism, and that he does not train people to become terrorists are as hollow and phony as his fanciful tales of genies and teleporting himself through time and space like a character in a bad science-fiction film. The evidence is powerfully on display, along with a real flesh and blood Gilani, in the "Soldiers of Allah" training video.

In the video, Gilani warns of the dangers of the video falling into the hands of the enemy. "You should see that it is a dangerous personal property and you do not make any other illegal copies," he states. "You do not make any copies of this film so that it doesn't fall into the hands of the enemies of Islam. It can, you know, be quite serious."

The "Soldiers of Allah" tape was made available to PRB Films by a known and respected law enforcement official, who confirmed that U.S.

Intelligence is aware of the film. It has been authenticated independently, and the portions filmed in Hindi have been professionally interpreted.

In the film, after Gilani's introduction, the footage switches to a training segment that instructs jihadists how to use stealth and camouflage to sneak up on unsuspecting targets. It shows jihadists simulating attacks and murders on guards, stand-ins for citizens and military personnel. Then it provides instruction in shooting high-caliber and low-caliber weapons, how to use ropes and garrotes to strangle victims, how to hijack cars, how to wire and detonate explosives and other guerilla-warfare techniques.

In another training segment, an instructor sitting in a forest setting identified as Kashmir holds up a training book to about 20 jihad students. On a table in front of him is an assortment of weapons, which he identifies as Russian-made Kalashnikovs, Israeli-made Uzis, Mannlicher pistols, garrotes and more.

The instructor begins the lesson by saying: "Today, I want to teach you how each team works against Jews and Israelis ... what kind of work this is going to be." He instructs his students not to use the biggest gun available. "Point gun at me," he tells a student whom he has called forward. " When you point the gun, I will just push it away from me. With this big gun, you can miss the first shot, so make gun smaller ... Use both hands ... keep gun straight ... point and shoot. Now? Point and shoot ... no need of aiming ... shoot madly and randomly. When you hit once and you see him not dead, then shoot him from close quarters ... don't stand there, keep going ... don't turn back."

The techniques Gilani teaches in the video are identical to those used in 2001, perhaps just months after the video was produced, against the peaceful villagers living in the mountains of Kashmir.

Another training segment in the video shows Gilani with an instructor demonstrating the creation of bombs and fuses. Speaking in both Hindi and English, the instructor states:

" ... Like this, you know ... and you put in a mark, some sort of mark, so then you know exactly, this one has to be kept here, about this much, and then this is snugged in. Now it is knocked. Now then you have to crimp it. It is kept with one hand, one finger on the other side and two fingers on the north. Push it up and push it down. Then it is snugged and you take the crimper and just take it off like that. Keep it away and squeeze it. Now, this can be taped here. This can be taped here ... tape isn't necessary ... Pen knife, not blade, but good penknife, jack-knife, tape ... so you can tie these things up here with this tie here. You can make a hairpin to be very short. You can make a hairpin like this ... here, so then it is between the two so it is not intimate contact. Otherwise, you can tie a reef knot here and have this so the blasting current will follow both ways."

While the instructor speaks, Sheikh Gilani leans in to get a better look. "If there is some breakage here, then it will get in on the other side. But normally we have two firing systems ... one can be put here, one can be put here. Now how many charges we have? One, two and three. This is half a kilo? Half a pound?" A students answers, "yes."

The instructor concludes, "You put a plastique on top of the blasting cap, so we can all know the time." The group then explodes the homemade device in a nearby creek, to the sounds of "Very good. Ok."

In another segment, Gilani is seen giving instruction to students. Oddly out of place is the sound in the background of a baby crying—a sound typical of the training compounds located on American soil. "I hope you understand, all these things here have to be practiced and learned," Gilani tells his students. "I want you to understand; if any calamity comes upon you in combat, you need to understand that it will be taken care of. You will be paid 7,000 if you agree to it and if it's ok with you.

'Tigers And Lions'

"I give you my word," Gilani continues. "Give me a paper with any doubts or fears and I will take care of it personally. You are my brothers and sisters. We are one family. I'll take care of all your concerns. We will train you to be like tigers and lions."

Gilani's appeal to his students is rewarded with a loud group cheer of "Long live Gilani!"[10]

At the conclusion of the training portion of the video, Gilani reappears on screen seated inside a house, flanked on each side again by leaders identified as representing the Muslims of the Americas. Gilani states, without faltering or any hedging, that Muslims of the Americas "is comprised of training camps to establish Soldiers of Allah."[11]

"As you know," Gilani states, "we have already established a fabric of an organization under the auspices of Muslims of the Americas Incorporated. Our organization is called Soldiers of Allah. Remember, this is our own organization and it is from the holy book. The name has been derived from the holy book, Soldiers of Allah."

Gilani is referring to the numerous references in the Quran and other ancient Islamic writings that command Muslims to fight unbelievers. One verse, for instance, states that "jihad (holy war) is ordained for you (Muslims), though you dislike it, and it may be that you dislike a thing which is good for you and that you like a thing which is bad for you. Allah knows, but you do not know."[12]

Gilani explains that his "Soldiers of Allah fight for the oppressed people. Soldiers of Allah fight for the sake of Allah ... Therefore, you will be seeing this documentary, where Soldiers of Allah went into war-torn Afghanistan ... in Kabul, in Ghazni, in Jalalabad ... we're going. I won't say all the time, but there are skirmishes, there are ambushes, there are bombardments, there is shelling. The Russians have left, but they have left their agents, who are ruling Kabul and one or two more cities."

Then Gilani refers to a 1982 jihadist insurgency in Afghanistan that he orchestrated. "As you know," he states, "in 1982, we organized a jihad campaign and we said that we must attack Kabul to finish the battle. And we plan to raise the army of 12,000."[13]

Remember, Gilani was already spreading his jihadist wings in the early 1980s. When the Soviets invaded Afghanistan in order to impose a Marxist regime there, the United States sided with the Islamic insurgents, with then-President Jimmy Carter choosing what he believed was the lesser of two evils. When President Ronald Reagan took office in 1982, he continued the policy of siding with the Afghan insurgents. The United States joined with terrorist nations including Pakistan and Saudi Arabia to oppose Soviet domination. Around 1982, Islamic organizations from other countries joined forces to begin fighting the Soviets in Afghanistan. Notable among them was a young Saudi jihadist named Osama Bin Laden, along with one of his devoted jihadist cohorts, Sheikh Mubarik Ali Gilani, who was making a big name for himself in Brooklyn, New York.[14]

Toward the end of the "Soldiers of Allah" video, Gilani claims that his soldiers are neither "a terrorist nor a mercenary," but they "fight for the oppressed people ... Soldiers of Allah fight for the sake of Allah, seeking His happiness without expecting any reward at any time."

Finally, Gilani implores recruits to join the Soldiers of Allah. "You are most welcome to join one of the most advanced training courses in Islamic military warfare, special training, if you wish," he states in English. "You can get in touch with the commanders (whose names he lists) and anybody in the Muslims of Americas in the United States, Canada, Trinidad or in Pakistan. You are most welcome," he states again. "We will train you so you can defend yourself."

He concludes by promising that more terrorist training videos will be produced in the future. To date, however, no more have become public. Yet it is widely suspected that many homegrown terrorists who have been in the headlines in recent months have received their training overseas, possibly in one of the numerous training compounds funded and established by Sheikh Gilani, their terrorist fervor piqued, perhaps, by a glimpse of the "Soldiers of Allah" video.

The Ultimate Takeover

In early January of 2010, some members of the Hancock, New York, compound owned by Sheikh Gilani's Muslims of the Americas—the same group Gilani praises in his "Soldiers of Allah" video—disappeared. Law enforcement officials confirmed that the compound had been under investigation for engaging in a massive tax-return fraud plot in which money was raised illegally to send to their terrorist leader in Pakistan, Sheikh Gilani.[15]

The question is: Where did the men go? Are they with Gilani in Pakistan? Are they receiving specialized terror training at one of Gilani's numerous camps in the United States, Canada or the Middle East?

Gilani is no fool. In addition to training his followers to engage in armed combat with the infidel, he also provides them with additional, valuable training in tax fraud and welfare scams. According to the law enforcement sources, many of the missing men from the Hancock compound were receiving tax training in order to file false returns and collect taxpayer money to fund their terror operations. Friendly mosque members from New York were giving the followers storefront tax outfits run by Jamaat Al Fuqra. There, the Hancock members would file false tax returns and collect 24-hour rapid returns. A large referral fee would reportedly be sent to the imam of the New York mosque which provided the storefront, with the remainder sent overseas to Gilani's bank accounts.

What does all this mean? It is proof that Sheikh Gilani—from his comfortable, secluded existence in Pakistan—still has the same goal that jump-started his jihadist career: To defeat the infidel. Hand in hand with that goal is the desire for lots of American money. Whether he uses violence or white-collar fraud, it doesn't matter to Gilani and his followers.

The end game is an Islamic takeover of America.

This photo, taken from Al Fuqra's "Soldiers of Allah" guerilla training video, shows trainees practicing their strangling technique.

Sheikh Gilani is shown with gun in hand in his "Soldiers of Allah" training video, aimed at recruiting Islamic jihadists.

Sheikh Gilani is clearly seen in the Soldiers of Allah guerilla training video he produced in the 1990s. It was obtained by Christian Action Network by a former law enforcement official.

Still from an MOA/Al Fuqra training video, showing American Muslim women involved in guerilla training.

Still from an MOA/Al Fuqra training video, teaching combatants how to engage in hand-to-hand combat.

"They communicated with Pakistan and other jamaats ... Fuqra had various radios with an international beam where they could communicate directly with Pakistan ... They had their radio towers and guard towers set up out at Trout Creek Pass (in Colorado); all this equipment with the dials set for the Middle East."

Susan Fenger, lead investigator of the Jamaat Al Fuqra Colorado case in 1993.

CHAPTER 5

The Gang That Couldn't Shoot Straight

THE ASTROZON SELF STORAGE COMPANY IS STILL IN OPERATION in Colorado Springs. Advertising the first month's rent for just one dollar, their customers come and go on a daily basis—moving their possessions in and out of storage, arranging and rearranging, and sometimes hiding their treasures from prying eyes.

By August 29, 1989, the owner of Astrozon had placed a padlock on one of his rented lockers. He was concerned that the renters had not paid their bill for some time, so he padlocked it to prevent them from getting back in until their bill was paid in full.

Watching the news one morning that August, he was struck by the headline story: A rash of burglaries in the Colorado Springs area was still unsolved. This got the owner of Astrozon thinking about his locker with back rent due. Could the renters be the thieves the police were searching for? They were "suspicious," he concluded, coming and going at all hours, and now they seemed to have abandoned the locker completely.

He called the Colorado Springs Police Department and told them he had a tip—an unpaid storage locker that may contain stolen goods. A detective arrived at Astrozon within the hour and, after listening to the owner's story, put a call in to the Colorado Springs District Attorney's Office for permission to enter.

"Can I see inside?" the detective then asked the owner of Astrozon. "Sure," answered the owner, and he opened the padlock.

What immediately struck the detective was the immediate, visible presence of mercury switches. A mercury switch is commonly used in homemade bombs; it contains liquid mercury to connect electrodes within a glass tube, which ignites a flow of electricity that triggers an explosion. In his cursory search, the detective also found a number of documents that referenced alarm systems and weapons inventories, and he noticed that some of the documents appeared to be written in Arabic. The detective knew he had stumbled upon a treasure trove of evidence pointing to Islamic terrorist activity. He walked out of the unit and instructed the owner of Astrozon to lock it up; he would be back.

Within a few days the detective returned, accompanied by police officers and investigators with the Intelligence Unit of the Colorado Springs Police Department. Some accounts said FBI agents were also present. Documents found in the locker on the second visit included maps with overlays depicting locations and routes of major electric, gas and telephone lines throughout Colorado, all of them potential terrorist targets. Also among the items found was a "targeting packet" with photographs and a detailed description of a planned bomb attack against a Hare Krishna Temple in Denver, Colorado. Investigators later learned that the bombing had taken place five years earlier exactly as outlined in the packet, causing more than $150,000 in damage to the temple.[1] Also seized were weapons, bomb-making components, including the mercury switches spotted a few days earlier, electric wiring and timers.

Investigators obtained a search warrant to more thoroughly scour the locker, and they returned again on September 14, 1989. Accompanying them this time were members of the Colorado Department of Labor and Employment, the State Attorney General's Office Bomb Unit and K-9 Unit, the White-Collar Crime and Terrorism Unit, the Colorado Department of Revenue, Liquor and Tobacco Enforcement Unit, and the FBI. They found 30 pounds of explosives, three large pipe bombs wired and ready to detonate, shape charges, bomb-making instructions, handguns with obliterated serial numbers, silencers, instructional material on guerilla warfare, documents indicating potential targets, newspaper clippings of a triple homicide of East Indians in Washington State and much more.[2]

Membership Applications

Also found were applications from numerous American citizens, entitled "Talibeen Fuqra Jamaat," filled out and requesting membership in Jamaat Al Fuqra. "One of the membership requirements of the Fuqra was that you should have Army training and bring your own weapons," said Susan Fenger, chief investigator of the case. When investigators examined the applications, answers ranged from "Yes, I have one rifle and one 9mm," to "I have served in the Army" or "I served in the Air Force."[3]

More damning evidence was also found, including a plan to kill the imam of a mosque in Arizona (see Chapter One). Although authorities immediately contacted police in Arizona who, in turn, notified the imam of the threat against his life, the grisly murder was carried out just two weeks later exactly as outlined in the plan found in the storage locker. In all, 279 locker items were seized and catalogued.[4]

It seemed like a slam-dunk case; here was obvious evidence of murder, forgery, bomb making, guerilla training and more. The renters of the storage locker were obviously terrorists, or connected to terrorists— quite a remarkable and disturbing revelation for the all-American resort town of Colorado Springs.

After the investigation got under way, the FBI began to jokingly refer to the terrorists as "The Gang That Couldn't Shoot Straight." They had left a trail of their activities a mile wide, the agents said. How stupid could they be? The FBI refused to even call them terrorists. They laughed at them as if they were bungling fools.

But from the moment Susan Fenger was called in on the case, she knew this was a serious underestimation of a group of deadly terrorists. "If you go back to records from ATF, (there were) 14 or 17 fire bombings and 13 or 14 murders you could tie this group to," she said in a 2007 interview. "This is definitely not The Gang That Couldn't Shoot Straight. A lot of the things they did were stupid, like keeping all this documentation, but now they don't do that anymore.

"What I had were pieces of a puzzle," she said. "And all we needed was for someone to put those pieces together."[5]

It was Fenger who put them all together. In a manner similar to the famous Al Capone case, when "untouchable" Elliott Ness finally put Capone away by proving tax fraud instead of pursuing a murder case against him, Fenger was able to prove that Al Fuqra members had been committing white-collar crimes for a decade, most of them involving worker's compensation fraud in Colorado, in order to fund their terrorist-related activities. The final charges brought, and subsequent convictions, would fall under the heading of racketeering and white-collar crime.

In early 1990, the FBI approached Susan Fenger with a request. Fenger was the chief criminal examiner for the Colorado State Department of Labor and Employment at the time. She was a forensics expert in, among other things, handwriting, and she knew how to track financial fraud. The FBI agent walked into her office in Denver and handed her a paper with some names on it.

"They were worker's compensation claims, and he wanted to know if I could run those names against records within my department and get back to him if I saw anything that looked suspicious," said Fenger. "I ran the names ... and I thought it very odd that the handwriting of a man named Woods appeared in the Pierre file, and Pierre was in the Woods file. So I thought that was interesting ... suspicious." Furthermore, Fenger found that the witness to Woods' supposed accident, a James D. Williams, Jr., listed the same home address as Woods on the claim form.

Fenger told the FBI agent about her suspicions concerning the Pierre/Woods file, and the agent returned to her with a list of several thousand more names. "I put together a cross-match, and I cross-matched all those names and Social Security numbers against our system, which was worker's compensation and unemployment claims," said Fenger. Numerous fraudulent claims jumped out.

All of the names presented by the FBI were names of Al Fuqra members, said Fenger. "At that point, the agent wanted to meet with my director, and he told my director at the agency that these people were allegedly terrorists."[6]

As the implications of the case began to sink in, the FBI suddenly announced they were "pulling out." They said the U.S. Attorney's Office had decided it was not worthwhile to pursue a worker's compensation fraud case in federal court.[7]

Then-Governor Roy Romer was furious. "I don't want terrorists here in Colorado. What are you going to do about it?" he asked Fenger.[8] He appointed her as chief investigator and insisted that she pursue the case above all others. It was up to Fenger now to make the case.

"This requires a real financial crime investigation. That's my specialty," Fenger recalls telling the Governor when she agreed to spearhead the investigation. "I know how to trace the funds. Also, I'm a forensic documents examiner, which has always been my specialty from the beginning."

The governor said, "Anything you need, just ask for it."

Fenger replied: "I need to carry a gun."

Following The Money Trail

It would take Fenger two years to build her case and gain indictments against five suspects. She began by searching through worker's compensation claims from thousands of Al Fuqra members. A pattern began to emerge that showed Al Fuqra members filing claims for accidents occurring on work sites. Fake construction companies were set up with Fuqra members listed as employees. Accident claims would be made, with hundreds of thousands of dollars awarded through the state government—claims that Fenger eventually proved were bogus.

By executing dozens of search warrants on banks, Fenger proved that Al Fuqra members were laundering the money and eventually funneling it back into their terrorist activities. The scam began with the setting up of fake companies, then false identities for employees were established; the employees were actually Al Fuqra members. The workers took out insurance, and then faked injuries on the job. In some cases, there were real injuries that were treated, but they were not received on the job, as Fenger would later prove. False claims, signed by Al Fuqra members claiming to be witnesses, were filed and huge sums of money were awarded.

Once the money came in, it was laundered in several ways. It would be deposited in a first account, then the account holder would write checks to a bogus company for "services rendered." That money would be divided up and redeposited in several more accounts under different names. From there, money orders and travelers checks would be issued, and payments would be made for a variety of purposes, including purchasing weapons, paying mortgage installments on land in Colorado owned by Al Fuqra and other items. Money would also be directed to the Al Fuqra headquarters in Hancock, New York, which openly operates as Muslims of the Americas. Fenger was able to follow the money all the way from Colorado to New York, to Pakistan and ultimately to Sheikh Gilani himself.

Fenger also cross-referenced all the stated income against IRS records, and none of the Al Fuqra members had reported any income or paid taxes, even though they were drawing hundreds of thousands of dollars worth of taxpayer money through fraudulent claims.

Fenger went even further in her investigation. As a forensics expert, she visited all the local hospitals near where the suspects lived and subpoenaed their medical records. What she found at the local hospitals in Colorado confirmed a new aspect of the case. Some members of Al Fuqra were receiving injuries—but not on the job. They were injuring themselves during commando training.

"We made the identifications through radiographic, or x-rays," she said. "What they were doing was injuring themselves while they were practicing karate and commando training in the mountains ... This radiographic identification was the first time it was used in a criminal case in Colorado"[9]

Shopping For Property

Fenger unearthed another interesting tidbit of information. She tracked down a realty company in the area of Buena Vista, Colorado, that had sold land near the compound to Sheikh Gilani himself in the early 1980s.

"I found the realty company that dealt with him, and all they could tell me was that he was a big, overweight fellow, and that he smelled very bad," Fenger said. Gilani, accompanied by one of his American wives, "had a terrible body odor." The real estate agent "said that was the worst thing about working with him." It is reported that he purchased the property, but sold it quickly thereafter. All of those records have been turned over to the FBI, Fenger said.[10]

After two years of research and following the money trails, Fenger determined that five members of Al Fuqra in Colorado illegally collected and cashed $355,000 in checks from the Colorado worker's compensation insurance fund. In the summer of 1992, a grand jury handed down indictments against five Fuqra members involved in the scam. In October, in order to arrest the men, Fenger and her investigators led a raid on a 101-acre compound which they had learned through their investigation was owned by Al Fuqra. It was located in an area known as Trout Creek Pass, outside Buena Vista, Colorado, about 90 miles west of Colorado Springs and the Astrozon storage locker.

The Trout Creek Pass Compound

"I had 64 different law enforcement officers with me," Fenger recalls when the raid began at dawn. "A SWAT team and the bomb squad went in ahead of us ... then the rest of the law enforcement officers, with me in the lead, leading the way. I showed (them) where to turn off, leading the rest of the law enforcement officers, and there was a train of us (going) down the highway."[11]

They found even more damning evidence at the compound, including a large cache of weapons, 5,000 rounds of Chinese ammunition, rifles, knives, bows and arrows, along with some illegal weapons. Investigators also checked the mines that crisscrossed the compound, including a man-made cave, and found assault weapons, 40,000 rounds of ammunition and survival gear. Also found were books on commando training, firearms training, gun magazines and applications for "Soldiers of Allah," another name used by Jamaat Al Fuqra, from American citizens across the United States wanting to join the terrorist group.

In the hidden, man-made cave investigators also found the property that had been stolen during burglaries in the Colorado Springs area.

At the time of the raid, there were only about 20 people on the compound, including four of the five wanted men. Most of them were women and children, living in poor, overcrowded, dilapidated conditions. "The women kept telling the children we were there to kill them," said Fenger. "They were very quiet. They were just talking to their children, telling them how evil we were, what devils we were, and that we were there to kill them."[12]

Four of the five wanted men, Vicente Rafael Pierre, James D. Williams, James Upshur and Edward McGhee, were arrested during the October, 1992, raid. A fifth suspect, Chris Childs, fled into the mountains as the raid got under way, and he has not been seen or heard from since.

The local and state media had a field day with the raid, accusing Fenger's squad and the governor's office of harassing a "poor group of Muslims who had left the city in quiet and peace, away from the city life, to raise their own animals, raise their children, and were peaceful people," said Fenger. "All the newspapers were giving the Governor and Attorney General ... a bad name."

Firebombing In Denver

Fenger was told by the state Attorney General's Office to make the case that terrorism had been committed. The negative press, sympathizing with the Muslims who lived at Trout Creek Pass, was beginning to hurt the Governor and all the investigators involved in the case. So Fenger once again employed all her investigative and forensic skills to build a case for terrorist activity, not just welfare fraud. She focused on a packet of information found in the Astrozon storage locker that detailed a bombing in Denver at a Hare Krishna temple that occurred in the mid-1980s. Thankfully, the Denver Police and Fire Department had kept all the records on that case, so Fenger was able to piece together the evidence from Denver with the plans found in the storage locker.

Sifting through dozens of boxes of evidence on file in Denver, Fenger found writings from Sheikh Gilani himself expressing hatred for Jews, Hindus and Muslims who didn't agree with him. The boxes also contained photos of numerous synagogues and temples, including the Hare Krishna temple that was bombed. But Fenger again came up against a brick wall when she tried to obtain FBI evidence that had been collected during their initial investigation of the Denver firebombing.

"I had to fight with the FBI to turn this stuff over to me," she recalls. "They let me look at it in pieces during that year. Finally I got them to turn it over to me; I got custody of everything; they weren't doing anything with this stuff." Finally, she was able to put her second big case together.

Ultimately, James D. Williams, one of the men charged during the raid at Trout Creek Pass for involvement in the worker's compensation fraud, and another Al Fuqra member, Edward Flinton, were charged and convicted with conspiracy to commit murder in the Hare Krishna firebombing. Flinton was considered a Fuqra "mastermind" who developed assassination and bombing plans nationwide, including a 1983 hotel bombing attempt in Portland, Oregon, the 1984 firebombing of the Hare Krishna temple in Denver and the 1990 murder of Imam Rashad Abdel Khalifa in Tucson, Arizona. In 1993, authorities indicted Flinton for conspiracy to commit murder in connection with the Hare Krishna temple firebombing. After hiding out as a fugitive for years with his family, he was finally arrested in 1996 at the Holy Islamville Al Fuqra compound in York, South Carolina. He was arrested and is imprisoned in Colorado, scheduled for release in 2015.

"These guys in prison all do their time real well," said Susan Fenger. "They're on good behavior in prison. The whole idea is to get in and get out, to get back to work."[13]

Martin Mawyer in front of a large, man-made tunnel at the now abandoned MOA/Al Fuqra compound in Buena Vista, Colorado. A large cache of weapons was uncovered hidden in a tunnel at the compound in 1989.

Professional Security International

The company known as Professional Security International (PSI) was a major player in the Colorado Al Fuqra case. Fenger and her investigators learned that numerous Fuqra members were employed by or associated with PSI over the years, and it was the central facilitator of money laundering and money transfers. It was also the central information source for planned terrorist activities by Al Fuqra. Amazingly, investigators learned that PSI, which established the appearance of legitimacy, was able to negotiate security contracts with the federal government and international airports that house sensitive information.

"PSI and similar security businesses frequently exist wherever Fuqra members are active," stated investigators with the U.S. Department of Justice in a 2005 report entitled, "Identifying the Links between White-Collar Crime and Terrorism."(Appendix E)

Customs records showed that Al Fuqra members traveled to Pakistan under the guise of working for PSI, carrying money to set up a security agency in Pakistan. "They actually carried (the money) to Gilani," said Fenger, "and we were able to prove that amount of money going through different bank accounts in different states" ended up in Pakistan.

James D. Williams was listed as president of PSI. Through research, investigators learned he was also the leader of Sector 5 of Muhammad Commandos (Sector 5 being the Colorado "jamaat" of Al Fuqra). He was also named as the owner of McClane's Carpenter & Home Builders, another fake contracting business involved in the worker's compensation fraud, and was named as the purchaser of the Trout Creek Pass compound, the money having been laundered through various bank accounts before he made payments on the land. He was ultimately convicted of conspiracy to commit first-degree murder in the Arizona imam case, along with racketeering and forgery in the worker's compensation scams.

Williams was arrested in the Trout Creek Pass raid, but escaped and remained a fugitive until 2000, when he was caught in Lynchburg, Virginia. He was returned to Colorado and a year later he was sentenced to 69 years in prison. At the time of his second capture, Williams was living at the Red House compound in rural Virginia, close to the city of

Lynchburg. From at least the mid-1980s through 1990, Williams was also the main leader of the Colorado Al Fuqra compound.[14]

What has become of the other men arrested during the raid at the Trout Creek Pass compound? Vicente Rafael Pierre was sentenced to just four years of probation in July of 1993 for his part in defrauding the Colorado worker's compensation fund and was permitted to return to his home in Pennsylvania. The sentencing judge described Pierre's role in the fraud as minor, and further pointed out that Pierre had not taken part in any actual terrorist attacks. In 2001 Pierre was arrested in Virginia, along with his wife, Traci Upshur, for obtaining firearms by fraud. Because he was convicted as a felon in 1993, he was not allowed to own any firearms. He was living at the Red House Al Fuqra compound at the time. He was sentenced to two years in prison and has not been heard from since.

James Upshur and Edward McGhee have not been heard from in recent years. It is believed they served several years in prison, behaved themselves, were released, and then disappeared. What happened to Chris Childs, whom Fenger described as "the one who got away" as the raid began at Trout Creek Pass? At this writing, no one seems to know.

The Four Faces Of Al Fuqra

Fenger's research resulted in the discovery of what she calls the "four faces" of Al Fuqra. First, there is the Sufi militant lifestyle they lead on the compounds, which are also called "baits." They raise families in a communal setting, teach their children at home, garden and raise their own food and live in contented isolation from the rest of the world. "That is the face they put to the public," said Fenger.[15]

Then there is the second face, which focuses on their income. The common sources of income from all the Jamaat Al Fuqra compounds are food stamps, welfare, worker's compensation, student loans and subcontracting as construction workers. Al Fuqra Muslims living at compounds throughout the nation have devised multiple other sources since then, including drug and arms trafficking. In almost all the cases, there are no income-tax reports filed and no taxes paid on the income.

The third face is the establishment of front organizations like Professional Security International and other security-related firms, that appear to operate as legitimate companies. They are used to gain access to sensitive targets in the United States and to gain firearm permits. Through PSI and other phony security firms, Al Fuqra members also communicate to Sheikh Gilani in Pakistan, as well as other terrorist "jamaats" (communities).

The fourth face is terrorism. It includes the covert activities that have been carried out at the many Al Fuqra compounds across the nation, such as combat and jihad training, stockpiling weapons, making explosives and surveilling targets. Once trained, the "soldiers" carry out undercover commando assignments against their targets: Hindus, Jews, Christians, other Muslims, and anyone who disagrees with them. Every terrorist act conceivable has been committed, including murder.(Appendix F)

Hurricane Katrina

Years after the Colorado worker's compensation scam and revelation of numerous white-collar crimes committed by Al Fuqra, the group's front organization, Muslims of the Americas, was in business again taking advantage of American citizens. In 2005, following Hurricane Katrina, Muslims of the Americas (MOA) formed a group it called "Hands to Hands Social Services Agency," ostensibly to help Katrina victims. Funds donated to Hands to Hands have been traced back to its Pakistani leader, Sheikh Mubarik Ali Gilani, funneled through the Al Fuqra/MOA headquarters in Hancock, New York.

When contacted, one of the Hancock officers admitted that "some money" collected for Katrina victims had been sent to Gilani in Pakistan, and that Gilani "sometimes directs where the money should go."[16] Amazingly, Hands to Hands is still in operation, with an active web site that is still soliciting donations at www.handtohand.org.

Lessons Learned

In the early 1990s, as the Colorado Al Fuqra case was coming to an end, an FBI agent paid a visit to Susan Fenger's office. Fenger had spearheaded a two-year-long investigation into the Muslim camp, their members, fraudulent activity, theft and terrorist activity. She was in the process of successfully prosecuting the top four suspects and had managed to shut down the terrorist camp where most of the activity took place. Susan Fenger's hard work had not only paid off, but it also exposed the existence of a vast network of terrorist activity operating beneath the radar in neighborhoods throughout America.

The FBI agent walked into Fenger's office and told her bluntly that Sheikh Mubarik Ali Gilani, the leader of Al Fuqra, had placed a $50,000 bounty on her. She had become a marked woman.

"They advised me that Fuqra had put a bounty on the FBI woman," she said. "That's what they called me, the 'FBI woman,' because I had been working with all the FBI agents." But Fenger was not with the FBI, even though she worked with their task force to help make her case. Gilani "was angry that he had to put up bond for all these guys, to bond them out (early in the case). It cost him a fortune to put up all these guys' bonds" and he wanted Fenger dead. He was willing to pay a little more to punish her for exposing his network of terrorist-training camps.[17]

Ironically, although the FBI did not conduct the investigation, they scooped up all the evidence at the end of the trial and it has never been seen again, not since the verdicts were handed down in 1993. This "norm of secrecy" within the FBI has perpetuated the view of the FBI as the "black hole of intelligence information; everything goes in and nothing comes out."[18]

The FBI, Fenger confirms, still has Al Fuqra on their radar and they are watching them, [19]although they will not officially confirm the existence of any investigations into Al Fuqra and its front organization, Muslims of the Americas.[20]

All these years later, Fenger still believes the goals of Al Fuqra are the same. "Based on my knowledge of the group and my knowledge of what other law enforcement agencies are continuing to do, the group's goals have not changed," Fenger said in a 2007 interview with Christian Action Network. "Their methodology, perhaps, has changed, as to how they go about accomplishing their goals."

Sheikh Gilani started Al Fuqra—now more commonly known as Muslims of the Americas—camps "for training purposes, and as enclaves for these different groups," Fenger added. Gilani "wanted them to live together, just like Jim Jones ... if you remember, he purchased land in Guyana to bring them together under his control. The more he could keep people away from civilization, the more he could control them."

Fenger has confirmed that while Jamaat Al Fuqra compounds appear to be quiet in recent years, they are spreading throughout the world, with jamaats planted in the Caribbean, Indonesia, Malaysia and other international locations.

"I place Gilani along the same type as a person like Jim Jones and David Koresh," said Fenger. "He has the same kind of ability to con, and has those kinds of leadership qualities that people follow ... In a way, it's bigger than a cult. They all work together.

"They want to return to the times of caliphas," Fenger added, when the Ottoman Empire ruled the world and everyone lived under Sharia law.

Explosives material and weapons found at the MOA compound in Buena Vista, CO, during a raid in 1992.

"Call me God."

Note left for police by beltway sniper John Allen Muhammad.

"I play the stupid fool. Look at how I act and speak. Everybody underestimates me. It gives me the edge I need to study, conquer and overcome."

Beltway sniper Lee Boyd Malvo, writing to a fellow inmate in prison.

CHAPTER 6

The Beltway Snipers

KIP BERENTSON, RETIRED SERGEANT WITH THE U.S. ARMY, remembers watching the news about the Beltway Snipers who terrorized the Washington, D.C., region in October of 2002. After a multi-week killing spree that left 10 dead and another three wounded in the beltway region, the snipers were arrested and identified as John Allen Muhammad, 41, the leader and elder of the two, and his 17-year-old murderous protégé, Lee Boyd Malvo.

Berentson was horrified, but not all that shocked, when he heard the news. As the headlines played on TV, Berentson opened his wallet and pulled out a dog tag and piece of paper. On the paper was scribbled the name "John Allen Williams." The dog tag contained Williams' Army ID number.

"In the back of my mind, I knew our paths would cross," Berentson told the Seattle Times after Muhammad's conviction. "That face has been in my mind for 11 years."[1]

For years Berentson felt that Muhammad was a ticking time bomb. During Muhammad's service in the Persian Gulf War, when Berentson was his superior officer, Muhammad was suspected of throwing a thermite grenade into a tent where 16 of his fellow soldiers were housed. Made of aluminum mixed with a metal oxide, and packing a blasting heat up to 1,200 degrees, thermite grenades are used to destroy equipment during battle. Berentson was in the tent at the time of the grenade attack and remembers that all 16 men ran out coughing and gagging but were amazingly uninjured. The grenade went off near a staff sergeant with whom Muhammad had fought earlier that day, Berentson told investigators. Muhammad was led away in handcuffs and eventually transferred to another company pending charges.

Although it was widely believed that Muhammad was guilty of throwing the grenade and nearly killing 16 of his fellow soldiers, he was never indicted or court-martialed, and he finished out his Army stint without further episode.

Seeing Muhammad's face on the news years later, Berentson was overwhelmed with anguish and guilt that he could not have stopped him. But Berentson could not have known that just one year after being discharged from the Army, Muhammad would join the Nation of Islam. Moreover, his penchant for violence would be fueled to the boiling point in subsequent years through his association with an obscure group of Muslim extremists known as Muslims of the Americas (MOA), the front organization for the radical terror group Jamaat Al Fuqra.

At this writing, years after the Beltway sniper attacks, the media is still reluctant to label the two killers as jihad-inspired Muslims. There are numerous psychological profiles of both snipers which attempt to explain their descent into violent madness. Some say Muhammad was disenfranchised from white society and his explosive final chapter was inevitable. Others say his sniper murders were a ruse to create havoc while he tried to regain custody of his children. Even those who see the obvious link to radical Islam focus more on Muhammad's connection to the Nation of Islam, failing to appreciate that Muhammad had shifted his allegiance to Jamaat Al Fuqra prior to the sniper killings. This was an important shift, because Jamaat Al Fuqra is the sworn enemy of the Nation of Islam and its leader, Louis Farrakhan, and Al Fuqra advocates a more violent jihad against its enemies.

"Muhammad gravitated to an organization at odds with the Nation of Islam and aligned with the Wahhabist sect of Islam associated with Al Qaeda, Osama Bin Laden and Sheikh Rahman (ringleader of the first World Trade Center attack in 1993)," writes Christian M. Weber, contributing editor for Soldiers for the Truth. "In America today, one organization fits that bill—Al Fuqra."[2]

But to really understand why Muhammad recruited the young and impressionable Malvo and then went on his murderous rampage, it's important to explore his earlier life and, most of all, why he walked into the welcoming arms of the Muslims of the Americas.

The Making Of A Sniper

While the young Lee Boyd Malvo may not be the brainwashed victim that many portrayed him in the immediate aftermath of the sniper attacks, it is undeniable that Muhammad was the mastermind and leader of the two. Muhammad's early upbringing in Louisiana was dominated by physical abuse, and in some cases even torture, at the hands of his relatives. In court testimony his defense team argued that Muhammad, who grew up as John Allen Williams, was brutally beaten multiple times by the relatives in whose care he was left following the death of his mother when he was just a toddler.

"Our life was pure hell," said Aurolyn Marie Williams, one of Muhammad's sisters. "We just got beat. I wouldn't wish the life I had ... on my worst enemy."[3] She told authorities that all six Williams children were beaten with electrical cords, switches and hose pipes. On more than one occasion a brutal uncle used to shock Muhammad by forcing him to touch the sparkplug on the lawnmower while he pulled the cord.

"We didn't know anything but beatings," confirmed Muhammad's oldest sister, Bessie Williams. "We were raised like animals."[4]

After high school, Muhammad got married and joined the Louisiana Army National Guard. Although his military career seemed promising at first because of his strength, agility and keen marksmanship, his behavior started to fray around the edges. He was court-martialed twice, once for failing to report for duty and another time for hitting an officer.[5]

The year 1985 was an eventful one for Muhammad. He separated from his first wife, joined the Army, remarried to a woman named Mildred Green and also converted to Islam. At the time, he was stationed in Washington State, where he and Mildred and their growing family lived. He excelled at shooting and ultimately would serve in Germany and the Middle East, where the thermite grenade incident occurred.

In the early 1990s Muhammad was drawn into the Nation of Islam. Some reports state that while stationed in the Gulf he read *The Autobiography of Malcolm X*, the story of the ex-con who became the most famous militant leader of the Nation of Islam. The group is strictly an American amalgamation, blending black nationalism, a sprinkling of doctrine from the Jehovah's Witnesses and some Islamic teachings. It teaches that the black man is the "god of the universe," the father of civilization, and the white man is the devil,[6] hence the cryptic note left by Muhammad for police claiming, "Call me God."

Muhammad joined the Nation of Islam while still in the Army and stationed in the United States. It is believed that he legally changed his name from Williams to Muhammad in October, 2001, just a month after the September 11 attacks.

Despite the thermite grenade incident, Muhammad was honorably discharged from the Army in 1994, having received numerous military decorations during his Gulf War service, including the Southwest Asia Service Medal, the Kuwait Liberation Medal and the Saudi Arabia Liberation Medal. He had also received mechanic training in the Army, and, following his discharge, he opened his own auto shop. The shop failed, however, and so did a karate school that he briefly opened.

Nation of Islam

By the mid to late 1990s, Muhammad was a regular member of the Nation of Islam. He began dressing in a suit and tie and attended weekly meetings of a Nation of Islam study group in Seattle, Washington. His Black Muslim comrades in Seattle greeted each other as "god," foreshadowing the note he later left for police during the sniper killings.[7] In 1995 he helped provide security for the Million Man March on Washington, organized by Farrakhan's Nation of Islam.

Throughout the 1990s Muhammad, whose work history was becoming erratic, was somehow able to travel not only throughout the United States, but also to the Caribbean and Canada on numerous unexplained trips. "Muhammad did quite a bit of traveling and always seemed to be able to get money," one law enforcement officer said after the sniper arrests.[8] Later, when word got out that Muhammad and Malvo were connected to Muslims of the Americas/Jamaat Al Fuqra, his travels, especially to the east coast, Canada and the Caribbean, and his unexplained access to funds, began to make sense. Jamaat Al Fuqra members have traveled the world on jihadi business, yet many of them hold no real jobs. Investigators have learned that their main method of financing is scamming the American welfare system, ID fraud, and establishing front companies to obtain and launder money. Muhammad, while later living at a homeless shelter in Seattle with Malvo, was able conduct his travel arrangements from the shelter. Muhammad and Malvo were also known to have traveled to California, where the largest Muslims of the Americas compound existed at the time in the Sierra mountain foothills, known as Baladullah (city of God). The 1,000-acre compound even maintained its own airport. (See chapter 15)

"Not many men at the shelter got phone calls from travel agents," reported the Seattle Times. "It was as if Muhammad was using the shelter as a base of operation."

In 1999, Muhammad's second wife Mildred filed for divorce, striking a devastating blow to Muhammad's desire to control and mold his children. He began to threaten her, demanding visitation, and by the next year she had obtained a restraining order against him. But just weeks after the order was obtained, Muhammad kidnapped his three children and fled to the Caribbean island of Antigua.

It is in the Caribbean, where a strong Muslim presence thrives and where Jamaat Al Fuqra operates additional guerilla training compounds, that Muhammad is believed to have made his break from the Nation of Islam and connected with Al Fuqra, a move which fueled his growing thirst for a more radical and violent outlet to express his Islamic faith.

In Antigua he also met a 14-year-old teenager who would become his partner in the beltway sniper killings, Lee Boyd Malvo.

The Trigger Man

Malvo was born in Jamaica, the son of Una James, described as an "itinerant mother."[9] Muhammad, who was hiding out on Antigua with his three children to avoid losing custody of them, earned some money trafficking in false passports and immigration visas. He may have learned the trade from fellow Muslims living in the Caribbean, since ID fraud is a hallmark of the MOA and its sister group, Jamaat Al Fuqra.

Malvo's mother, "who was consumed by a desire to live in the United States,"[10] was one of Muhammad's customers in Antigua. She paid Muhammad for a false ID and headed to Florida, planning to bring her son there once she was settled.[11]

Malvo, though just a boy, was a well-mannered, clean and muscular young man, but he was frequently on his own while his mother tried to eke out a living in Antigua. With his mother now illegally in the United States, Malvo became close with the man who had helped his mother escape the island, John Allen Williams, soon to be known as John Allen Muhammad. Neighbors on Antigua reported that Malvo lived with Muhammad and began calling him "dad."[12]

Muhammad returned to Seattle with his three children, still hiding from the authorities, and enrolled them in school there under false identities. In early 2001, Malvo entered the United States illegally, using fraudulent IDs provided by Muhammad, and joined his mother in Miami. In a disturbing irony, Malvo and his mother were detained by immigration officials in late 2001 for being illegal immigrants, but they were released on the promise that they would attend immigration hearings.

Around the same time, Muhammad's ex-wife Mildred located him in Seattle, and he was forced to surrender the children, losing custody to Mildred. She quickly fled with the children to Maryland and went into hiding, but Muhammad was not alone for long. Malvo left his mother and joined Muhammad in Seattle, where they began a bizarre existence together, living mostly in homeless shelters and gaining a reputation as a dangerous and disturbing pair.

The two lived together at the Lighthouse Mission for the homeless in Bellingham, Washington, which is about an hour and a half north of Seattle. Following the snipers' arrest, *The Free Republic* reported that their acquaintances considered them homosexual lovers. One man who exercised with the pair at the local YMCA commented: "It was a gay relationship ... Muhammad put his arms around Malvo and (was) seen kissing him on several occasions. There were quite a few gay guys at the YMCA and if any of them looked at Malvo, Muhammad would get furious. He often felt the young man's muscles after a workout and said Malvo was his pride and joy. He told the young man, 'Allah is going to be proud of you. You must be strong to do his work.' The kid was totally in Muhammad's power."[13]

Whether or not Muhammad and Malvo had become homosexual lovers is unclear. What is clear is that after the September 11, 2001, attacks had been carried out, Muhammad was increasingly in touch with radical jihadists, and his protégé began weapons and combat training in earnest. Their base of operations in Washington State is no coincidence. Al Fuqra has a history in Washington State; Hindu and Sikh religious institutions were bombed in Seattle and Tacoma, Washington, by Al

Fuqra members, just a year before Muhammad, then known as
John Allen Williams, was stationed nearby at Fort Lewis.[14]

A few days after the 9/11 attacks, Muhammad, who was living at
the mission in Bellingham, wandered into the Horseshoe Restaurant, a
popular local eatery and tavern. He sat at the bar and listened while
some locals sipped their morning beers and expressed outrage at
Osama Bin Laden. One of the locals said the United States should bomb
the hell out of Al Qaeda. Muhammad interrupted.

"In a calm, even tone, he told the men that the CIA had sponsored
a lot of terrorism in the world, and that the U.S. was itself a terrorist
state," the *Seattle Times* reported. "The group glared at the stranger who
interjected himself into a private conversation. One man came unglued.
He was a local fisherman and crabber named Drew Sandilands ... If anyone had reason to, it was he: His cousin was the airline pilot of one of
the jets that was hijacked and slammed into the World Trade Center.
Sandilands told Muhammad to get out or he would 'get his ass wh-
upped.' Another man in the group, Tracy Ridpath, held Sandilands
back. As calmly as he had walked in, Muhammad walked out into daylight and out of trouble. Sandilands followed him outside, but
Muhammad was already gone. The fisherman later told his buddies that
he had a feeling Muhammad was a terrorist."[15]

By this point Muhammad was fully radicalized, and his jihadi contacts were urging him on to violence.

East Coast Connections

Red House, Virginia, is a remote country location with thousands
of acres of woodland to hide in. The most notable landmark is the court-
house in nearby Appomattox where Lee surrendered to Grant, thus end-
ing the Civil War. Hidden in the woods in Red House, along a road
named "Sheikh Gilani Ln," is a 100-acre Muslim compound that served
as a perfect hideout for the Beltway Snipers during their killing spree. It
is believed that Muhammad and Malvo also had frequent contact and
support from the Red House compound prior to the killings, raising the
possibility that MOA may have helped fuel and fund their murders.

Other east coast connections are evident. The FBI investigated the
snipers' affiliation with the radical Dar Al Hijrah mosque in Falls
Church, Virginia, which is known to have provided shelter to at least

two of the 9-11 hijackers. Muhammad and Malvo are known to have attended jumah (Friday prayer services) there, yet the FBI has gone silent on this possible link.

The link goes even further than it appears. The Dar Al Jijrah mosque frequented by the snipers was founded by members of the radical Deobandi movement, another offshoot of Al Qaeda and connected to Jamaat Al Fuqra. One of the Deobandi's most influential "missionaries" was Sheikh Mubarik Gilani, who eventually established dozens of compounds based on the militant Deobandi principles and called the compounds Muslims of the Americas. They were, of course, only front compounds for the terrorist group Jamaat Al Fuqra.[16]

Another east-coast connection with the snipers was focused in Maryland. By late 2001, Muhammad had broken from the Nation of Islam and was associating with Muslims of the Americas/Jamaat Al Fuqra. The pending shootings in the area of Silver Springs, Maryland, were focused around the Ahmadiyya Muslim community, an offshoot Islamic group greatly reviled by Jamaat Al Fuqra and its leader, Sheikh Gilani.

The Ahmadiyya group is also known as United Submitters International. The group has twice been targeted by Al Fuqra in the United States. In 1983, a leader of the Ahmadiyya sect was shot to death in his home in Michigan. Hours later, the Ahmadiyya mosque in nearby Detroit was firebombed. Two Fuqra members, William Cain and Calvin Jones, were found burned to death inside the mosque, along with the gun that they had presumably used to kill Ahmad. And in 1990, an Egyptian Ahmadiyya imam, Rashid Khalifa, was stabbed to death in his Tucson, Arizona, mosque by Al Fuqra assassins.

Investigators have theorized that the snipers may have received assistance from Al Fuqra in Red House, Virginia, to not only create a reign of terror against America, but to punish the Ahmadiyya community in Maryland for breaking away from Al Fuqra's radical beliefs.

Boys' Camp

One statement made by Malvo after his arrest went unnoticed by many in the media, but it is yet another clue that the snipers were either active Al Fuqra recruits, or sympathizers. Malvo testified that Muhammad had plans to "set up a camp to train children how to terrorize cities."[17] This startling revelation fits perfectly with the operational structure of MOA. At this writing, residents of MOA camps are now into the fourth generation; they are almost all black Americans, usually born of poor, young black women and raised from birth to be jihadists. Muhammad's plan was to recruit young boys, take them to Canada, where Muslims of the Americas had and still has a strong presence, and form a training camp where an army of Islamic jihadists would be molded.

It is exactly what the MOA have been doing in the United States, Canada, the Caribbean and in other countries, yet the national media, law enforcement and many of our congressional representatives refuse to acknowledge it.

In fact, the clues were everywhere, but they were ignored. While the snipers were living at the homeless mission in Washington State, the shelter's executive director, Rev. Al Archer, concluded that Muhammad was dangerous and that he was linked to Islamic extremists. Nearly a year before the sniper killings, he contacted the FBI, but they did not respond.

"After I got to know Muhammad better, I suspected him of being part of a terrorist organization," Archer said. "I called the FBI in October, 2001, but tragically, they didn't listen to me."[18]

For months Muhammad and Malvo trained for what was to come. They practiced their shooting skills on old tree stumps. Muhammad imposed on the young man a spartan exercise program and a special diet, one that consisted of honey and crackers, to help train for life on the road.

The killing was about to begin.

The Murders

Police believe Muhammad and Malvo committed their first killing in February of 2002, on the opposite end of the country from their future beltway killings. On that day they knocked on the door of the home of Isa Nichols in Tacoma, Washington. Nichols had kept the books for Muhammad when he ran a mechanic's service, and she had sided with Mildred in the recent custody dispute. She had also helped police track down Muhammad and their three children when they were in hiding in Seattle.

Nichols was out on an errand when the knock came. Her 21-year-old niece, Keenya Cook, answered the door and was shot in the face, dying instantly. It was a revenge killing and not Islamic inspired, but it established that both men were ready and willing to kill. Within the radical Muslim community, "honor" beatings and killings are encouraged to make a statement and preserve the "honor" of the attacker.[19]

The next victim was a golfer who was shot from a distance in Tucson, Arizona, in March of 2002. Malvo bragged to a friend prior to the Beltway shootings that Muhammad had shot the golfer, Jerry Talor. The link was confirmed when authorities proved that Muhammad and Malvo were visiting Muhammad's sister in Tucson at the time of the shooting. She lived just a few blocks from the golf course. There was no firm terrorist motive this time, just the urge to get in some practice shooting for the slaughter ahead.

Muhammad and Malvo began living like vagabonds, formulating their killing plan. They took a bus to Baton Rouge, Louisiana, and stayed with some of Muhammad's friends in August. They already had their sniper rifle, a Bushmaster .223 stolen from a store in Tacoma, Washington. In Baton Rouge they told everybody their final destinations were Washington, D.C., and, eventually, Jamaica. This was apparently true, because during the Beltway murders they demanded that 10 million dollars be placed in a bank account in Jamaica. When that was done, they would stop the attacks.

In September of 2002, Muhammad and Malvo made their way to Trenton, New Jersey, and, on the one-year anniversary of the 9-11 attacks, they purchased the now-infamous blue 1990 Chevrolet Caprice for $250. While Muhammad registered the car at a New Jersey Motor Vehicles office, Malvo called in a phony bomb threat to the same office one year to the very minute that the first jetliner hit the World Trade Center.

During the month of September in 2002 the snipers did a lot of traveling, leaving a bloody trail along the way. It is believed they killed six people that month, possibly up to nine or more. There were shootings in Maryland, Alabama, Louisiana and Georgia, but they were not yet connected by law enforcement. They had already created a shooting hole in the trunk of the Caprice, where it is believed Malvo hid while Muhammad did most of the driving. Malvo, now 17, was no longer an innocent. He had been trained to kill, and it is believed he was the trig-german on most of the shootings.

Early in the evening of October 2, 2002, a 55-year-old man was shot and killed in the parking lot of a grocery store in nearby Wheaton, Maryland, kicking off the Beltway shootings, where another 10 people would die and three more would be shot and injured.

It was not "random chance that the killing spree started on October 2, the anniversary of the conviction of World Trade Center bombing ringleader Sheikh Omar Abdul Rahman in 1995," wrote terror expert Christian M. Weber.[20]

The next day five people were shot and killed as they went about the ordinary activities of their lives—one mowing a lawn, one mailing a package, one crossing a street, two filling their cars with gas. By October 4, America woke up to the reality of another horrifying episode of ter-rorism with no end in sight. Yet for months, even years afterward, the connection between the sniper attacks and an obscure Muslim sect with dozens of legally established American compounds would not be made.

Throughout the ordeal Muhammad and Malvo left notes for au-thorities, and at one point even called the police asking them to state on TV: "We have caught the sniper like a duck in a noose." They also de-manded $10 million to end the killing, to be deposited in a bank ac-count in Jamaica, where radical Islamic activity thrives.

The attacks came to an end on October 24, 2002, when Muhammad and Malvo fell asleep in their Chevy Caprice at a rest stop near Myersville, Maryland. A motorist and an attendant at the rest stop noticed the pair and the car, which matched descriptions released by the media, and they called police. In the back seat was the Bushmaster rifle. (Appendix G)

The case was easily made. The snipers, in one of their notes left for police, took credit for a shooting in Alabama. What the snipers did not know was that Malvo had left a fingerprint at the scene. Immediately af-ter the snipers left the note for police, investigators traced the finger-print to Malvo and then quickly made the connection to his companion Muhammad. Before they were found asleep in the Chevy Caprice, police already had a good idea of who they were looking for.

During the days and weeks that followed, the national media made no mention of "Islam," "Muslim," or "terrorism." Muhammad was described as an ex-soldier, a former Army combat engineer and a Gulf War veteran who was an expert marksman. Malvo was usually described as an illegal alien from Jamaica, a misguided youth and clueless dupe of Muhammad. The overriding news theme was that the Beltway Snipers, as they became known, were disenfranchised, lone serial killers unassociated with any official terrorist group.

Soon reports began to surface that Muhammad had been a member of the Nation of Islam. Some reporters learned that the FBI was also investigating the snipers' link to Jamaat Al Fuqra and rumors that they had used the Red House, Virginia, compound, as well as an Al Fuqra compound in Commerce, Georgia, to hide out during their killing spree.

To counteract what should have been the obvious conclusion that Muhammad and Malvo were Muslim terrorists, the Council on American-Islamic Relations (CAIR)—a Muslim Brotherhood-founded organization—issued a statement demanding that the media avoid linking Islam with the snipers.

"Police reports indicate the suspects acted alone, based on their own motivations," the CAIR statement read. "There is no indication that this case is related to Islam or Muslims. We therefore ask journalists and media commentators to avoid speculation based on stereotyping or prejudice. The American Muslim community should not be held accountable for the alleged criminal actions of what appear to be troubled and deranged individuals."

A willing media readily agreed to comply.

Malvo Talks

In a shocking phone interview from prison in July, 2010, Lee Boyd Malvo claimed that he and Muhammad killed 42 people during their killing season in 2002. He also said that there were at least three other snipers involved in the scheme, ready to kill in other regions of the country, but they backed out at the last minute. Investigators labeled Malvo's comments as "ridiculous" and have refused to reveal they are investigating the claims.[21]

Yet Malvo's interviews with investigators—and even more so his prison drawings—have provided a significant window into the minds of both Malvo and Muhammad and the terrorist mindset that motivated the two. A number of detailed, violent drawings, replete with anti-

American and anti-Semitic comments, were made by Malvo while in prison, proving that he was every bit as murderous as Muhammad or any other Islamic terrorist. Included in his portfolio of drawings are the following:

- A detailed depiction of the White House in the crosshairs of the scope of a rifle with this caption: "You will weep and moan & MORN. You will bleed to death, little by little. Your life belongs to Allah. He will deliver you to us." To the side of the White House, another caption says: "Sept. 11 we will ensure will look like a picnic to you."
- A self portrait of Malvo peering through the scope of a rifle while exclaiming, "Allah Akbar" and the following verse: "Many more will have to suffer/Many more will have to die/Don't ask me why."
- An etching of Malvo and Muhammad together with the words: "We will kill them all. Jihad."
- A sketch of Osama Bin Laden with the caption: "Servant of Allah." The sketch is labeled as Bin Laden, but also bears an eerie similarity to photos of the leader of the Muslims of the Americas, the group that hid Malvo and Muhammad: Sheikh Mubarik Ali Gilani.
- An image of the World Trade Center with a jet flying into it and this caption: "You were warned."
- Drawings of Islamic dictators Saddam Hussein and Muammar Gaddafi, along with the verse: "Our minarets are our bayonets/Our mosques are our baracks (sic)/Our believers are our soldiers."
- A drawing of a man who resembles both Bin Laden and Gilani, with the verse: "Say not of those who die in Allah's cause that they are dead, they are living tho ye perceive it not. Islam the only true guidance, the way of peace. Do not take our kindness for weakness."
- A depiction of words from Surah 2:190 in the Quran: "Fight in the cause of Allah those who fight you and slay them wherever ye catch them."[22]

At this writing, Lee Boyd Malvo is in his mid-twenties and is serving six consecutive life sentences for murder without parole. Muhammad, who remained mostly quiet during his murder trials and while on death row, was executed by lethal injection in November, 2009.

It is impossible not to notice the similarities between Malvo's drawings, the jihadist declarations he made, and those of Sheikh Mubarik Gilani, the Pakistani cleric who founded and still leads MOA/Jamaat Al Fuqra, which provided sanctuary for the two assassins in 2002.

Gilani, who also fancies himself a poet, wrote:

"We pray to the beat of a submachine gun. Come join my troops and army, says our Sheikh Gilani. Prepare to sacrifice your head, a true believer is never dead. Say 'Victory is in the air,' the infidel's blood will not be spared."[23]

The so-called "Beltway Snipers" before their killing spree, John Allen Muhammad, right, and Lee Boyd Malvo.

Jailhouse drawings of Beltway sniper Lee Boyd Malvo.

Jailhouse drawings of Beltway sniper Lee Boyd Malvo.

"The possibilities were stupefying. New York would be struck by a series of powerful explosions that would bring the city to its knees. First, bombs would go off in the Holland and Lincoln tunnels, trapping thousands of commuters deep below the Hudson River in the ultimate claustrophobic horror. The lucky ones, those closest to the explosions, would die instantly. The unlucky would be shredded by flying glass and metal or crushed by falling debris, then burned alive."

Tom Morgantha writing in *Newsweek* about the thwarted "Day of Terror."

CHAPTER 7

The Original Ground Zero

FOR MOST AMERICANS, THE ATTACKS ON SEPTEMBER 11, 2001, brought Islamic terrorism into painfully sharp focus. Prior to that day, terrorist attacks by Muslims were infrequently mentioned in the news, dismissed as aberrations, incidents of petty crime or foreign activity in remote lands that had little to do with America. They were quickly forgotten. After 9-11, however, our national conscience was altered forever; it is estimated that there have been more than 16,000 acts of Islamic terrorism throughout the world since 9-11.[1]

Yet in the decade preceding 9-11, terrorist activity was simmering. There were, in fact, dozens of Islamic-inspired terror attacks in North America alone, many of them deadly, with several potentially catastrophic plots thwarted just in the nick of time. This chapter will examine several of those plots, schemed up with the aid of an obscure group known as Jamaat Al Fuqra, a.k.a. Muslims of the Americas, the group which still exists today, unmolested, in the form of dozens of Muslim compounds on American soil.

These were the original Ground Zero targets.

1991: The Canadian Fuqra Plot

Some would call Canada the original "ground zero" target of Islamic terrorism in North America, following a failed plot to kill more than 4,500 Hindus and Indians in the area of Toronto in the fall of that year. The plot was uncovered when several members of the terror group

Al Fuqra were stopped as they tried to sneak across the Canadian border from the United States.

The men, most of whom were originally from the Caribbean where Al Fuqra had—and still has—a large presence, included a black man named Barry Adams, who also went by the name of Tyrone Cole, among other aliases. Before trying to sneak across the border into Canada, several of the terrorists, including Adams, had lived for a few years in Texas under American aliases, trying to blend in and establish American identities. Detaining them at the Niagara crossing, border agents found a sheet of paper in their vehicle with the statement: "Dying as a soldier of Allah." Agents also found disturbing evidence with the men, including aerial photos, videotaped interiors, entry plans, instructions for building bombs, diagrams showing ways to plant explosives around natural gas lines and more.

The documents found also included assignments for a "hit team," a "guard team" and a "recon team," which detailed how the attackers would enter one building through the window of a men's restroom and how a woman could hide a bomb in the women's restroom. Border agents also found homemade videos of the defendants. Another document gave a hint of the conspirators' ideological motives, describing at what hours the largest number of Indians could be killed at the two targets.[2]

There was clear evidence that this was not a small-scale plot, but rather had been planned for months in minute detail. Questioning the men for several hours at the border, investigators soon learned that they, along with other accomplices soon to be arrested in Canada, planned to attack thousands of Hindus and Sikhs in Toronto while they celebrated the annual Festival of Lights, known as Diwali. This five-day festival in Hinduism and Sikhism is one of the most important festivals of the year and is celebrated by families through traditional activities together. The targets were the India Centre Cinema, with a capacity of 500 people, and the Vishnu Hindu Temple, with a capacity of 4,000, both in Toronto. The terror plot was set to climax at the two separate locations one after the other. One decade before the 9-11 attacks, the planned Toronto attacks would have killed 1,500 more people than the worst terror attack ever carried out.

Investigators would also learn that the conspirators, totaling five in all, were members of, or frequent visitors to, a Muslim community called

Hasanville, a rural enclave in Ottawa, Canada, purchased just one year before for the Muslims of the Americas/Jamaat Al Fuqra. All of the conspirators were followers of Sheikh Mubarik Ali Gilani, the Pakistani cleric who had made a name for himself in Brooklyn during the preceding decade preaching jihad and recruiting black Americans from prison to join his militant crusade against unbelievers.

One of the five men spilled his guts during the investigation and admitted they all worked for Jamaat Al Fuqra and were followers of Gilani. In an interview taped by the Canadian Broadcasting Company during the investigation, Gilani, from his base in Pakistan, admitted that "one or two of the men" charged in the conspiracy had studied with him in Lahore, Pakistan, but he insisted that Al Fuqra did not exist, and that he does not advocate violence. To this day Gilani denies the existence of the very organization he created.[3]

A book seized by police titled *Mohammedan Revelations*, contained a passage written by Sheikh Gilani: "The mission of this Jamaat Al Fuqra is to lead Muslims to their final victory over Communists, Zionists, Hindus and deviators."[4]

Three of the men, including Barry Adams, were convicted in 1994 of "conspiring to commit mischief endangering life." They were sentenced to 12-year prison terms in Canada, while two others received two-year prison terms. Another Muslim comrade was let go. None of the terrorists were convicted for conspiracy to murder, despite the overwhelming evidence that death and mayhem were their intent.

Barry Adams and his comrades served their prison terms well. Adams, in particular, was singled out for his exemplary behavior, although he was denied early release in 1998. After 12 years, the three men were quietly released and deported from Canada in 2006. At first, Canadian authorities refused to say where the men had gone, but it was later learned they were sent back to their homes in Trinidad and the Dominican Republic. In May, 2006, the Trinidad Express confirmed that two Trinidad and Tobago citizens "who were jailed in Canada for involvement in acts of terrorism" had been deported back to Trinidad and Tobago.[5]

The entire plot targeting 4,500 Canadian citizens was easily forgotten ... until the fall of 2010, when it was revealed that Barry Adams was not living in Trinidad, as authorities believed, but was thriving as the

leader of the Muslims of the Americas (MOA) headquarters in
Hancock, New York.

Not only is Barry Adams—a plotter of the foiled Canadian mas-
sacre—alive and well, but he is also the highest-ranking member of Al
Fuqra in the United States, second only to its founder and leader, Sheikh
Gilani in Pakistan. At Gilani's death, it is understood that Adams will
lead Jamaat Al Fuqra in the United States.

1993: World Trade Center Bombing

Most Americans know that the 9-11 World Trade Center attacks
were not the first assault on the Towers; they were the biggest and deadliest, but not the first. In February of 1993, Muslim terrorists planted a
truck bomb in the basement of the towers that detonated, killing six
people and wounding more than 1,000. Involved in the successful 1993
World Trade Center bombing and an unsuccessful series of attacks
planned elsewhere a few months later was Clement Rodney Hampton-
El, a former U.S. military fighter and member of Al Fuqra, trained, in
part, by the CIA.

Hampton-El has been referred to as the "Frankenstein created by
the CIA." Hampton-El even referred to himself as Rambo. "Many people have come here to see who this Rambo is after all," he told one interviewer following his trial. "I tell them it's something they will have to decide in their own mind."[6]

One observer noted: "We created a whole cadre of trained and motivated people who turned against us. It's a classic Frankenstein's monster
situation."[7]

Hampton-El grew up wanting to fight. As a young man radicalized
into Islam at New York City and New Jersey mosques, he volunteered to
fight with the in Afghanistan in the 1980s when they were fighting
Soviet aggression with the aid of the United States. The mujahideen, or
jihadists, received training and weaponry mainly supplied by the CIA.[8]
Estimates are that from 1985 to 1992, 12,500 foreigners were trained in
bomb-making, sabotage and urban guerrilla warfare in Afghan camps
the CIA helped to set up. Since the fall of the Soviet "puppet" regime in
Afghanistan, another 2,500 are believed to have passed through the
camps. Tragically, they are now run by an assortment of Islamic extremists, and at one time were ruled by Osama Bin Laden.[9]

Hampton-El would later testify that after making a reputation for himself overseas as a fierce jihadi fighter, he was summoned to the Saudi Arabian embassy and allotted a budget of $150,000 to recruit and train American servicemen as fighters. He was told the money was being supplied by wealthy Saudis who were sponsoring jihad operations in Bosnia, a reference to Osama Bin Laden and his backers.[10]

"These moneys, a small portion would be given to me to establish a training program," Hampton-El stated. "The remaining would be given to people who went to Bosnia to help the people to support their families, to pay their bills, etc., here in America."[11] The day after the meeting at the embassy, Hampton-El was given a list of U.S. soldiers who were completing their tours of duty to recruit as potential jihadists. Not coincidentally, Sheikh Gilani was also busy at this time recruiting and training jihadists, most of them American blacks, to fight in Afghanistan and Bosnia.

The Saudis had other jobs for Hampton-El, as well. Early in 1993, prior to the World Trade Center bombing, he traveled to Europe, where he received large amounts of cash from wealthy Saudi donors who were trying to protect their identities and brought it back to the U.S. "Some of the money went to fund terrorist training and operations on U.S. soil, some of it was earmarked for Bosnia," writes one reporter.[12]

Hampton-El, like many of the Muslim volunteers in the Afghan war, acquired the reputation of being a "zealous troop" who did not avoid "fierce combat." The fighters' policy was to take no prisoners. One expert on Afghanistan described them as having "the reputation as some of the most brutal fighters in the war, and they deserved it. They kept themselves apart from the Afghans and were disliked for it. They regarded themselves as superior."[13]

After he was wounded in the Afghan war in 1988, Hampton-El returned to the United States and received treatment at Long Island College Hospital. Interviewed by a researcher seeking information on wounded fighters, Hampton-El stated that he desperately wanted to go back to Afghanistan to have "another chance at martyrdom and paradise."

Back in his Brooklyn neighborhood following the Afghan war, Hampton-El became known as "Dr. Rashid," a reference to his Muslim name, Abdul Rashid Abdullah, which he adopted while living in and attending mosques in Brooklyn—among them the Al Farouq mosque where Sheikh Gilani preached. Hampton-El fought drug dealers and dispensed medical advice and became known as something of an oddball for wearing a ninja-type outfit to patrol the streets as a vigilante. He also became increasingly more radicalized in his Islamic faith, and it is around this time that he may have first made contact with Jamaat Al Fuqra. It is known that Sheikh Gilani had a loyal following in Brooklyn mosques. Hampton-El, already an expert fighter, later continued his jihad training at a Fuqra camp near Harrisburg, Pennsylvania.

"Before I left on jihad (to Afghanistan) I had a super bad temper," Hampton-El said in his hospital interview. "I wanted to take care of business."[14]

Hampton-El had become something of a celebrity, known for his ninja outfits, vigilante spirit and for being a firebrand speaker on Islam. There are reports that during this time the FBI was monitoring Hampton-El's activity and knew he was training at an Al Fuqra camp, but they did nothing about it.[15]

Hampton-El became even more militant in 1980 when author Salman Rushdie published his *Satanic Verses*, a book which the Islamic world considered blasphemous against the prophet Mohammed. Hampton-El participated in a demonstration in New York against the book and in favor of the fatwa (edict) pronouncing a death sentence on the author. (The fatwa was lifted, but is back in effect today, offering a reward to any Muslim who carries it out; Salman Rushdie continues to live in hiding in Great Britain.)

Hampton-El "had established himself as a go-to guy for guns and other jihad supplies, such as explosives and detonators. He paid for weapons from gun shows, local stores and freelance sellers ... Rashid made deals with Al Fuqra."[16]

Through training with fellow jihadists and at the Jamaat Al Fuqra camps he frequented, Hampton-El became an explosives expert. By 1993, Hampton-El was in league with a cell of jihadists based in New York and New Jersey, under the umbrella of Al Qaeda with ties to Al Fuqra and its terror training facilities. The cell was plotting a number of attacks against the United States. The first would take place on February 26 at the World Trade Center.

The epicenter of the attack was the parking garage beneath the Twin Towers, where just after noon a massive eruption blew out a nearly 100-foot crater several stories deep and several stories high. Six people were killed almost instantly. As people poured out of the towers, many panic-stricken and covered in soot, smoke and flames streamed upward into the buildings. More than 1,000 people were injured in some way, many with crushed limbs. The terrorists later confessed that their plan was to so seriously damage one of the towers that it would fall over into the other tower, bringing both of them down. Eerily, that scenario is very close to what ultimately happened in 2001, yet by that time the terrorists had figured out a better way to accomplish it, using airplanes.

The small band of attackers had left the bombs, which Hampton-El helped to create, in a rented truck in the parking garage. The FBI, which, it was later learned, knew that Islamic terror activity was on the rise and may have known about the imminent attack on the World Trade Center, was immediately on the scene. In the rubble, investigators uncovered a vehicle identification number on a piece of wreckage that matched a rented van reported stolen the day before the attack. Soon three Muslims were in custody, and a storage locker containing bomb-making chemicals—enough to wipe out a small town—was found.

In the course of the trial it was revealed that the FBI had an informant, Emad Salem from Egypt, who claimed he had informed the FBI of the plot to bomb the towers as early as February 6, 1992, a year before the attack.[17] It was Salem who had been in contact with Hampton-El about the explosives used at the World Trade Center bombing. The information ultimately led to Hampton-El's arrest in June of 1993.

Of note is that Salem was also a member of the notorious Al Farouq Mosque in Brooklyn, the same mosque where Sheikh Gilani staged his coup in the 1980s against the Dar-Ul-Islam sect and planted his flag for Jamaat Al Fuqra. It has since been the stage for a number of notorious Islamic terrorists and was a major recruiting office for Al Qaeda. It is still in existence today on Atlantic Avenue in Brooklyn. Salem testified later that he had offered to spy on the mosque for the FBI, but they did not accept his offer.

The big shock for investigators after Hampton-El's arrest was not so much that he was a member of another splinter group of Al Qaeda, the then-obscure Jamaat Al Fuqra. After all, the FBI had known about Al

Fuqra for nearly 13 years and still viewed it as a group involved in heresy disputes between Islamic sects and other religious groups, not broad terrorist conspiracies.

No, the shock came when Hampton-El and other World Trade Center bombers revealed that they were planning a massive "Day of Terror" which would have killed hundreds of thousands of people in July, 1993, had it been carried out.

1993: Day of Terror

What many Americans don't know, or have easily forgotten, is that the 1993 World Trade Center attack, as horrific as it was, was only one in a series of Islamic assaults planned for the same year by the same group of Muslims that would have killed multiple thousands. This second plot, the unsuccessful "Day of Terror," was uncovered as investigators were continuing to unravel leads in the first World Trade Center bombing.

The results of the investigation were shocking: The terrorists planned to bomb a series of New York landmarks simultaneously, including the U.N. building, the Holland and Lincoln tunnels and the Javits Federal Plaza, which houses the FBI offices in New York City. The group also intended to simultaneously kill Egyptian President Hosni Mubarak, U.N. Secretary-General Boutros Boutros-Ghali, New York Senator Alfonse D'Amato and New York State Assemblyman Dov Hikind, an outspoken supporter of Israel. The plot was unveiled when, acting on a tip from their undercover informant, FBI agents stormed a warehouse in Queens, New York, and caught several members of the terrorist cell in the act of assembling bombs. Hampton-El was arrested within a day at his home in Brooklyn.

"The possibilities were stupefying," wrote one journalist following the Day of Terror investigation. "New York would be struck by a series of powerful explosions that would bring the city to its knees. First, bombs would go off in the Holland and Lincoln tunnels, trapping thousands of commuters deep below the Hudson River in the ultimate claustrophobic horror. The lucky ones, those closest to the explosions, would die instantly. The unlucky would be shredded by flying glass and metal or crushed by falling debris, then burned alive in the uncontrollable gasoline fires that would surely break out next. Two more explosions would follow: at the United Nations building on Manhattan's East Side and at the Jacob Javits Federal Building near City Hall. Swamped by multiple catastrophes, police, fire and ambulance crews would be stretched beyond their limits. New York would panic."[18]

Just eight years later, the terrorists' learning curve would advance so significantly in the art of terror that they would accomplish that ultimate panic by totally collapsing both Twin Towers with hijacked airplanes.

Hampton-El received a 35-year sentence in 1995 for seditious conspiracy, bombing conspiracy and attempted bombing. He was never convicted for his role in the first World Trade Center bombing. Now in his early 70s, Hampton-El has traded his ninja threads for a prison jumpsuit and is serving his sentence in Colorado's Supermax prison alongside Ramzi Yousef, a 9-11 conspirator; Terry Nichols, one of the Oklahoma City bombing conspirators; the Unabomber and other dangerous terrorists.

Hampton-El was not the only member of Jamaat Al Fuqra involved in the Day of Terror plot, although it is impossible to know how many other conspirators were schooled in the art of jihad at any of the Fuqra training camps. Earl Grant was arrested a few days after Hampton-El in Philadelphia and charged with conspiracy to transport explosives. He received three years' probation and was released.

Lessons Unlearned

The attempted Canadian bombing, the first World Trade Center bombing, the Day of Terror plot and dozens of other acts of terrorism are examples of obvious lessons the American people and our representatives have refused to learn—despite evidence that could not be clearer.

The resolve of Islamic terrorists, coupled with the FBI's reluctance or refusal to share their information or act upon it, are fomenting another disaster waiting to happen.

The real tragedy of these plots are the nearly 3,000 victims of 9-11 and other victims who have followed them—attacks which could have been prevented. The victims cry out from their graves not only for justice, but also for vigilance against the very plotters who lived among us then and live among us still. Many of them are terrorists in the making right now, living and training for jihad in Jamaat Al Fuqra camps across the country, funded by the American taxpayers through stolen welfare money. These terror camps are right now, as this is being read, breeding hatred for the very country and its citizens who give them the freedom and funding to plan their own executions.

Wreckage from the first World Trade Center bombing in 1993.

Clement Rodney Hampton-El, a member of MOA/Al Fuqra and one of the planners of the original World Trade Center bombing in 1993.

Sheikh Mubarik Ali Gilani, founder and leader of Muslims of the Americas and Jamaat Al Fuqra.

A still taken of Sheikh Gilani, taken from the "Soldiers of Allah" guerilla training video.

Photo of bullet-riddled American flag, used for target practice at an MOA/
Al Fuqra compound in Wayne County, Pennsylvania.

A resident of the Red House, Virginia, MOA/Al Fuqra compound attacks
the front of our car when we attempted to show leaders of the camp the
guerilla training film, "Soldiers of Allah."

This road sign announces the entrance to the Red House compound in rural Virginia.

Police were called when Christian Action Network attempted to show the guerilla training film, "Soldiers of Allah" to residents of the York, South Carolina, compound.

View of a portion of the York, South Carolina, MOA/Al Fuqra compound. The large building in the center was declared a shrine in 1996 after a fax from Sheikh Gilani was received there, prompting "a perfected (sic) shaped rainbow (to appear) on the ceiling of the room where the fax machine sat" containing the names of Allah and the prophet Mohammed.

An aerial view of a portion of the Commerce, Georgia, MOA/Al Fuqra compound.

115

Aerial view of the Red House, Virginia, MOA/Al Fuqra compound.

Aerial view of the Hancock, New York, MOA/Al Fuqra compound, showing a guardhouse at the entrance road. The compound is the headquarters for MOA.

Aerial view of Muslim cemetery on the Hancock, New York
compound of MOA/Al Fuqra.

The entrance sign at Holy Islamville in rural York County, South Carolina,
also advertises the International Quranic Open University, founded
by Sheikh Gilani. The university teaches students to perform miracle
healings using "quranic healing."

Informant Ali Aziz, front right, with members of the Hancock, N.Y., MOA/Al Fuqra compound and FBI agents (front row, center). Aziz lived secretly among MOA members for eight years.

FBI agents attended a picnic at the New York headquarters of MOA/ Al Fuqra in 2005 to celebrate the Muslim Boy Scouts of America. FBI Agent Philip Irizarry sent the following note to the camp following the visit: "I just wanted to thank you again for a great day yesterday. It was a pleasure presenting to the boys ... I have attached the pictures we took memorializing the event and we look forward to the graduation in August, Inshallah ... Salaams on our behalf."

"Although terrorist groups are in many ways similar to traditional organized crime groups, (they are) unique in the following ways: Members are driven by their belief systems, and money is not raised for the benefit of individual members; it is used to promote the group's cause ... Members of the Fuqra group have raised money by taking advantage of a variety of social services programs, including worker's compensation, public health care, welfare and food stamps programs."

U.S. Department of Justice[1].

CHAPTER 8

Muslims of the First State

THE ARREST OF EIGHT PEOPLE ON CHARGES OF TRAFFICKING IN counterfeit goods wasn't considered a very big story when it broke in March of 2007, but it jumped off the page when I read it.

The 7-million-dollar counterfeit scam involved the operation of a wholesale counterfeit clothing business and pirated movies and music by individuals in four states. Under various store names, the counterfeiters sold fake brand-name merchandise at low prices. I knew that Muslims of the Americas (MOA)—and other terrorist and terrorist-related groups—had a history of financial fraud, welfare scams and tax fraud, with the money often laundered and funneled into more dangerous criminal activity, including drug dealing, illegal arms sales, assassinations and other forms of terrorism.

One of the accused, Ronald Roundtree of Lynchburg, Virginia, lived less than 10 minutes from our offices. He is well known for his association with Sheikh Gilani and has lived both in the city of Lynchburg and at the MOA compound in Red House, Virginia. Roundtree was also known as Muhammad Talib.[2] Several of his wives, who had lived with him in a polygamous marriage at the MOA camp in Red House, were also detained in the original arrest.

Another name also popped up on the list of counterfeiters: William Statts of Dover, Delaware, who was charged with conspiracy to traffic in counterfeit clothing and pirated movies and music.

At the time, this new name meant nothing to me; he was just another unidentifiable person among of a host of mysterious names, aliases and associates within the Sheikh Gilani terrorist empire. Soon, however, the name of William Statts would solve one of the biggest and most controversial questions surrounding Muslims of the Americas.

Was MOA recognized by the IRS as a tax-exempt organization?

During our first two years of investigation, we came across numerous, seemingly endless, news and law enforcement reports stating that MOA was a tax-exempt organization. But how could this be? Just think of the public outrage if the American people learned that the IRS gave a tax exemption to a terrorist organization.

It just became too shocking to think that an organization with a 20-year history of violence, terrorism, criminal scams, drug running, gun running, fire-bombings and murder could really be tax exempt. The question of a tax exemption for MOA could not be easily ignored, especially if true. More important, it could not be repeated as FACT if untrue.

I searched the IRS web site. MOA was not listed. I called the IRS; they had no record of giving Muslims of the Americas a tax exemption. I plunged our organization into months of investigative legwork to find the truth. After a year of research, we had no evidence that the IRS had given a tax exemption to MOA.

Tax Exempt

Then two things occurred almost simultaneously. The first happened when I learned of an organization calling itself "Muslims of the First State," which claimed to be doing business as Muslims of the Americas. It was listed as a tax-exempt organization. Furthermore, the IRS verified that Muslims of the First State was, indeed, tax exempt.

But was this the same organization as Sheikh Gilani's Muslims of the Americas? It was difficult to determine at face value. The organization had no tax filings with the IRS, having listed itself as a church. And the only public information about the group was its president's name, Brent Garfield, and that it was incorporated in Dover, Delaware.

I had no sooner discovered this information when a Virginia State law enforcement officer told me to watch the news. He said something big was about to happen regarding Sheikh Gilani's terrorist organization.

About a week later, news broke of eight people arrested by the FBI in a 7 million dollar counterfeit ring. Having been tipped off by law enforcement that this was an MOA bust, I knew each of those arrested was working within the Gilani terrorist empire.

When I looked up the address for William Statts, one of the accused counterfeiters listed in the FBI indictment, it was listed as 329 W. Loockerman St., Dover, Delaware. The address was nearly identical to that of Muslims of the First State, which was 331 W. Loockerman St. The addresses were close, separated by just two digits, but not an exact match. There could be no room for error in determining whether the two were connected. The gravity of accusing the IRS of giving a tax exemption to an international terrorist organization was of such high import that we could not make a mistake, no matter how logical the connection appeared on paper.

It is important to understand the benefits of being a tax-exempt organization, especially if that organization files as a church. All tax-exempt groups are immune from paying taxes. But after that, it gets complicated. Some tax-exempt groups can lobby Congress. Some cannot. Some tax-exempt groups must file an annual report with the IRS. Some do not. In certain cases, donations to a tax-exempt group are deductible for personal income-tax purposes. Some are not. In some cases, states require a tax-exempt group to be audited by a certified public accountant. Other states do not demand this audit. The IRS codes governing tax-exempt groups are voluminous, difficult to comprehend and exacting.

However, if you file as a church, then forget about all these burdensome regulations, rules, filing requirements, annual reports, pesky IRS agents and audits. Just put the money in the bank and spend it as you wish.

The reason churches are exempt—not only from taxes, but from prying government eyes—is because of this clause in the First Amendment to the U.S. Constitution: "Congress shall make no law respecting an establishment of religion or prohibiting the free exercise thereof..."

There have been legal challenges brought by the IRS against a few churches which claim a religious exemption, but only sporadically and very cautiously. Even these periodic legal cases never challenge whether a church can be tax exempt or free of government supervision. They have basically challenged whether or not the so-called church is really a religious institution. For example, the IRS won a legal battle against a "church" calling itself "The Church of Sunday Night Football" for obvious reasons. To put it simply, if a religious entity has a long history of being an established religion (such as Christianity, Islam, Buddhism, etc.), the IRS will not challenge its right to claim tax-exempt status. This is important to understand because Muslims of the First State seemingly has a religious history and would not necessarily raise alarms within the Internal Revenue Service.

The danger of giving tax-exempt status to a terrorist organization that claims to be a church is easily recognized.

Contributions to a church are tax deductible. And though the IRS may be aware of the contribution, (especially if the donor claims the deduction on his personal taxes), the IRS will not know how the church spends that money. The church is not only free from paying all taxes (state, local and federal), but it does not have to report to any government agency its income, expenditures, acquisitions, donor names, bank accounts, administrators, board members or employees. Imagine the dangers of this lack of government oversight if the so-called "church" is really a terrorist organization.

Holy Land Foundation

The case of the Holy Land Foundation is an example of how easily a tax-exempt Islamic group can funnel money into terrorism. In 2004 a federal grand jury brought a 42-count indictment against the organization with charges that included conspiracy, providing material support to a foreign terrorist organization, tax evasion and money laundering. In 2009, the founders of the Holy Land Foundation (HLF) were sentenced to life in prison for funneling $12 million to Hamas.

The successful government prosecution of the Holy Land Foundation, however, may give us a false sense of hope that a terrorist-sponsoring group, masking itself as a benevolent religious institution, can be brought to justice. There are important differences and observations to be made between the Holy Land Foundation and Muslims of the First State.

First, it must be made clear that it was not easy for the federal government to bring charges against the Holy Land Foundation (HLF). The organization was founded in 1989 and its founders were not successfully prosecuted until two decades later, even with suspicions about the group funneling money to Hamas arising almost immediately, in 1990. It then took another 11 years before HLF was listed as a *Specifically Designated Global Terrorist* by the U.S. Department of Treasury's Office of Foreign Asset Control. Another three years passed before indictments were handed down in 2004. Then another three years followed before a trial of its leaders could begin in 2007. That trial was quickly declared a mistrial by Judge Joe Fish because jurors could not reach a verdict. Then another year went by before the second trial could begin in 2008. Then, finally, 20 years after the formation of HLF, its founders were convicted in 2009. Not easy.

The Muslims of the First State "church" presents even greater problems for the IRS and other federal agencies which might want to investigate the so-called "church." The one thing both Muslims of the First State and the Holy Land Foundation have in common is that both became front groups for terrorist organizations: The Holy Land Foundation became a front for Hamas; Muslims of the First State became a front for Muslims of the Americas.

But there are important differences. The Holy Land Foundation was listed with the IRS as a charitable organization, meaning it had the responsibility of filing a Form 990 with the IRS detailing its income, expenditures, activities, grants, investments, non-cash contributions, board members and many other filing requirements. Even a relatively small tax-exempt organization can find itself answering or providing 30 pages of detailed information to the IRS. Because a charitable organization is under the intense scrutiny of the federal government, it is much easier for the IRS to red-flag certain income, activity and expenditures as suspicious.

Muslims of the First State, on the other hand, is listed with the IRS as a "church," and therefore is not responsible for government filings whatsoever. This makes it nearly impossible for the government to track the organization. They can deposit money; spend money; make acquisitions; receive non-cash contributions; conceal the names of their board members, associates and employees; and open up numerous bank accounts—all without government oversight.

It doesn't take much imagination to put two and two together when federal investigators bust a 7 million dollar counterfeit clothing ring in which one of the accused may also be connected to a tax-exempt church called Muslims of the First State—which also claims to be doing business as "Muslims of America."

As a side note, even though Sheikh Gilani's organization is officially known as Muslims of the Americas, it is oftentimes shortened by the media and some of its own members to simply Muslims of America. That being said, one cannot assume that any group calling itself Muslims of America is necessarily associated with Sheikh Gilani. It's just too ubiquitous a name. For this reason, it became important to make sure there was no mistake in the connection between Muslims of the First State and Gilani's Muslims of the Americas.

Connecting The Dots

To remove all doubt, it meant we had to travel to Dover, Delaware, and connect the dots.

Delaware is known as the best state in the nation to form a corporation. The fees are extremely low, the paperwork is light, and the process can be accomplished in one day. Furthermore, Delaware has no sales or personal property tax, and the physical presence of a corporation is not required to incorporate in Delaware. It made perfect sense for Sheikh Gilani to form a tax-exempt corporation there.

At the Delaware Division of Corporations, I located the incorporation papers for Muslims of the First State. The organization was officially formed in September of 1998 under the name Muslims of the First State, Inc. Nearly a year later, it sought to be recognized as a tax-exempt corporation for "charitable, religious and educational purposes."

Under Article IV, its mission was (1) to promote the practice of the Muslim faith, (2) to carry out acts that accomplish this purpose, and (3) "to solicit, receive and administer funds, grants and property for the above purposes ..."

But it was Article V that brought us one step closer to connecting the dots between Muslims of the First State and Muslims of the Americas. William Statts, who was charged in the 7 million dollar counterfeit ring and, as a result, was now a known member of Sheikh Gilani's terrorist organization, was listed as a member of the Board of Directors for the "church." William Statts was already on his way to amassing a lengthy criminal record, including arrests and convictions for felony thefts, possession of illegal firearms, drug trafficking and fraud. Yet here he was listed as a director of a tax-exempt "church."

It was becoming clear the IRS had given a tax exemption to a front group for Sheik Gilani's terrorist organization in the same manner the IRS had given a tax exemption to the Holy Land Foundation as a front group for Hamas.

Still, we had to be sure, though the evidence was mounting.

It was impossible to interview William Statts; his whereabouts was unknown after his arrest. Our best hope was to find Muslims of the First State in the Dover, Delaware, area and start asking questions. The mosque listed several addresses on its various filing forms with the State Division of Corporations, but each address proved futile. One building was empty. Another had been converted into a garment store. Another had been converted into a day care center. Still another was occupied by a man with a live-in girlfriend. Neighbors vaguely remembered a mosque in their area, but knew little or nothing more. We visited a prominent Muslim leader in Dover. Although he was familiar with Sheikh Gilani, he knew nothing about a mosque called Muslims of the First State. We talked to the local FBI. We spoke with the county Sheriff's Department. They knew nothing. We were coming up empty.

Our last hope was to find the president of Muslims of the First State, Brent Garfield, who was also listed as a board member. We had a home address that he poorly, almost illegibly, scribbled on one of the state filing forms. Unsure if we had the correct street address or even the right unit number, we visited a slum area with ill-kept buildings and vagrants loitering throughout the neighborhood. It was mid-afternoon. Eyes were fixed on us the moment we drove up, not only from the street, but from within the apartment buildings. Pulling out camera equipment only served to draw more attention to us.

A Knock On The Door

We knocked on the door of what we hoped was the apartment of Brent Garfield, but there was no answer. We knocked on a neighbor's door. A young woman answered and told us there was a man living in the unit next to her; she wasn't certain of his name but knew he worked at the Domino's Pizza up the street. We visited the Domino's store and learned that Brent Garfield, indeed, worked there, but was out of town on a medical emergency that would keep him away for several days.

Though we felt relief that we had Brent Garfield's correct address, we were also disappointed that we were going to have to travel back to Virginia and then make another trip to Delaware to actually confront him. And we would have to do this without any assurance that he would be at his home on the next trip. But the issue of a terrorist organization having an IRS tax exemption, especially a tax exemption that does not require any government oversight, was too important to ignore. The amount of funds that could be laundered through this tax-exempt group to buy or sell drugs, illegal weapons, operate counterfeit schemes or fund terrorist operations could literally be in the millions—and the IRS would never know. There are absolutely no reporting requirements for a church, not even a bank account.

During our second trip we spent two heat-soaked days knocking on Brent Garfield's door with no answer. The Domino's Pizza was of no help. He had quit his job. Not knowing his whereabouts, we reluctantly prepared to leave the next morning, once again failing to gain incontrovertible evidence that Muslims of the First State was a front group for Muslims of the Americas.

My staff and I packed that morning, checked out of our motel and met at a local diner for breakfast. Though frustrated at not being able to meet Brent Garfield, we discussed the evidence we had linking the two groups. Perhaps we had enough: William Statts was a director of Muslims of the First State and was also arrested in the FBI bust of a counterfeit ring that involved members of Muslims of the Americas. We also knew that William Statts listed a home address that was just two digits apart from the one-time headquarters of Muslims of the First

State. We also knew that Muslims of the First State claimed to be doing business as Muslims of America, which is often an abbreviated form for Muslims of the Americas.

Was this enough? Maybe. But I still felt uncomfortable. If we were somehow proved wrong, it could jeopardize the perceived integrity of all our other research, information and investigation into Sheikh Gilani's terrorist organization. After all, we were already claiming that there were approximately several dozen Islamic terrorist camps scattered around the United States. This was going to be controversial enough. But then to say that they are tax exempt would be pushing the absurd into the incredulous. There could be no room for doubt or error.

As we paid our breakfast tab, we discussed making one final attempt to knock on Brent Garfield's door. It was out of our way back to Virginia, and we had just knocked on his door the previous night with no answer. And we were already discouraged enough that we didn't really want to add a reminder to our unsuccessful trip by making another fruitless journey to a slum area where, by this time, we were beginning to look like undercover FBI agents. But we made the trip anyway.

There was more scurrying about in the neighborhood when we pulled into the low-rent, subsidized housing project. Our silver Armada was becoming well known by the residents at this point. And I think the neighbors were also becoming curious to see if Brent Garfield would ever answer his door when we knocked upon it. We knocked. There was no answer. Perhaps there was a collective and disappointed sigh throughout the entire project that he did not answer. Curiosity, even among the neighbors, was peaking. We decided to write a message on a piece of paper asking Garfield to call us when he returned home. Our interviewer, Jason Campbell, walked the sheet of paper up to the doorway to perch it between the screen door and the entrance door when, all of a sudden, the door opened.

We were all shocked when a very sleepy, confused-looking man stood in the entryway. Brent Garfield is white, in his mid-thirties, with a beard dyed red in the classic tradition of venerating the prophet Mohammed. Jason explained our purpose for the visit, and Brent invited him into his home. "This is a bad neighborhood," he told Jason, ushering him into his living room.

When asked about Muslims of the First State, Brent Garfield said, "I was part of it, but that was like years ago. I don't know, about six years ago." Jason asked if he would go on camera to talk about the tax-exempt group, but he declined, saying, "I can't go on without permission."

Permission From Whom?

"I am a member of Muslims of America," Garfield said, explaining that he needed permission from his MOA superiors to go on camera to talk about Muslims of the First State.

Obviously, this did not shock us. Even off camera, he said very little about the tax-exempt group. Garfield admitted he knew the accused counterfeiter, William Statts, who was also a board member of Muslims of the First State. But Garfield wouldn't admit that Statts was an MOA member. "You have to ask *him* that," he told Jason.

Garfield said he established the tax-exempt organization to "have a place of worship." The reason the group had several locations in the area was because they failed to pay rent. "They were just centers we had established for prayer."

There was little else he would say or admit to regarding Muslims of the First State.

But Garfield did say he had been a member of MOA for 15 years, that he had traveled from camp to camp inside Gilani's tightly controlled compounds and was welcomed at them all. But he was by no means a leader inside the Gilani empire.

"I'm not a leader of anything. Ever since I've been a Muslim, I've been part of the community," he said, referring to Muslims of the Americas.

Rather than talk about the tax-exempt group, Garfield wanted to spend time defending Sheikh Gilani.

"He (Gilani) teaches us to follow the Sunnah, and it's against violence and is actually to reach out towards Christians and Jews, which is why I chose to speak to you."

Garfield failed to mention that Gilani repeatedly calls Jews "human satans."

"I've been taught in this community from the very beginning to obey the laws. This is our country," he said. "Obey the laws. Be the best community. Be the best husbands. Be the best fathers. Be the best brothers. Open your hands to the non-Muslims and the Christians and the Jews."

He claimed people are kicked off the compounds for drinking. "The good people continue to build, the bad people go to jail," he said. "People that commit crimes do need to go to jail."

It was quite apparent that Garfield was well versed in the Gilani spin machine regarding criminals inside the camps. When members are arrested for various crimes, Gilani claims, they are simply infiltrators, sent by Gilani's longtime enemies (Dar-ul-Islam, in particular) to bring harm, embarrassment and shame upon his peaceful camps.

"So over 20 years it's been weeded out," Garfield said. "These criminal individuals have been weeded out and gotten arrested. They were criminals before he (Gilani) came."

Some crimes, of course, can't be blamed on Gilani's former enemies. William Statts and six other MOA members arrested in the 7 million dollar counterfeit ring were recent and prime examples of dedicated Gilani followers committing crimes. But Garfield dismissed these criminal elements. "When people left to join this community, they brought their baggage with them," he said.

One of those with "baggage," however, was his own board member of the Muslims of the First State, William Statts. Garfield would only say of his former friend and board member: "If he committed a crime, he needs to go to prison."

We learned very little from Garfield about the activities of Muslims of the First State. But we now knew it was set up by a 15-year member of Muslims of the Americas. This was the evidence we needed to verify that Muslims of the First State was a front group for Muslims of the Americas. The fact that William Statts, who was accused in the $19 million counterfeit scheme, was also an MOA member and a board member of the tax-exempt group, was now simply icing on the cake.

Even the little Garfield told us about Muslims of the First State could not be trusted information. He started the conversation by saying he was a "part of it," but it was "like years ago. I don't know, about six years ago."

For Garfield to say he was just a "part" of Muslims of the First State, would be like Bill Gates saying he is just a "part" of the Microsoft Corporation." Besides admitting he filed for the IRS tax exemption, Brent Garfield's name has been listed on various filing forms for Muslims of the First State as a board member, treasurer, secretary, president and CEO. His name does not escape a single official title of the organization. Claiming that he was just a "part of it" was evasive and simply laughable.

Discrepancies Arise

As mentioned above, Garfield also claimed it was nearly six years previous to our meeting that he was a "part" of the organization. We met him in 2007. That would mean he had ceased his activity with Muslims of the First State somewhere around 2001. Yet his name appeared on a 2001 state filing form as CEO and president of the organization. His name would appear again on a 2005 state filing form, listing himself as the organization's treasurer/secretary, indicating he was at least involved with the organization within two years of our interview—not six.

There were other discrepancies. According to a form filed with the State Division of Corporations, Brent Garfield dissolved Muslims of the First State on January 1, 2003. Yet the form wasn't officially filed until January 21, 2005, more than two years later. Why, a reasonable person would ask, did it take more than two years for Garfield to finally (and officially) notify the State of Delaware that he had dissolved Muslims of the First State? Raising further intrigue was why the Internal Revenue Service *still* listed Muslims of the First State as an official non-profit, tax-exempt organization in 2007, more than four years since it had been dissolved?

When asked about the two-year delay in notifying the state of the dissolution and why he never notified the IRS that he had dissolved the corporation, Garfield said he simply "forgot." This is not only unlikely, but an absurd and pathetic excuse. Garfield shut down the corporation listing himself as treasurer/secretary, a title that does not have the legal authority to dissolve the tax-exempt organization. That power is reserved exclusively for the board of directors. The corporation's bylaws clearly state: "The control and disposition of its property and funds shall be vested in the Board of Directors of the Corporation."

Garfield would have us believe that somehow he "forgot" for more than two years that he dissolved a corporation on New Year's Day 2003 and then, when he did remember in 2005, he forgot to tell the IRS. To understand the significance of what this means: Garfield's "church," even after it was dissolved, could continue to operate as a non-profit organization—receiving all the tax benefits, deductions, deposits and expenditures afforded such a "church"—even though it was a corporation that did not exist. A more likely scenario is that something happened between Jan. 1, 2003, and Jan. 21, 2005, that Garfield wanted to cover up. He wanted Muslims of the First State to disappear in the eyes of state and local authorities after Jan. 1, 2003. But—and this is important— Garfield did not want the "church" to disappear in the eyes of the IRS. He wanted the newly dissolved Muslims of the First State to continue to operate as a tax-exempt entity.

The Potential For Fraud

Failure to notify the IRS that the "church" was dissolved makes it easy to see the potential for fraud, deception and diversion. Garfield (or anyone else connected with Muslims of the First State) could continue to set up tax-exempt bank accounts throughout the country, even after the dissolution of the company. All that was needed was for Garfield to present the bank the Employer Identification Number. These newly created bank accounts could go unreported to the IRS because, very simply put, they *don't have to tell* the IRS the location of their banks or their bank account numbers.

It does not take much of an imagination to understand the benefit to a terrorist organization which can travel around the country setting up tax-exempt bank accounts whose funds, receipts and expenditures are not only unreported, but untraceable to the IRS. A bank in Arizona, for example, won't know that Garfield dissolved the corporation in Delaware as long as Garfield presents the bank its Employer Identification Number, which was still valid since Garfield had failed to notify the IRS of its dissolution.

To make matters worse, once the bank account is established, the bank will never know if the corporation loses its tax-exempt status. Why? Because the IRS does not even know the bank account exists. Remember, a church does not have to notify the IRS of any money matters.

When I complained to Garfield that for more than two years he failed to notify the IRS that he dissolved Muslims of the First State, he told me he would call the IRS and notify the agency. During the next several months I frequently checked with the IRS to see if Garfield had honored his word. Not surprisingly, he had not. I then called him, giving him a final ultimatum: If he did not notify the IRS that Muslims of the First State had been dissolved, I would file a formal complaint with the IRS. Within days the "church" had been removed from the IRS rolls as a tax-exempt organization.

The dangers of giving a terrorist organization tax-exempt status should be obvious to all. But those dangers are compounded when the IRS designates such an organization as a tax-exempt "church," which has no fiscal accountability, no forms to submit to government agencies, and no legal requirement to track money received or spent. There should be no mistaking the sinister motives of MOA member William Statts: The same man who was accused in a 7 million dollar counterfeit ring was also a founding board member of a tax-exempt "church" connected to a terrorist organization.

Muslims of the First State is no longer in existence, but the lure of having a tax-exempt church, with its ability to hide and launder funds, is never far from the thoughts and minds of Gilani's terrorist empire. Therefore, it came as no surprise when we later learned that Muslims of the Americas now has another tax-exempt church at its disposal, called Ikhwanul Muslimun, Inc., located on the property of its headquarters in Hancock, New York.

But what makes this tax-exempt church different from Muslims of the First State is that it is part of another notorious terrorist organization called The Muslim Brotherhood.

"Allah is our goal; the Prophet is our guide; the Quran is our constitution; Jihad is our way; and death for the glory of Allah is our greatest ambition."

Muslim Brotherhood creed[1].

CHAPTER 9

The Muslim Brotherhood

IF YOU TYPE THE WORDS "IKHWANUL MUSLIMUN" INTO THE IRS web site in search of charities, you will learn that Ikhwanul Muslimun, Inc. is a tax-exempt organization filing as a church, and located on a 70-acre terrorist training camp in Hancock, New York—the same camp owned by Muslims of the Americas. It was registered with the IRS in 1974, yet, when contacted, the IRS claims to have no supporting or founding documents for the group. They know nothing more about them other than to confirm that they pay no taxes.

When you type the same name into the Google search window and hit the "I feel lucky" button, you will immediately be taken to the main web site for the Muslim Brotherhood (www.Ikhwanweb.com). "Ikhwanul Muslimun" is literally translated "Muslim Brotherhood" in Arabic. The Muslim Brotherhood, with proven links to terrorist outfits, therefore owns a tax-exempt "church" on a compound owned and operated by another Muslim organization with links to terror, Muslims of the Americas (MOA).

What does this connection between MOA and the Muslim Brotherhood really mean? The obvious answer is that the so-called peaceful MOA—which is known to be a front group for a radical terror group called Jamaat Al Fuqra—is working in cooperation with another known terror group, the Muslim Brotherhood. So cooperative are they, in fact, that they live together side by side in the rural New York enclave, educate their children together and share the same mosque. At this sprawling New York compound they are, in essence, one and the same.

The much more worrisome question is: Why are both groups allowed to operate in tandem and unfettered on American soil, without having to pay taxes or divulge their income sources? Why are members of both groups, with their known terrorist backgrounds and current affiliations, allowed to carry out their jihadist plans with no apparent obstruction from law enforcement, while the IRS, the FBI and other law enforcement agencies simply look the other way?

The answers are complex and have roots in American and world history.

In one sense, the link between MOA and the Muslim Brotherhood is not all that surprising. The Muslim Brotherhood, with its many tentacles and back-door connections, may, in fact, be tethered in some way to nearly all Muslim groups operating within the United States. The following groups, among many others, are known to be associated with, or initially formed by, the Muslim Brotherhood:

Hamas—One of the deadliest and most overt Islamic terrorist organizations in the world, Hamas was formed in 1987 by the Muslim Brotherhood as a Palestinian support group. Officially listed by the U.S. government as a terrorist organization, Hamas has killed thousands of people in terrorist activity since its founding.

The Organization of the Islamic Conference (OIC)—The OIC is the second largest intergovernmental organization after the United Nations. It has sponsored numerous pro-Sharia resolutions in the United Nations, including a resolution considered in 2010 that would make it a punishable offense globally to blaspheme the religion of Islam. The OIC is the umbrella organization for every Muslim nation in the world, encompassing some 57 odd states (which includes Palestine as a state). In 1990 the OIC enacted a treaty called the "Cairo Declaration," stating that the OIC and its member states define "human rights" as Sharia. The OIC is currently attempting to assume greater control of the Internet in order to implement its goal of a universal ban on "blasphemy" of Islam.

The Islamic Society of North America (ISNA)—This group's goal, as stated in its 2010 handbook, is to establish the Al Jamaah, or Islamic State, which "has the authority to enforce Sharia's political, educational, criminal justice system." Muslims of the Americas and the ISNA have jointly participated in conferences to promote Islamic issues. These conferences are frequently attended by sympathetic members of Congress and other public officials.

The North American Islamic Trust (NAIT)—This group is funded by Saudi Arabia and is today considered the financial center or "bank" of Muslim Brotherhood activities in the United States. The NAIT holds the titles to the majority of the mosques and Islamic centers in America.

The Council on American-Islamic Relations (CAIR)—This group is an advocacy group for Muslim Americans, and works to improve the image of Islam in America. It is a well-known front group for the Muslim Brotherhood, whose co-founder, Omar Ahmad, stated: "Islam isn't in America to be equal to any other faiths, but to become dominant. The Quran, the Muslim book of scripture, should be the highest authority in America, and Islam the only accepted religion on Earth."[2] Founded in 1993, CAIR typically files lawsuits against Americans and American institutions when they make statements that CAIR deems insulting to Islam.[3] CAIR was also an unindicted co-conspirator in the Holy Land Foundation case (see more information below).

The Muslim Public Affairs Council (MPAC)—Founded in 1988 as another Muslim Brotherhood front group, MPAC's purpose is to improve the public relations and "civil rights" of Muslims in America. It has a history of publicly supporting known terrorists and terrorist organizations. Shockingly, despite its terrorist connections, a 2010 report proved that MPAC is regularly invited to attend meetings with U.S. governmental groups, including the Civil Rights Division, the FBI, Department of Homeland Security, and other agencies.[4]

The Muslim American Society (MAS)—This group is now partnered with the ISNA and is the original Muslim Brotherhood in the United States. In 1992 the MAS renamed itself, and described its mission as promoting "Islam as a total way of life." Chapters can be found on hundreds of colleges campuses, where "Brothers" are recruited for jihad.

Given all these interconnections between Muslim Brotherhood front groups, mosques, terrorist training camps and terror activity in America and abroad, it's not all that surprising to learn that MOA has a connection to the Muslim Brotherhood. After all, MOA's founder and leader, Sheikh Mubarik Ali Gilani, who has been linked to Al Qaeda along with the Muslim Brotherhood, has stated his goal is to "purify Islam through violence." The Muslim Brotherhood, which takes a more political and stealthy approach, has the same goal: to "purify" Islam.

A Violent History

The Muslim Brotherhood was founded in 1928 by a young Egyptian named Hasan al-Banna who wanted to start an Islamic revival following the collapse of the Ottoman Empire. Al-Banna, like Sheikh Gilani of today, believed in the strict form of Islam and the imposition of Sharia (Islamic) law.

Al-Banna began training his followers for jihad. His group, the Muslim Brotherhood, grew quickly and became involved in Egyptian politics, as well as the Palestinian resistance to Israel. In 1948 a follower of Al-Banna shot and killed Egyptian Prime Minister Mahmud Fahmi Nokrashi. Al-Banna was assassinated one year later, presumably by government loyalists.

In the next two decades the movement grew and spread well beyond Egypt. The Brotherhood was legalized in Egypt in 1948 as a religious organization only, but was banned again in 1954 when it insisted that Egypt be governed under Sharia law.

Another Brotherhood follower, Abdul Munim Abdul Rauf, attempted to assassinate Egyptian President Gamal Abdel Nasser in 1954. Rauf was executed, along with five other Brotherhood members, yet in the aftermath thousands of Brothers fled to Syria, Saudia Arabia, Jordan and Lebanon to foment terror groups there.

In the 1950s, key leaders of the Muslim Brotherhood came to the United States after fleeing the chaotic conditions of Egypt. They settled in Indiana, Illinois and Michigan and began to hatch a plan to re-establish the global Islamic state (caliphate) and implement Islamic Sharia law in the United States.

Meanwhile, in Egypt, Nasser's successor, Anwar Al Sadat, was friendly to the Muslim Brotherhood, and promised them that Sharia Law would be implemented in Egypt. Sadat released all of the Brotherhood prisoners but made the fatal mistake of signing a peace agreement with Israel in 1979. Four Muslim Brotherhood members assassinated Sadat in 1981 during a parade in Cairo. In addition to Sadat, 11 others were killed and 28 were wounded, including the young vice president of Egypt, Hosni Mubarak—who later took control of the nation, banned the Muslim Brotherhood, and was ousted 30 years later, in 201,1 in a revolution many believe was instigated by the Muslim Brotherhood.

Back in the United States, the Muslim Brotherhood was gaining a foothold. The plan they formulated in 1987 to realize their goal of establishing a caliphate and implementing Sharia had five phases[5]:

Phase One: This was the phase of discreet and secret establishment of leadership. Throughout the 1960s, 1970s and 1980s this was successfully fulfilled.

Phase Two: This was the phase of the Muslim Brotherhood's gradual appearance on the public scene by using public activities to introduce themselves into American life and to appear legitimate. "It greatly succeeded in implementing this stage," states John Guandolo, a former FBI agent and writer on Islamic issues. "It also succeeded in achieving a great deal of its important goals, such as infiltrating various sectors of the government, gaining religious institutions and embracing senior scholars, gaining public support and sympathy."[6]

Guandolo ominously states that Phase Two also succeeded in establishing a secret shadow government within our government.[7] "Many Muslim advisers to the U.S. government are Muslim Brothers or sympathetic to the Muslim Brotherhood cause," Guandolo says. They are "advising the U.S. national leadership and our national security apparatus on how to respond to the events in Egypt and elsewhere."[8]

Phase Three: The is the escalation phase, which occurs prior to the final stages and calls for open confrontation with the leaders and institutions of the United States, mostly through use of mass media. This phase is currently in progress and obviously being employed successfully as most media outlets express support for Islamic issues.

Phase Four: This phase involves open public confrontation with the government by exercising political pressure. It is the aggressive implementing of Phase Three, escalation. This phase also involves the use of weapons training both domestically and overseas "in anticipation of zero-hour."[9]

Phase Four is in its initial stages and is making noticeable inroads. The Oklahoma lawsuit cited previously is just one example, along with a 2011 decision by a Florida judge who announced he will allow Sharia law to be used in a private arbitration agreement.

Another example is the U.S. Treasury Department adopting and encouraging Islamic financing principles. In 2008, under President George W. Bush, the Treasury held a seminar on Islamic finance to educate government and private-sector bank officials in Sharia law banking principles. Speakers included an array of Islamic "experts" with ties to radical terrorist groups.[10] The seminar was, in effect, a type of Trojan Horse, with the gates of the city opened wide by our own government.

In a memorandum written by the Muslim Brotherhood, the group's "organizational shift" is clearly outlined.

"Understanding the importance of the organizational shift in our movement work, and doing jihad in order to achieve it in the real world ... serves the process of settlement and expedites its results. The first pioneer of this phenomenon was our prophet Mohammed (sic), God's peace, mercy and blessings be upon him, as he placed the foundation for the first civilized organization, which is the mosque, which truly became the comprehensive organization. And this was done by the pioneer of the contemporary Islamic dawah (call to Islam), Imam martyr Hasan al-Banna, may God have mercy on him, when he and his brothers felt the need to re-establish Islam and its movement anew, leading him to establish organizations with all their kinds: economic, social, media, scouting, professional and even the military ones. We must say that we

are in a country (the United States) which understands no language other than the language of the organizations, and one which does not respect or give weight to any group without effective, functional and strong organizations. "[11]

Another fact worth noting about Phase Four is that it involves terror training on American soil. Clearly, the numerous training compounds owned by Muslims of the Americas fit into this phase. The FBI has known for decades that both the Muslim Brotherhood and MOA have been training jihadists on American soil. The existence of both organizations—flagrantly established as tax-exempt "churches" at the same compound in Hancock, New York—is proof that Phase Four is being carried out jointly and cooperatively by both groups.

Phase Five: This final and last stage is when Muslims seize power to establish their Islamic caliphate, within which all parties and Islamic groups will be united under Sharia law.

Holy Land Trial

In the annals of America's greatest courtroom dramas, the O.J. Simpson trial may rank at the top for its theatricality alone. The Lindberg kidnapping trial, the McCarthy trials, the spectacular Al Capone tax evasion case, Patty Hearst—even the Lindsay Lohan hearings—are known in minute detail to most Americans. Yet few know about the Holy Land Foundation trial, which proved conclusively the existence of a vast terrorist network in the United States which, in turn, was funneling millions of illegally gained dollars to the Palestinian terror group Hamas. For the vastness of the scheme alone, the Holy Land Foundation trial, which was settled in 2008, should rank number one on our list of important American trials.

The Holy Land Foundation was the largest Islamic charity in the United States, headquartered in Richardson, Texas. After the trial, it was proved that the Foundation was in reality a front group for the Muslim Brotherhood, yet, inexplicably, the Muslim Brotherhood was never prosecuted, nor have any of its numerous sister organizations been shut down.

The Holy Land Foundation purported to offer "practical solutions for human suffering through humanitarian programs that impact the lives of the disadvantaged, disinherited, and displaced peoples suffering from man-made and natural disasters." Their primary area of focus was on Palestinian refugees, according to its web site at the time—but it was actually funding Hamas to the tune of more than $12 million.

It took the federal government more than seven years to build a case and bring charges. The case began when, in 2001 following a lengthy investigation, the Department of the Treasury designated the Holy Land Foundation as a "Specially Designated Global Terrorist" and froze its assets. Federal indictments were handed down in 2004, charging conspiracy, providing material support to a foreign terrorist organization, tax evasion and money laundering.

The indictment alleged that the Holy Land Foundation provided more than $12.4 million to individuals and organizations linked to Hamas from 1995 to 2001, when their assets were frozen. The indictment also named seven specific officers of the Holy Land Foundation. Five of the seven were arrested; two others fled and are still considered fugitives.

In 2007 a mistrial was declared when jurors could not come to a unanimous decision, but a retrial in 2008 proved successful for the Justice Department, and the Holy Land Foundation was found guilty, along with five of the defendants. During the course of the trial, CAIR—the Council on American-Islamic Relations, founded by the Muslim Brotherhood—was named an unindicted co-conspirator, along with the NAIT and MAS.

"CAIR officials have met or regularly meet with current and former U.S. Presidents, members of their respective administrations, members of the United States Congress, governors, mayors, members of state legislatures and county commissioners," according to the CAIR web site, which also admits they frequently attempt to place their own interns within the U.S. government. "Several CAIR affiliates have received proclamations and citations from mayors and county commissioners. The organization itself has received praise from congressmen and women to top military officials such as General Wesley Clark ... CAIR also regularly meets with national, state and local law enforcement officials, including the Department of Homeland Security."[12]

The Holy Land Foundation sued the U.S. government, challenging its designation as a terrorist organization. CAIR also sued, demanding that its co-conspirator designation in the Holy Land Foundation trial be expunged. Both legal challenges failed, and in 2010 the FBI stated that it had formally cut ties with CAIR. The fact that the FBI ever had any ties to CAIR, or that it had cooperated with them on Muslim issues, is the most shocking revelation to emerge from that announcement.

Although the Holy Land Foundation is now defunct, CAIR—its parent organization, and itself just a front group for the Muslim Brotherhood—continues to operate from its base on Capitol Hill, manipulating members of Congress, the media and Muslims throughout the United States as it transitions from Phase Three to Phase Four in its plan to establish a global caliphate.

Shadow Government

Within the realm of Islamic issues and domestic terrorism, the FBI clearly has a major role to play. We can assume that the FBI has ulterior motives when it initiates détente with the Muslim Brotherhood and other terrorist groups operating on American soil, chief of which would be to encourage information sharing that may lead to a tip-off that terrorist activity is in the works. In building these bridges, however, is our government allowing a shadow government to be created?

Consider the following:

In 2010, representatives from ISNA, the Muslim Brotherhood front group, joined "interfaith leaders" from the National Interreligious Leadership Initiative for Peace in the Middle East (NILI) at the White House and State Department. ISNA also hosted a one-day "strategic planning meeting" for attendees.

Abdul Rahman al-Amoudi, now in prison on a variety of charges, is a Yemeni emigrant who served as Islamic adviser to President Bill Clinton. The founder of the American Muslim Council (a Brotherhood front group), he also met with George W. Bush while he was a candidate to discuss anti-terrorist laws. He was involved in the selection process of

Muslim chaplains for the U.S. military and acted as a consultant to the Pentagon for more than a decade. In 2004 he pleaded guilty to charges of illegal financial transactions with the Libyan government, unlawful procurement of citizenship and impeding administration of the IRS, as well as having a role in a Libyan conspiracy to assassinate then-Saudi Crown Prince Abdullah.[13]

In 2010, U.S. Homeland Security Secretary Janet Napolitano and her senior staff secretly met with a select group of Muslim, Arab and Sikh organizations, among them members of the Muslim Brotherhood. One critic of the confab commented: "Through the so-called partnership between the jihadi-sympathizer networks and U.S. bureaucracies, the U.S. government is invaded by militant groups."[14]

Thanks to the Obama Administration and its bailout bonanza, every American taxpayer became a stockholder in AIG, the American Insurance Group, which also runs the world's most publicly funded Sharia-compliant insurance businesses. Under the headship of Treasury Secretary Timothy Geithner, AIG retains advisory boards of Sharia experts who tell the companies which investments are permissible (halal) and which are forbidden (haram).

Muslim extremists, led by the Muslim Brotherhood, administer, in effect, a shadow government within our government—a thinly disguised form of stealth jihad.

Together Again

Despite announcing, following the Holy Land Foundation trials, that it was cutting ties to the Muslim Brotherhood, the FBI has continued its relationship with them and other radical Islamic groups. We know this because the Muslim Brotherhood is listed as the tax-exempt owner of a "church" on the terror-training compound in Hancock, New York, owned by Muslims of the America. And we know that the FBI regularly visits the MOA camp, as if the two groups were dearest friends, to keep dialogue open between them.

How do we know these visits and get-togethers occur? In recent years a photograph surfaced of a picnic on the grounds at the Hancock camp. Pictured were FBI members enjoying the food, surrounded by members of the camp, specifically the Muslim "boy scout" organization founded by MOA leader Sheikh Mubarik Gilani. Pictured among the Scout leaders, flashing a wide grin, was a young Egyptian Muslim named Ali Abdel Aziz.

What his fellow camp members never knew was that Ali was an undercover agent for the New York Police Department. He could identify every visitor at the picnic and which law enforcement agency they worked with. Now out of the shadows, Ali's story is a prophetic one, like the canary in the coal mine. In exclusive interviews that were carefully and secretly arranged, we met with Ali to hear his chilling story ... and his warnings to Americans.

Ali's dramatic story can best be understood by first understanding a central theme of Islam: the coming of the Mahdi, the Islamic version of the messiah.

"The one who will come after me is Imam Mahdi ... He will be followed by ... our friend and great Sufi master, Jesus, son of Mary. We will tell the world who he is and how he lived. As a matter of fact, he's still living in the first heaven; he's 33 years old and I know him. I have met him."

Sheikh Mubarik Ali Gilani.

CHAPTER 10

The Coming of the Mahdi

WINSTON CHURCHILL, WRITING IN 1899 OF HIS EXPERI-
ences as a soldier fighting for the British in the Sudan,
described the now infamous Battle of Omdurman.
When the dust settled at the battle's end, the combined English and
Egyptian forces had killed more than 10,000 "Dervishes"[1]—Islamic
fighters who ruled a brutal, extremist, Islamic regime in the region.
The battle was a rout for the British forces.

"The Dervishes fought manfully," recalled the young Churchill.
"They tried to hamstring the horses. They fired their rifles, pressing the
muzzles into the very bodies of their opponents. They cut reins and
stirrup-leathers. They flung their throwing-spears with great dexterity.
They tried every device of cool, determined men practiced in war and
familiar with cavalry; and, besides, they swung sharp, heavy swords
which bit deep. The hand-to-hand fighting on the further side of the
khor lasted for perhaps one minute. Then the horses got into their
stride again, the pace increased, and the Lancers drew out from among
their antagonists. Within two minutes of the collision every living
man was clear of the Dervish mass. All who had fallen were cut at with
swords till they stopped quivering, but no artistic mutilations were
attempted."[2]

Churchill continued: "Some realization of the cost of our wild
ride began to come to those who were responsible. Riderless horses
galloped across the plain. Men, clinging to their saddles, lurched help-

lessly about, covered with blood from perhaps a dozen wounds ... Two impressions I will, however, record. The whole scene flickered exactly like a cinematograph picture; and, besides, I remember no sound. The event seemed to pass in absolute silence. The yells of the enemy, the shouts of the soldiers, the firing of many shots, the clashing of sword and spear, were unnoticed by the senses, unregistered by the brain. Several others say the same."[3]

Churchill records, and history confirms, that the British army defeated the Dervishes, who were also known as the Mahdist Army, at the Battle of Omdurman in what could only be called a stunning victory of technology over manpower. The outgunned Dervish Mahdists were no match for the British and Egyptian troops. More than 9,700 were killed, 13,000 wounded, and 5,000 captured. The British and Egyptian troops lost only 47 men, with 340 wounded. With the Dervish Mahdist Army destroyed, the Sudanese war was deemed officially over.

"Thus ended the Battle of Omdurman," wrote Churchill, "the most signal triumph ever gained by the arms of science over barbarians. Within the space of five hours the strongest and best-armed savage army yet arrayed against a modern European Power had been destroyed and dispersed, with hardly any difficulty, comparatively small risk, and insignificant loss to the victors."[4]

The Mahdist Rule

This combined British/Egyptian victory in 1898 ended nearly 15 years of rigid Islamic domination of the Sudan under what is now referred to as the Mahdist rule. For centuries prior, the people of the Sudan had lived in a state of alternating war and peace with surrounding governments, religions and foreign intervention. Prior to the Mahdist wars, the Sudan was under Egyptian and Turkish control. Political corruption and spending fueled instability in the region, and in 1873 the British government stepped in to assume responsibility for all of Egypt's fiscal affairs, including the affairs of the Sudan.

Although already unstable, the region became even more inflamed when a revolt broke out in the Sudan led by a religious leader named Muhammad Ahmad ibn Abd Allah (Ahmad), a Muslim cleric who claimed he was the Mahdi—the "guided one," the promised messianic redeemer of the Muslim people who will, according to tradition, usher in the end times. It is to the Mahdi, the Muslims believe, that Jesus will bow as the battle of the end times gets under way.

Ahmad was born to a Sudanese family that claimed to be descendants of the prophet Mohammed. He showed an aptitude for religious study and Islamic Sufi mysticism. Ahmad was awarded the title of sheikh, or scholar, and began to preach a strict adherence to the Quran; any deviation among his growing cadre of followers was considered heresy and was dealt with severely.

In 1881, Ahmad announced his claim to be the long-awaited Mahdi, but not everyone recognized his claim. Egyptian officials, fearing his power and ever-growing number of followers, tried to have him arrested. In response, Ahmad declared a jihad.

"I am the Mahdi," he proclaimed in his jihad, "the successor of the prophet of God. Cease to pay taxes to the infidel Turks and let everyone who finds a Turk kill him, for the Turks are infidels."[5] His followers, the Dervishes, rallied behind him, and Ahmad prepared to take control. Out of sheer terror, most of the Sudan fell under Mahdist control with Ahmad at the head of the Dervish/Mahdist army. In a devastating loss for the British, the Mahdists took control of the city of Khartoum in central Sudan; the British retreated and left the Sudan in the hands of Ahmad and his Mahdist Dervishes. It quickly transformed into a brutal regime, which dictated that everyone must join and become a believer and subsequently declare Ahmad as the Mahdi, or be destroyed.[6] Under Ahmad's rigid Islamic leadership, the Mahdists controlled the Sudan for the next 15 years, until 1898 when the British and Egyptian forces, with the young Winston Churchill in the ranks, defeated them at the Battle of Omdurman.[7]

Following the overthrow of the Mahdist regime, the Sudan was governed as a British colony from 1899 through the 1950s, technically with an Anglo-Egyptian government administered by a Sudanese governor. In the 1950s a series of civil wars broke out, eventually leading to the independence of the Sudan from Great Britain and Egypt, but also establishing numerous internal Islamic wars. The relentless in-fighting among tribes and Islamic sects has resulted in the deaths of millions of Sudanese by both famine and war. This international trag-edy is still exhibited in the humanitarian crisis in Darfur, where mil-lions of people are displaced and suffering due to the ongoing conflict.

Throughout its tumultuous history, the people of the Sudan have been victimized by brutal warlords and their followers bent on estab-lishing a rigid Islamic state. At the core of many of these bloody skir-mishes is the concept of the Mahdist state—with the long-awaited Mahdi as its leader.

Who Is The Mahdi?

In Shia and Sunni ideology, the Mahdi—which literally means "guided one"—is the prophesied redeemer of Islam who will stay on Earth anywhere from seven to 19 years, depending on various inter-pretations and sects. Prior to the day of judgment, the Mahdi will "rid the world of wrongdoing, injustice and tyranny"[8] alongside Jesus.

In Islamic teaching, Jesus is revered as a prophet of Allah and is frequently called "the son of Mary." Muslims believe the man Jesus ex-isted, but that He did not die on the cross, nor is He the Son of God. Muslims believe the Mahdi will rule in the end time with Jesus as his subordinate.

All Muslims are expected to believe in the doctrine of the Mahdi, but the Sunni and Shia branches differ in their views. Most followers of Shia Islam follow the theory of the Twelfth Imam, an actual person who was known as Muhammad al-Mahdi, and whose return from "occultation"—a type of centuries-old invisibility and incubation pe-riod—is anticipated at any time.

Often referred to as "Twelvers," these Shia Muslims believe that the coming Mahdi is literally Muhammad al-Mahdi, who was born in 869 and was considered the twelfth legitimate imam and descendent of the prophet Mohammed. Tradition states that he was hidden by Allah at the age of five, and is living in a state of occultation, "awaiting the time that (Allah) has decreed for his return."[9]

The Twelfth Imam will return as the Mahdi with "a company of his chosen ones," and his enemies will be led by the Antichrist and the "Sufyani"—an evil, end-times character often mentioned in Islamic writings. The two armies will fight "one final apocalyptic battle" when the Mahdi and his forces will prevail over evil. After the Mahdi has ruled Earth for a number of years, Jesus will return and will bow to the Mahdi, according to Islamic tradition.[10]

Writings (commonly referred to as the hadith) of the prophet Mohammed state: "A group among my Ummah (community) will continue to fight for the truth until Jesus, the son of Mary, will descend, and the imam of them will ask him to lead the prayer, but Jesus replies: 'You have more right to it, and verily Allah has honored some of you over others in this Ummah,'" a reference to Jesus' acquiescence to the leadership of the Mahdi.[11]

Not all Sunni Muslims believe the Mahdi is the Twelfth Imam come back to life, but they agree he must be a descendant of Mohammed. All devout Muslims believe the Mahdi will have the name of Mohammed, will rule earth as a fore-runner to Jesus' return, and that he will establish an Islamic worldwide caliphate—an Islamic Sharia-compliant government.

The Islamic hadith also encourages the doctrine of the Mahdi. "The Mahdi is the protector of the knowledge, the heir to the knowledge of all the prophets, and is aware of all things," the prophet Mohammed is believed to have written. "In the time of the Mahdi, a Muslim in the East will be able to see his Muslim brother in the West, and he in the West will see him in the East."[12]

"He is a person with broad forehead, small nose, big eyes, and glittering and evenly spaced teeth," according to another of the hadiths. "Upon his right cheek there will be a mark resembling a pearl that illuminates his face like a star."

Another hadith claims that the prophet Mohammed himself predicted the coming of the Mahdi. "This world will not come to an end until one person from my progeny rules over the Arabs, and his name will be the same as my name," Mohammed stated in another hadith.

"Al Mahdi will be from my progeny. His forehead will be broad and his nose will be high. He will fill the world with justice and fairness at a time when the world will be filled with oppression. He will rule for seven years."

Muslims throughout the world may differ on the specifics of what the Mahdi will look like, where he will appear and who he will be, but they are in agreement about one thing: The Mahdi is coming. And according to Sheikh Mubarik Ali Gilani … he is already here.

The Mahdi Is Here

In 2009, a young Muslim man living among the Muslims of the Americas—Sheikh Gilani's front group in the United States for a radical terrorist group known as Jamaat Al Fuqra—traveled from the Hancock, New York, camp known as Islamberg into New York City to pick up the latest issue of the *Islamic Post*, a newspaper published by Gilani for his followers and other Muslims worldwide.

After stopping at the print shop in the city, the young man, Ali Abdel Aziz, loaded up his car with newspapers to distribute. Before returning to the compound in Hancock, Ali glanced at the latest issue and its headlines. A shocking story caught his eye: Sheikh Gilani claimed he had met the Mahdi. Driving to a secure phone, Ali called his government contacts; Ali was an informer, living undercover with Muslims of the Americas, and he knew that the story he had just read was the equivalent of an earthquake for Sheikh Gilani's followers.

"I was shocked that these camps weren't shut down … with the information I gave them," Ali said later. "This Mahdi thing is scary, it's very scary. Because I know the rest of the story. When Gilani comes out and said he knows the Mahdi … I was shocked. I got the feeling that the government is scared."[13]

Why was this information so shocking? Many people throughout history have claimed to be the Mahdi, or to have known who the Mahdi was. Although the Mahdist state which ruled in the Sudan in the 1800s was the longest and bloodiest in modern history, there have been other Mahdist uprisings. In the last century alone there have been numerous claims to the Mahdi throne, and thousands killed in the name of establishing an Islamic Mahdist caliphate. In 1979, one such revolution occurred in Saudi Arabia when Muhammad bin abd Allah al-Qahtani was proclaimed the Mahdi by his brother-in-law, Juhayman al-Otaibi. Otaibi led more than 200 militants to seize the Grand Mosque in Mecca, ultimately resulting in the deaths of more than 300 people during a two-week-long siege.

What Ali knew, upon hearing Sheikh Gilani claim to have met the Mahdi, was that Gilani was warning the world of a pending battle. Whether Gilani believed his own claim or not, he was issuing a clear warning to the world: Prepare for the end.

In the *Islamic Post* article Gilani stated:

"The one who will come after me is Imam Mahdi, whom I've introduced to some of my followers. He's in his thirties and will appear when he's 40. He will declare himself during hajj at Mecca, putting an end to falsehood and lies. He will be followed by Jesus, son of Mary, who will descend in Palestine at the minaret of the Dome of the Rock, joining Muslims and Christians as one. This will bring to an end all the machinations of (Christian Action Network[14]) and their cohorts. I cannot. If they want to raid all Muslim villages, then let them go ahead. They will be killing their own citizens.[15]

Gilani continued: "We will tell the world who (Jesus) is and how he lived. As a matter of fact, he's still living in the first heaven; he's 33 years old and I know him. I have met him. When he descends, he will still be 33 years old."

Gilani, the article stated, "ascended along with the Khalifahs and Talibs in the higher realms of the non-physical world and there, as directed, he introduced once again Hazrat[16] Imam Mahdi and told his Khalifahs and others to inform the world about the expected arrival of the promised Mahdi."[17]

The "Mahdi was introduced to a few followers of the Imam of the Muslims of the Americas, Sultan Syed Mubarik Ali Shah Gilani," the article continues. "Hazrat Imam Mahdi was introduced to the Imam Gilani's followers by Imam Gilani himself, but at that time it was kept a secret. During the blessed month of Ramadan[18], however, El Sheikh Gilani has now declared that the matter must now be made public."[19]

The Sixth Sultan

Why would the Mahdi, the promised redeemer of the Islamic world, present himself to Sheikh Gilani, a reclusive, elderly Pakistani cleric who has been trying to keep a low profile ever since it was learned that *Wall Street Journal* reporter Daniel Pearl was on his way to meet Gilani when he was kidnapped and ultimately beheaded?

The sheikh himself has answered that question. Gilani calls himself the Sixth Sultan Ul Fuqr (fuqr is a reference to "spiritual poverty"). His sultanship, he claims, is of the Qadri Order; the fifth sultan was a man named Hazrat Faqir Sultan Bahu, a Sufi poet, cleric and Islamic "saint" of 17th century Pakistan.

"He (Fifth Sultan Bahu) was the greatest teacher and propagator of faqr, which is the shining guiding star in his teachings," gushes one Islamic web site.[20] "(Bahu) may be considered one of the greatest Revealers in the history of Sufism."

Following in his footsteps is Sheikh Gilani, who claims to be the next in line to the title of Sultan Ul Fuqr. Gilani has also stated that his young son, who died at the age of five, was the Seventh Sultan Ul Faqr. Because of Gilani's self-proclaimed elevated position within the Islamic world and within Sufism, the Mahdi chose to present himself to him alone.

One of Sheikh Gilani's followers further describes the meeting between Sheikh Gilani and the Mahdi in this way in the *Islamic Post* article:

"My Murshid Kamil (Gilani) walked into the room and we stood. He was smiling as we all were. Then he asked if we knew who the man was, chuckled and said, 'You have just met the Mahdi.' After the introduction, Imam Mahdi presented our Murshid with gifts. Our Murshid smiled at this and commented, 'You have completed your studies.'

"Imam Mahdi was neither tall nor short. He was average height. He had a bright complexion. His beard was neatly shaped. He was handsome and had a mature disposition. He looked to be in his mid to late thirties ...

"Muslims the world over should prepare themselves to receive him. In simple terms, this means to turn back to Allah, seeking forgiveness, and striving to be good Muslims. People should remember that Imam Mahdi will only appear at the Baitullah Shareef.[21] He will not appear to anyone else before the appointed time. Any other claim is false. However, Sheikh Gilani confirms that it is not a matter of decades for physical appearance, rather just a matter of years."

When Ali, the undercover agent living at Islamberg in New York, read the article in the *Islamic Post* about the appearance of the Mahdi to Sheikh Gilani, he understood the gravity of the sheikh's claims. "I know the rest of the story," Ali said with alarm. "I can't really let you know what I know."

The warning from Gilani, through his followers, is clear, however:

"People should work extremely hard, stand firm and rest assured that what they are being told is right," stated the article in the *Islamic Post*. "Now, more than ever, is the time to leave aside all unIslamic activities and turn back to almighty Allah in repentance and dua ... El Sheikh, head of the Qadri order, has done his duty in conveying this information; it is entirely up to people to accept or reject it.

"The tide is about to turn. The world will change forever and for good. The end time has started."

Only One Group Will Get To Heaven

The myriad of competing Islamic sects and claims to superiority are well documented. Among the most well known are the divisions between Sunni and Shia Muslims, exemplified by the antipathy between Iran, which is predominantly Shia, and Iraq, its bitter enemy, which has a Shia majority but has been ruled by Sunnis. (Sufis, of which Gilani is an adherent, are considered a more religious, mystical subcategory within the Sunni discipline.)

In addition to differing somewhat on the doctrine of the Mahdi, the Shias and Sunnis disagree over who should be the leader of the Islamic world, based on the lineage of the prophet Mohammed. The differences today are generally political, however, involving disputes—

usually bloody ones—over which group will control a border or region, and which sect will dominate the other. Most of the Islamic world falls within the Sunni category, more than 80 percent, and that includes Sheikh Gilani and his thousands of American followers.

Yet despite these distinctions, which are not unimportant to the Shias, Sunnis and multiple sub-sects within them, the Sunni label is the least important one for Sheikh Gilani. Because he knows that not all of the competing Muslim groups can claim the mantle of leadership and therefore lay claim to the one true sect within Islam, Gilani has preached that his brand of Islam—and those who follow him under the names of Jamaat Al Fuqra, Muslims of the Americas, Soldiers of Allah, Muslims of the First State, Muhammadin Soldiers, or any of the other incarnations—will be the only ones to make it to Islam heaven.

While most non-Muslims focus on the Sunni vs. Shia divide, what often goes unnoticed is the Muslim belief that there are not two, but 73 competing groups within Islam. As foretold by the prophet Mohammed, only one of the 73 groups—the true believers—will go to heaven.

"Muslims will divide into 73 groups," the prophet Mohammed is quoted as saying in his last sermon, as recorded in the Hadith. "All will be in Hell, except one. The one me and my companions are on today."

Sheikh Gilani insists he and his followers are the true believers, true followers of the prophet Mohammed, and it is their duty to "purify Islam through violence."

Ali, the undercover agent who lived among the Muslims of the Americas, shudders at the realization that Gilani controls his followers by convincing them he is a direct descendant of the prophet Mohammed, that he has met the Mahdi and that his group is the only one in all of Islam that will go to heaven.

"Gilani tells them that they are the one group," says Ali. "All the other Muslims in the world are no good. They are not following (Islam). 'You have to follow me. I am the descendent.' This is how he brainwashes these people. The people are poor, off the streets, oppressed, not educated, and you go to someone like that and you say you are the chosen one, 'you have to follow me.' And that is how he controls several different continents."[22]

Warning To The World

In 2009, Sheikh Gilani warned that the end is coming. "It is not a matter of decades for physical appearance (of the Mahdi), rather just a matter of years."

Gilani also reiterated his mission, and his warning, in a 2011 "New Year's Message" posted on the web site of one of his American compounds in York, SC, known as Islamville. "As promised in the Holy (Quran) and Bible, Allah shall raise messengers and imams from the family, descendants of Abraham. I am one of those who have been raised and, of course, when Allah chooses a member of the family of the Holy Last Messenger ... and backs him with miracles, he serves as an ambassador of the Holy Last Messenger ... and is given capabilities of granting audience of the Holy Last Messenger ... to the most loyal and sincere seekers, and this is my mission."

Gilani also claims the rainbow is his symbol of salvation, even nonsensically implying he may responsible for placing the rainbow in the sky. "The rainbow, which people have been seeing ..." he writes, "is my sign of authority, a symbol of salvation and success and ultimate triumph."

Finally, in his rambling new year's message, he warns of the coming Mahdi. "The promised Mahdi, who will be from the family of the Holy Last Messenger ... will appear soon. I have met him non-physically ... Imamate itself is an institution without boundaries or borders. It rules hearts and reaches people, not land. Neither followers nor myself seek ruling government positions."

Gilani writes of a 1975 "meeting" with the prophet Mohammed, presumably one of those "audiences" which Mohammed personally granted to Gilani in the mystical realm. During the meeting, Gilani claims Mohammed singled him out to "propagate Al-Islam"—establish an Islamic worldwide state.

"In 1975 ... the Holy Last Messenger ... called a very large congregation where he was honoring guests and walis. Surprisingly, my companion at that time, Mian Abdur Rashid, a columnist at the Daily Nawa-I-Waqt of Lahore, was also given admission for the simple reason he had doubt about my mission. In an esoteric gathering we call Majlis of Noor of the Holy Last Messenger, The Holy Last Messenger ... tied a green turban on my head authorizing me to propagate Al-Islam. He also honored my companion with a white Imama. This occurred at tahajjud time, and when their spirits returned the first thing Mian Abdur Rashid asked was, 'Pir Sahib, what is the significance of the green and white turban?' I replied, 'The green is the color of Ahli-Bayt, and The Holy Last Messenger ... has confirmed my Wilayat (authority) and commissioned me as his Na'ib (second in command) to propagate Al-Islam.' The white imama was given as a token of honor to his guest since he was one of my companions."[23]

Sheikh Gilani may appear to be an addled Islamic fanatic, talking of spiritual meetings with long-dead prophets ... creating the rainbow as his own personal symbol ... transporting himself from one period of time to another to confer with long-dead Islamic leaders ... but to many who are close to him, he's crazy like a fox. In 2009, he posted an online rant in which he railed against those who question his motives. Despite decades of evidence—much of it documented by federal and state investigators—of his terrorist activities and associations, Gilani craftily insists he is worthy of praise, not rebuke.

'I Have Done My Duty'

"It's very strange," he writes, "that for the last 30 years I've been doing such noble work, reforming thousands of young men and women who were brought out of ghettos, stopping a life of crime and drugs. Don't I deserve a gesture of thanks from anyone? I have done my duty as a descendant of the Holy Last Messenger ... which is to guide people out of darkness into the light and showing the way to truth, salvation and success."[24]

Gilani's above statement is utter nonsense. Instead of helping the poor black Americans who flock to Gilani's compounds in hope of a sense of family and refuge, he has further enslaved them, assuming the role of cruel taskmaster over the compounds and imposing the harshest lifestyles on them. Testimony—which is provided later in this book—from Ali, the undercover agent who lived among Gilani's followers in one of the MOA compounds, asserts that the women and children in the camps are regularly beaten, raped, forced into illegal polygamous marriages and frequently held against their will. The young men are not only frequently recruited from prison because of their criminal past, which is useful to the group, but they are raised from birth to become criminals, learning at an early age how to scam the system in a multitude of ways.

So when Sheikh Gilani announced in 2009 that he had met the Mahdi, it's understandable that Ali became alarmed. Gilani's claim is not the senseless rambling of a foolish old man sequestered away in Pakistan. It is a stern warning to America:

"If Gilani tomorrow told everyone, set yourself on fire, everybody would burn themselves," Ali has revealed. "This has been going on for 30 years. And people praise him. They give him money. They kiss his feet. It's crazy. These people are slaves. I call them the modern warrior slaves."

The slaves, he adds, are building an army.

"The cops would never come ... It was like they were given the OK; like the police wanted to let them do their thing."

Allen Tucker, victim of Muslim violence, on the police department's lack of response.

CHAPTER 11

The Blueprint for Disaster

PUBLICLY, MUSLIMS OF THE AMERICAS (MOA) PRESENTS itself as a self-reliant community whose goal is to live quietly and peacefully in their faith. They claim to love America and even boast that America is "their country." Their primary aim is to be a haven for disaffected and troubled youth. That's the image they want to project—especially to the media, local politicians and, to a certain degree, neighboring law-enforcement agencies.

I have never seen an American flag on their property, but for the most part they have been successful in their public relations efforts. Their camps are surrounded by controversy, rumors and speculation, but the MOA leadership works hard to dispel any overt negative images that community leaders may have.

It is common for their camps to invite local sheriffs and even FBI agents onto their compounds for picnics and celebrations. Local politicians are frequently visited by MOA members at community meetings. In addition, MOA members have proven to be important votes in local elections, especially since these elections take place in small towns. The local media, which are sometimes non-existent in these isolated locations, are given supervised tours of their camps and entertained with grandiose stories of miracles, redemptive youth, self-sufficiency and community-service programs, including Muslim boy scout clubs, Muslim veteran groups and disaster-relief organizations.

Criticism of the camps is dismissed by MOA leaders as religiously or racially motivated—a predictable defense given that the majority of MOA members are either African-American or of foreign descent, mostly from Pakistan.

Though MOA leaders do their best to quell or diffuse any public image that is derogatory, their members are not shy about intimidating the communities in which they co-exist and fomenting fear in the hearts and minds of their neighbors.

Public officials speak about them in mere whispers, as if their words might prompt swift and terrible retribution if overheard by an MOA member. Most neighbors won't talk about them at all, others only behind closed doors. Some fear not only for their own lives, but even for the lives of their pets, which occasionally stray onto MOA land. Other neighbors build fences around their homes to keep MOA members off their properties. Some neighbors say local police fear going onto their compounds and often refuse to investigate their criminal complaints.

In one instance, a homeowner in York, South Carolina, said he called the police to report a missing electrical generator he was using to remodel his home. The man told the police he knew it was stolen by MOA members, whose property backed up to his house. The officer asked how he could be so sure. The man said, "Look at the tire tracks; they lead right down into their compound!" The officer refused, however, to enter the camp to probe the accusation.

This is just one example of many neighborhood complaints of stolen property near the South Carolina compound known as Holy Islamville—including missing animals—incidents the residents say police refuse to investigate.

When one neighbor complained to police too often about the compound, she found a six-foot grave built alongside her driveway, just a few yards into the woods. A couple of weeks later she was confronted by an MOA member who brandished both a gun and a knife at her.

Typically, when these wild stories begin to mount and cause public suspicion of the compounds, MOA will pick a day to open its camps to the public for all to come on a limited tour and examine their simple lifestyle and peaceful religion.

When MOA public relations' efforts are mixed into a cocktail of community fear and political correctness, these neighborhoods become numb and stupefied to the dangers of the MOA and the threat they pose to the nation. This mixture of political correctness, fear and self-serving propaganda can easily be seen as a recipe for disaster.

You don't have to look back too far in history to see that this story has basically played itself out before. Its blueprint can be found in a similar Muslim organization with a radical agenda, proclaiming itself to be self-sufficient, dedicated to helping troubled youth, instilling fear in the local community, yet receiving praise by community leaders, treated with kid gloves, and having many of their crimes ignored.

Your Black Muslim Bakery

If you've never lived in Oakland, California, you've probably never heard of this rather oddly named group: Your Black Muslim Bakery.

The media has given the organization very little attention. Even the 2011 murder trial of their leader was ignored by the major media outlets. Yet the story of this radical Muslim group is as fascinating, cruel, sinister and evil as any other criminal story the media regularly feed the American public. It involves sex, murder, cover-up, violence, fraud and even kidnapping and incest. But there has been almost no coverage about it in the mainstream media.

It's difficult to understand why most media outlets have chosen to ignore this national story, and I will not attempt to explain their silence. But what is known is that some who have attempted to write articles about Your Black Muslim Bakery have been threatened with death.

Reporter Chris Thompson, who was writing about Your Black Muslim Bakery for Oakland's *East Bay Express*, was threatened so often by the Muslim group that he had to work in a different county. He was followed by its members. Bricks were hurled through the windows of his newspaper building. Death threats were left on his voicemail.

The threats so intimidated the weekly newspaper that its editor and co-owner, Stephen Buel, said, "We stopped writing about the group."

When another reporter, Josh Richman, was writing a story for the *Bay Area News* about the Muslim group's alleged real estate scams, he received a call stating, "If you write that story, you're going to end up like your friend Chauncey."[2]

This was no idle threat. The assassination of another reporter, Chauncey Bailey, was Your Black Muslim Bakery's most high-profile execution.

On the morning of August 2, 2007, Chauncey Bailey was walking to his downtown office, where he served as the newly appointed editor of the *Oakland Post*, a weekly newspaper that had been serving the black community for nearly a half century. At the same time, a young 19-year-old African-American man was searching for him in a white Ford van. Devaughndre Broussard, a handyman for the Muslim group, would later claim he was "just being a good soldier" for the Bakery when he murdered Chauncey Bailey on his way to work.

Bailey was far from an unknown journalist in the Oakland vicinity. He had been writing in the area for more than 30 years, even spending time as an on-air reporter for KNTV in San Jose. Bailey's history as a newsman was wide and deep. From *UPI, Hartford Courant, Detroit News, Oakland Tribune,* even to commentator for a small local program in Oakland called Soul Beat Television, Chauncey Bailey seemed to be everywhere.

His credentials ran from the east coast to the west. And his killing was going to be big news, at least in Oakland. But this time, unfortunately for Bailey, he would be the subject of the news, rather than its reporter.

No one would reasonably suspect members of Your Black Muslim Bakery to be responsible for Bailey's murder. After all, Chauncey Bailey had defended the Muslim Bakery many times when the group came under any suspicion of criminal activity. He defended them both as a news reporter for the *Oakland Post* and as news director for Soul Beat Television.

Perhaps only Bailey knew, on that fateful morning, that this time it was different. He was about to ruffle the feathers of one of the most entrenched and powerful Muslim groups ever to establish itself in the Oakland area. Few knew the story he was preparing to write. But one who did know was Yusuf Bey IV, the current leader of the Muslim Bakery. And Bey wanted Bailey dead. The young handyman, Devaughndre Broussard, who would carry out the assassination, said he was under direct orders from Yusuf Bey IV to "take him out."

Bey IV was the son of Yusuf Bey Sr., the founder of Your Black Muslim Bakery, a man who, it was later revealed, fathered at least 42 children in the community.

Bey Sr. founded Your Black Muslim Bakery nearly four decades earlier as a bakery offering healthy alternatives to refined sugar, fats and preservatives. All the baked goods were prepared according to the Quran.

After arriving in Oakland in the early 1970s, Bey attended the Nation of Islam Mosque #26 in San Francisco, sharing many of its radical beliefs on black Muslim empowerment. He would eventually form his own congregation in the Oakland area, called the Nation of Islam Mosque #26B. Bey would assert in sermons that black men were a type of god and that the white man was the devil incarnate.[3]

Although the bakery's main location was on San Pablo Avenue, the organization sold its food in more than 150 area stores, with sales exceeding 6,000 loaves of bread and 300 cakes per week.

But the bakery was much more than a bakehouse kitchen.

Yusuf Bey boasted that he took troubled youth off the streets and put them to work. He reached out to ex-cons and impoverished ghetto youth, both male and female. He preached the Quran weekly on Soul Beat Television, the very TV station where Chauncey Bailey served as a news director. He preached self-reliance and racial pride. And he could provide a parade of youth, to anyone who would listen, to testify to the self-reliant virtues they learned from the Bakery.

'I'm A Cold-Hearted Criminal'

One such young man under Yusuf's care, who claimed on Soul Beat Television to have had a history of murder, robbery, assault, drugs and guns, would say, "I'm a cold-hearted criminal. And this dude (Yusuf) done went out of his way to help me get my business started. He done bought licenses. He done bought me trademarks. He done got my bank accounts started. He done did all my paperwork for me."[4]

Such glowing praise of Yusuf's success with teens prompted one state senator to praise Yusuf, saying, "The leadership you provide should be an inspiration to all concerned over the city's future."[5]

The Muslim Bakery owned dry cleaning stores, apartment buildings and even several security firms. Bey housed the unfortunate in his Section 8 housing and tried to start a health-care business to train female members to become nurse's aides and health-care providers. For many, if not most, Yusuf Bey stood as a beacon of success, hope, charity and perseverance for African Americans and Muslims in the city. One newspaper editorial gushed that Bey's life was "devoted to the development of economic self-reliance for Oakland's African-American community."[6]

The community praise heaped on this Muslim group was unprecedented and unparalleled in the Oakland area. But five years before Chauncey Bailey's murder in broad daylight, the horrifying truth of this Muslim group began to expose itself.

In September, 2002, Bey was arrested on 27 counts of the rape of four girls under the age of 14. And that was just the beginning of the nightmarish truth that would soon be revealed about the Muslim Bakery and its much-heralded Islamic leader, Yusuf Bey.

Though he had been arrested, many in the media continued to sing Bey's praises or simply to ignore the criminal history of the group. Even Chauncey Bailey, who would become a victim of the Muslim Bakery, came to the defense of Yusuf Bey after his arrest. In an article entitled "Accused Black Leader Given Support," Bailey found supporters of Bey who defended their leader. "It's a trick by the enemy because he's doing something positive," Arleta Bass told Bailey. "Jesus is the only one I know who is perfect," another supporter, Jayla Richardson, also stated.[7]

Chauncey Bailey, no doubt, believed in Yusuf Bey. During his time as news director of Soul Beat Television, where Bey preached a weekly sermon, Bailey would not allow the station to permit callers or guests to discuss or criticize Bey's arrest. This was an unusual and quite controversial position for a news director, who was responsible to present fair and accurate reporting, to take.

Notwithstanding this paradox, no one could seriously doubt Bailey's professionalism as a journalist.

Perhaps the only explanation for Bailey's defense of Bey is that they shared many things in common. Bailey was an African-American, as was Yusuf Bey. On the surface, both were examples of high-profile success stories for the black community. There was no doubt that Bailey was proud of his black heritage and culture, serving as news director for Soul Beat Television, which brought him into close contact with Yusuf Bey.

Regardless of his journalistic experience, honesty or dedication, it had to be unthinkable for Bailey to believe that the man he held in such high regard, who shared a television studio with him and represented the best of the African-American community could really be guilty of raping four girls under the age of 14. Bailey had to know the public damage all black Americans would suffer if these accusations were true.

No one could fault Bailey for believing in the constitutional principle that a person is innocent until proven guilty. The problem for Bailey was that Yusuf Bey was not innocent of the sex-crime charges, nor of other accusations that would soon be brought against him and the Muslim Bakery. Eventually, for anyone who knew Chauncey Bailey, the truth was going to come out even if Bailey himself had to report it. But that would still be five years after Bey's 2002 arrest.

Not everyone had been blind to the ugly and often terrifying truth about Yusuf Bey and his Muslim Bakery organization. The Oakland police knew. So did some in the media. As far back as 1994, the lies, brutality and hypocrisy of Yusuf Bey and his Muslim Bakery were evident for all to see, though few wanted to report on what they knew or saw. Whether due to fear, political correctness or zeal for the civil-rights movement, not many wanted to shatter the celebrated image of Bey and his Islamic organization.

But in 1994 everyone should have known the Muslim Bakery was cooking up more than cakes and bread.

A Troubled Family

Yusuf's son, Akbar Bey, was shot four times and killed by a local drug dealer. The 21-year-old was high on heroin and morphine at the time of his death. Far from simply being a victim of drugs, the younger Bey was described by police as "a little street thug" who often wore a bullet-proof vest. Three months prior to his killing, Akbar was arrested for carrying a concealed weapon and evading police.

Akbar Bey's murder was not some far-flung and isolated incident involving the Muslim Bakery in 1994. In the same year, Nadir Bey—a young man who worked so closely with Yusuf that he was allowed to take the family name—had his own run-in with the law. Reportedly upset that the owner of a renovated house would not reduce the sale price of the home, Nadir and several other Muslim Bakery soldiers entered the man's apartment and nearly beat him to death, then kidnapped him.

Nadir beat the man with an 18-inch police flashlight, stomped on his genitals, shoved his head into a toilet, kicked him in the chest, legs and abdomen, and eventually had to stuff a towel in his mouth to stop his screaming. At the conclusion of this violent torture, Nadir Bey kidnapped the man and had him stuffed into the trunk of the man's own car. After reaching the security gate of the apartment complex, the kidnappers decided to search the car before proceeding any further and they momentarily allowed the man out of the trunk. By coincidence, the victim spotted a police vehicle nearby and ran toward two officers, shouting for help. Only then was he who rescued.

Nadir Bey was arrested on charges of false imprisonment, robbery and assault. But Nadir argued in court that he was merely enforcing "Muslim discipline."[8] Apparently, the "Muslim discipline" defense carried some weight with the judge, and Nadir was sentenced to just six months of detention—to be served at home!

On the very day of this kidnapping and assault, 30 other Muslim Bakery members—armed with handguns—decided to take revenge on a man they claimed had stripped tires from one of their cars. When law enforcement was called into the ruckus, chaos ensued and the Muslim Bakery members found themselves in a fistfight with Oakland police officers who were wielding batons. Calm was eventually restored through the negotiating efforts of one the officers, and the riot ended. But when peace was restored, 30 Muslim Bakery members walked away free of any charges.

One of the few journalist critics of Your Black Muslim Bakery was Chris Thompson, a writer for the *East Bay Express*. He would later write about these violent incidents committed by Yusuf Bey and his Muslim Bakery.

"Virtually none of these arrests, confrontations and allegations received the scrutiny they deserved, and Yusuf Bey and his followers have been able to continue presenting themselves as role models for impoverished, fatherless children. In some quarters of the city, they've accumulated a populist moral currency that politicians and social workers could never hope to equal. They are, in a word, righteous," Thompson wrote.[9]

Even these cases were not isolated incidents of cruelty and criminality committed by the insanely sheltered Muslim group. Allen Tucker, who lived in one of the apartment buildings owned by Your Black Muslim Bakery, also encountered the violence of its members.

After his daughter was kicked by a 12-year-old boy who was the son of a Muslim Bakery member, he scolded the young lad by saying, "Don't be kicking my little girl, cause she's just six and you could seriously hurt her."

Soon afterwards, Tucker was confronted by four Muslim Bakery members, including the boy's father, Muhammad. The Muslim soldiers stomped the man to the point of unconsciousness. Even after he passed out, the men continued to beat him in the face. Tucker was left with a three-inch laceration on his leg, bruises around both temples, and a gashed lip.

The men were arrested, but all charges against the attackers were dropped—as usual.

In an interview with the victim, journalist Chris Thompson would report, "According to Allen Tucker, associates of the Bey family did much more than this one alleged beating." In fact, the Bey family terrorized the tenants with military drills in the parking lot and had violent confrontations. And the cops, Tucker claims, did nothing to stop it.

Tucker said tenants would often call the police over these violent confrontations, but "the cops would never come ... It was like they were given the OK; like the police wanted to let them do their thing," he said.[10]

An Expanding Empire

Meanwhile, during these years of unrestrained and lawless thuggery, Yusuf Bey was expanding the wealth of his criminal empire and taking advantage of law enforcement's willingness to turn a blind eye.

In a scheme that began in the 1980s and continued up to his death in 2003, Yusuf Bey drained the State of California of thousands of dollars each month, perhaps exceeding a million dollars total, in an unprecedented welfare fraud scam.

Beginning in 1981, Yusuf Bey, who claimed to have more than 100 wives, had one of his sisters-in-law successfully seek employment at the Alameda County Social Services Agency. He repeated this process again in 1988 by having another sister-in-law work at the agency. Eventually, the duties of these two women included determining who qualified for welfare. Together, they would help Yusuf Bey get approved for welfare checks to be sent each month to his more than 100 wives. The checks would then be deposited into his Muslim Bakery accounts.

Whenever welfare officials became suspicious of the checks being sent to Bey's numerous "wives," his sisters-in-law would tip him off. As a result, the "wives" would jump off the welfare rolls for a period of time before applying once again for welfare payments at a later date.

Bey would hold regular meetings with Bakery members to discuss strategies on facilitating the scam.

An important part of the scam involved forcing his "wives" to keep his name off the children's birth certificates. The "wives" would simply make up names for the fathers of their children. This also allowed the wives to hide Bey's income and help them qualify for public assistance. Once the children became old enough, they, too, would participate in the welfare fraud scheme.[11]

The scam began to unravel when three former wives came forward to testify against Yusuf Bey and Your Black Muslim Bakery. The wives, who remain unidentified due to threats against them, revealed to authorities much more about Yusuf Bey than just welfare fraud.

Horrifying Revelations

Bey was also accused of molesting his own children, even urinating into their mouths.

One Bakery member named Usman testified that he saw Bey sexually molesting a young boy in a bathroom. Upset with what he saw, Usman complained to some of the wives. "I couldn't believe it," he said. "I couldn't believe what I seen with my own eyes."[12]

A few days later, Usman was gunned down and killed. The wives said the murder was ordered by Yusuf Bey, Sr. as payback for disclosing the rape of the boy.

Bey's 2002 arrest, however, stemmed from impregnating a young girl who was placed as a foster child in his care. The accounts of this story are horrific; were it not for the courageous efforts of one determined woman, the sex crimes of Yusuf Bey might never have been discovered.

The woman, Tarika Lewis, was a part-time worker at Your Black Muslim Bakery married to a man who had three children from a previous marriage. Soon they would have a child of their own. She was originally attracted to the Muslim Bakery because she believed its message of empowerment—that black people could build something in the community, establish businesses and provide employment for many out-of-work African Americans.

But these hopes and dreams would ultimately fade as she watched the continued violence of Muslim Bakery members and their Islamic belief that men were allowed to beat their women.[13]

Yusuf Bey was known for controversial beliefs stemming from his Islamic faith. He once held a conference in which one speaker ranted about "no-good, hook-nosed Jews sucking our blood."[14]

Bey believed Islam gave man total domination over a woman. In a speech entitled, "Contract with the Devil," Bey endorsed the Muslim doctrine of honor killings, saying "There's a culture and a country in the East somewhere where if the girl fornicates, the brothers have to kill the daughter. Have to kill their sister."[15]

"When a man starts hitting a woman," Tarika Lewis told reporter Chris Thompson, "that was hard for me to comprehend. It was hard for me to stomach or sit around, pretending it was not happening."[16]

She would end up leaving the Muslim Bakery and divorcing her husband for unrelated reasons. Her husband's children were put in the care of Yusuf Bey, though Tarika tried to stay in touch with them, saying she had developed a motherly bond for the kids during her marriage.

Not surprisingly, the Muslim Bakery would have nothing to do with her. She was constantly told the children were not available. She could not even talk to them on the phone. And Bey threatened the children if they fled.

One day, however, she spotted her 13-year-old stepdaughter seated in the passenger seat of a van next to Yusuf Bey. She walked up to her stepdaughter and was surprised to see that she was in the late stages of pregnancy. By the girl's sad and embarrassed look, and knowing Bey's rumored sexual exploitation of children, she believed the father to be Yusuf Bey.

Tarika told her concerns to any government authority who would listen—Child Protective Services, the Social Services Agency, Oakland Police, lawyers, Christian and Muslim ministers. She got nowhere. Then, a few years later, she learned that another one of her stepdaughters was pregnant.

After eight years, two of her stepdaughters finally escaped Yusuf Bey's compound and he was arrested on allegations of rape and child sexual abuse.

Bey, however, would never live to meet man's justice; he died in jail of colon cancer shortly before his trial began in 2003.

Struggle For Power

After Bey's death, there was the anticipated power struggle for the organization's leadership. That role would eventually fall upon Yusuf Bey IV, who later orchestrated the murder of reporter Chauncey Bailey. But the younger Bey wasn't the Muslim group's first choice. That "honor" originally fell upon Carl Hambrick, a 51-year-old devotee of the organization who was so loyal to its founder that he was granted the "Bey" surname.

He became known as Waajid Bey and served as the Bakery's chief executive officer and Yusuf's personal confidant before assuming the group's leadership. He was Bey's handpicked man to succeed him.

But his reign was short-lived. Waajid Bey went missing on February 29, 2004, just five months after he took control. His badly decomposed body was discovered by a dog in a shallow grave on July 20. Though no one has ever been charged in his murder, police believed Waajid's assassination had something to do with his taking over the organization.

After his death, the leadership role went to Antar Bey. Antar was just 22 years old at the time he took the reins, but he would be dead by the time he was 23. On October 5, 2005, in what has been described as a botched car-jacking attempt, Antar Bey was shot in the back while trying to flee his pursuer. His widow, Amarreh Bey, said her husband had received death threats from his brother, Yusuf Bey IV, shortly before his murder and that shots had also been fired into their home.

The power struggle finally ended when Yusuf Bey IV took control after his brother's death. He immediately set out to make a name for himself and to assert his authority over the other Muslim Bakery soldiers.

Besides being accused of vandalizing an Oakland liquor store, smashing bottles and turning over shelves for selling alcohol to

African-Americans, Bey IV was also accused of attempted murder by trying to run over a bouncer of a San Francisco strip joint because Bey IV and his Muslim cohorts had been thrown out.

The younger Bey has also been accused of ordering the shooting deaths of Odell Roberson and Michael Wills in the summer of 2007. Bey ordered the killing of Wills simply because he was white.

But Chauncey Bailey wasn't killed for the color of his skin. Early on the morning of his death Bailey walked out of McDonald's, dressed in business attire and carrying a newspaper—a routine he followed virtually every morning. He walked one block toward his downtown Oakland office when a young man with a ski mask jumped out of a van.

The young man, Devaughndre Broussard, barely knew his victim. The first time he had even heard of Bailey was just the day prior to his violent confrontation with the reporter on the corner of 14ᵗʰ and Alice streets.

Broussard said he became aware of Bailey while watching a funeral video of the elder Yusuf Bey at the apartment of his son, Bey IV. Joined by another young man, Antoine Mackey, the younger Bey stopped the video when Chauncey Bailey appeared on the screen.

"That's the m*f* who killed my father and he's writing a story about the bakery right now."[17] Broussard said he and Mackey were under instructions to follow him from work later that day and figure out his routine.

"He wanted us to take him out before he completed that article," Broussard said of Bey IV. "I guess he understood the article was supposed to come out on Friday."[18]

Broussard said that he and Mackey were promised fraudulent IDs and a high credit card limit if they killed Bailey. The offer meant the two of them could "buy houses and cars without a job." Even without the promise of fake IDs, Broussard said he wanted "to be a good solider" for the Muslim Bakery.[19] With Mackey as the getaway driver, Broussard grabbed his short-barreled, pistol-grip shotgun and jumped in front of Bailey on that fateful Thursday morning.

He shot the reporter in the shoulder, then in the abdomen with his 12-gauge Mossberg. Bailey fell to the ground, dying. Broussard ran toward the getaway van but wasn't sure if Bailey was really dead. So he ran back to Bailey, reloaded the weapon, pointed the shotgun at the reporter's head, and fired a load of buckshot into his face. Bailey was pronounced dead at the scene.

Bey IV couldn't wait to see the slain reporter. Within 45 minutes of the shooting, he drove past the crime scene and would say, upon seeing the dead journalist lying on the bloody sidewalk, "That will teach them to f* with me."[20]

"Pow. Pow. Poof," Yusuf was recorded as saying in a secret jailhouse video recording, throwing his head back to mimic Chauncey's murder.[21]

In October, 2006, a year before Bailey's execution, Your Black Muslim Bakery filed for bankruptcy. Yusuf IV blamed Bailey both for his father's death (saying he caused his dad undue stress, thereby accelerating his colon cancer) and for writing articles that damaged the Bakery's reputation, even though Bailey had been a loyal friend of the Bakery for many years.

Reality didn't matter. Truth didn't matter. Islam did.

'God's Soldiers'

Yusuf Bey, Sr. had instilled in his followers the conviction that they were to be God's "soldiers," not unlike Sheikh Gilani's admonition to his own followers that they were to be "Soldiers of Allah."

Bey said of his Muslim followers: "These young men are soldiers. You cannot fool these young men of today. They were born with knowledge."[22]

From his jail cell the younger Yusuf said he sometimes believes he *is* God and that the natural disasters afflicting the earth are a result of his incarceration. Like his father, he also believes in the Muslim doctrine of plural wives. And it was his belief in Islam that led Yusuf Bey IV to order the killing of Chauncey Bailey.

The triggerman, Devaughndre Broussard, said that Yusuf used Islamic "rhetoric" to compel him carry out the murder. "He started hitting me with that religious (expletive)," Broussard said of Yusuf's instructions on Islam. "You can't just say you're a believer on your words alone. You gotta act upon your faith."[23]

Was Your Black Muslim Bakery an Islamic terrorist organization? Prosecutor Melissa Krum answered that question best in her closing augments against the leader of the Muslim Bakery, Yusuf Bey IV, during his trial on triple-murder charges.

"He terrorized our city," she told the jurors.[24]

Prosecutor Krum said the Bakery was run like a military organization with Bey at the top. She even showed jurors a video of Muslim Bakery soldiers performing military formation drills. Broussard testified that such drills were the culture of the Muslim bakery.

Dawud Bey, who also testified at the trial, said he was taught to be a "Black Muslim warrior." He said that Bey IV was the Muslim Bakery's commanding officer and that followers were required to salute him as if in the military.

When asked about Black Muslims killing whites, Dawud Bey said, "That's a good thing, in my opinion."[25]

Parallels To Muslims Of The Americas

Though not identical, there are many parallels between Your Black Muslim Bakery and Sheikh Gilani's Jamaat Al Fuqra, also known as Muslims of the Americas.

Both groups positioned their Islamic leaders as Muslim deities whose orders, religious views and actions were to be accepted with unquestionable loyalty and obedience.

Besides sharing a history in the United States spanning more than three decades, both groups reached into the Black Muslim empowerment movements to form the nucleus of their followers. Sheikh Gilani enlisted his original members from the controversial Dar ul-Islam movement, while Yusuf Bey recruited followers by brandishing the Nation of Islam sword.

Each leader also claims to take troubled youth, ex-cons, drug addicts and impoverished men and women off the streets to teach them the values, morals and principles of the Quran.

Yet both groups share a history of murder, assassination, fraud, drug running, threats, thuggery and unbridled control and discipline over their followers.

Both run their groups in military fashion. Your Black Muslim Bakery went as far as military formation drills and saluting its leaders. Jamaat Al Fuqra (the sister organization of Muslims of the Americas) has gone as far as having men and women, even children, dress in military uniforms, fire weapons, perform stealth training and form elite military groups.

Interestingly, both groups also created security firms. Your Black Muslim Bakery ran three security agencies, employing 65 people, which provided security for such entities as the Oakland Ice Center and the Marriott Hotel and Convention Center. The obtained security contracts at hotels, apartment complexes, schools and night clubs.

Security Firms As Fronts

Over the years, Jamaat Al Fuqra has run more than a half-dozen security agencies, including Dagger Investigation Services, Watchdog Security, Mills Security, 786 Security Companies and Professional Securities International.

One of its most active security firms, White Hawk Securities Services, sits squarely on Sheikh Gilani's 25-acre compound in Meherrin, VA. It claims to have 25 employees, $7 million in revenue, and claims it provides detective, guard and armored car services.

Former Colorado Criminal Investigator Susan Fenger said these security firms allow these Islamic terrorists "to obtain firearm permits," meaning they could purchase weapons not normally allowed to average citizens.

Fenger, who led the raid on Jamaat Al Fuqra's Buena Vista, Colorado, compound in 1992, is known by Gilani's Muslim group as "the FBI woman," even though she never worked for the federal agency. But her successful raid of the Buena Vista compound caught the attention of Gilani, who then put a $50,000 bounty on her head. (See Chapter 5)

In an interview conducted by Christian Action Network with Fenger, she explained the significance of these security firms for Jamaat Al Fuqra:

"Because they are security agencies," she said, "it is easier for them to get firearms. They have the perfect reason for it, and so they can apply to ATF and get the license for carrying and arming their people.

"They have gotten contracts with the Defense Department and other government agencies. That would have given them access not only to things like secret information or paramilitary or military information, but it also would give them access to documents such as birth certificates and things of that nature."

What is shocking, and perhaps the most difficult part to comprehend, is how the media, politicians and police officials simply ignore the behavior and crimes of these two groups and extol their so-called virtues.

In the case of Your Black Muslim Bakery, two Oakland police officers claimed they were told to "look the other way" when seeing crimes committed by the group.[26] One Oakland police officer, Sgt. Derwin Longmire, was even accused of helping the Muslim Bakery cover up its assassination of reporter Chauncey Bailey. Sgt. Longmire was suspended from the police force for his actions.

Whether Sgt. Longmire was an actual member of the Muslim Bakery who infiltrated the police force, or simply a devoted follower of Yusuf Bey, the facts may never be known. But what is known is that Jamaat Al Fuqra has infiltrated the local police in Sweeny, Texas, and Dover, Tennessee, where the group has Muslim compounds. In Sweeny, the terrorist group at one time had four members working inside the police force. In Dover, the head of the Jamaat compound was at one time the radio dispatcher for the police department.

America can now look back on Your Black Muslim Bakery and see the mistakes made by politicians, police officials, judges and the media regarding this Muslim criminal empire. It is a blueprint for the disastrous results that will occur if Muslim groups are viewed only from the eyes of political correctness.

In the case of Your Black Muslim Bakery, these disastrous results included incest, rape, financial fraud, kidnappings, murder, beatings and execution-style assassinations—all of which might have been prevented had politicians, the media, police and JUDGES taken their jobs seriously, rather than bowing at the altar of political correctness and fear of Islamic retribution.

Unfortunately, Your Black Muslim Bakery not only looks like it was a blueprint for disaster in Oakland, California, but a blueprint for an impending national disaster as government officials, law enforcement agencies and the press turn a blind eye to the dangers of Sheikh Gilani's ever-growing, expanding and entrenched American Jamaat Al Fuqra/Muslims of the Americas compounds.

After decades of ignoring the criminal empire of Your Black Muslim Bakery, it was easy for the media to look back and see the mistakes it had made.

A.C. Thompson, from New America Media, said, "Now we're kind of playing catch-up and excavating the past, and going back and looking at what happened during that time period when the media wasn't focused on the bakery, and a lot of times, law enforcement wasn't either."[27]

Will these unfortunate words be repeated again concerning Jamaat Al Fuqra and its Muslims of the Americas compounds scattered around the United States? Perhaps no one could tell us better than an individual who spent eight years inside Jamaat Al Fuqra as an undercover agent for the New York Police Department.

His name is Ali Aziz and he says the police already have "enough evidence to close these camps."

Your Black Muslim Bakery before their illegal operations were exposed. The empire was a blueprint for how to scam the welfare system.

"Do you know what are they gonna do to me? They are going to mistreat me. They are going to drown me. They are going to waterboard me. And then they'll say I was working for Muslims of the Americas… That's what will happen. I will be charged with espionage or as double agent."

Ali Aziz, undercover agent for the NYPD with Muslims of the Americas, talking about what could happen to him if he is deported to Egypt.

CHAPTER 12

The Jackal

AFTER OUR FILM "HOMEGROWN JIHAD" WAS RELEASED IN January 2009 exposing Sheikh Gilani's terrorist camps in the United States, our office began receiving many calls from individuals who claimed to have relevant information about Muslims of the Americas. Some of the calls proved to be legit, coming from neighbors of the camps, ex-law enforcement officials and a few private investigators. But others came from people of dubious backgrounds, questionable character and perhaps sinister motives. One person tried to represent herself as a CIA agent; another as a Department of Defense official. Some say they are highly placed in law enforcement, but claim they can't really disclose their true identity or police agency. We've heard it all.

It was not surprising, then, that eyes began to roll in our office when we received a call in early September, 2010, from someone speaking in a heavy foreign accent claiming to be an undercover agent inside Muslims of the Americas—someone who wanted to meet me personally. Of all the calls we had received, this one seemed most improbable and particularly dangerous. But our policy has always been to investigate every call, no matter how odd on its face, as long as we did not put ourselves in too much danger. This call was no different.

After the call passed a couple of internal reviews, it was determined that I should speak to a man calling himself Ali Aziz, an Egyptian national who claimed to have spent eight years as an undercover agent for the New York Police Department inside Gilani's terrorist structure.

This was a most frustrating call. Ali's foreign accent was extremely difficult to understand, especially over the phone. He was angry, emotionally wound up and speaking with such rapidity that at times his speech was nothing but a hurried blur. It was clear, however, that he wanted to meet with me somewhere in New York at a time and location to be disclosed later. Obviously, this was not going to happen without further information. Ali wasn't the first person to call our office seeking to meet with me, or the co-producer of our film, Jason Campbell, under some highly suspicious setting or arrangement.

I was on the phone with Ali for nearly two hours during that first phone conversation trying to understand the purpose of his call. I asked him to slow down, to repeat himself, to spell anything I couldn't understand. By the end of the conversation it was becoming evident that he might be exactly who he claimed to be—an undercover agent for the NYPD.

Of all the things Ali said, one thing stood out that made it highly probable that he was working for the NYPD. Ali asked me if I knew Detective David Bavasi. My answer was, "No. I never heard of him."

"Yes," he said. "You do know him. He called your home. He talks about you all the time. He left a message on your phone on his way to South Carolina when I was in his car. He said he wanted to stop by and see some of the film and photos you have on Muslims of the Americas."

"You mean Detective David Calla?" I corrected him.

"No," he was quick to reply. "Detective David Bavasi."

At that moment, I think we both realized we were talking about the same NYPD detective, who was going by two different names.

"Do you have a phone number for him?" Ali asked.

I did. But I asked him to give me his number first, as I wanted to be sure he wasn't just going to repeat my phone number back to me. He gave me the detective's phone number, which matched the one I had on file for Detective Calla.

This, by itself, did not prove he worked for Detective Calla. But knowing the details of the message that Detective Calla had left on my phone was an eye-opener that was hard to ignore.

During our years of investigating MOA, I had spoken to Detective David Calla several times by phone. He first reached out to me after learning our organization had aerial photos and film interviews of MOA members and their camps on our upcoming "Homegrown Jihad" documentary. He expressed a desire to review the film and photos, especially any film footage that was not going to be used in the final cut of the film. Detective Calla thought he might see or hear something that would have gone unnoticed by us.

We had literally hours upon hours of film and photos that would never make it into the documentary, and I told him he would need at least a couple of days to go through all the footage. It would be a laborious task, I told him, since much of the unused film would be uneventful, routine and even dull. Detective Calla seemed opened to the task, but told me he would have to wait until he received permission to make the trip to Virginia.

Nothing earth-shattering ever resulted from any phone conversation with the detective. Law enforcement has always been very tight-lipped about Muslims of the Americas. Detective Calla was as tight-lipped as any, except for telling me that the NYPD had an undercover agent working inside MOA at their Hancock, New York, headquarters. He never said who it was or for how long, of course. And I believe he only disclosed this information to make the point that not all law enforcement agencies were ignoring the dangers of this Muslim group.

During the summer of 2009, while I was traveling in Europe working on another film project, Detective Calla called my home and left a message. The detective said he was passing through Lynchburg, Virginia, and would like to stop by our office to review our film and photos. He didn't leave a date or time on his call. I phoned him upon my return from Europe only to learn he had left the message two weeks earlier. He told me that he had been on his way to South Carolina when he called, but had already returned to New York City. He would have to reschedule the meeting and review the film and photos at another time.

The fact that Ali knew Detective Calla's phone number, knew that he had called my home and left a message, knew the content of that message and also knew that Detective Calla was on his way to South Carolina when he made the call, helped convince me that Ali was probably working for the NYPD. I also remembered that Detective Calla told me the NYPD had an undercover agent inside the Hancock headquarters of MOA.

But out of an abundance of extreme caution, I left room for suspicion. Agreeing to meet someone I did not know, at an undisclosed location in New York, at an unknown time in the future by someone who also claimed to be an eight-year member of Muslims of the Americas, could prove to be a tragic meeting.

Meeting Arranged

We decided the best, and safest, approach was to meet with Ali's attorney before I had any face-to-face meeting with Ali himself.

Two members of my staff met with Ali and his attorney, Stan Weber, in a New York City office building near Ground Zero in late September. After a two-hour meeting it became clear that Ali did not present any harm to our organization and that his sole goal was to tell his story. With permission from Ali's attorney, we were granted an interview that took place in a conference room of Ali's apartment complex.

Ali began by saying he was a confidential informant for the NYPD—a rather hazardous occupation which usually involves a person agreeing to offer their services to law enforcement, such as infiltrating a criminal network, in exchange for avoiding prosecution for a criminal act.

Ali's story, as he told it to me, was not much different.

Ali arrived in the United States from Cairo, Egypt, around 2002 using a fake passport. Having gained a reputation in Egypt as a judo Olympian, Ali came to America wanting to train at the Olympic Training Center in Colorado Springs, Colorado. In addition, Ali claimed he needed to come to America to earn more money than he could possibly make in his home country to help his ailing mother in Egypt with her medical bills.

Unbeknownst to him, however, someone "ratted him out" on his fake passport and he was promptly arrested when he landed at America. A Colorado jury, after listening to a "choice of evil" defense (explained later in this chapter) found him not guilty. Several months afterwards, Ali was arrested again, this time by the U.S. Attorney General's Office, on similar charges.

In between these arrests, Ali came into direct contact with some members of Muslims of the Americas who lived in the area and attended martial arts training classes. While in jail on federal charges, he was recruited by the NYPD to use his connections to members of the group to infiltrate the organization. He agreed to the "deal," which involved a complicated plan of sending Ali back to Egypt, where he would re-enter the United States with a green card. The green card gave Ali permanent residence status to work and live in the United States.

But after eight years of infiltrating this terrorist organization, Ali had enough and wanted out. Ali would learn that it was not easy "quitting" a job as a confidential informant. It had consequences. One of those consequences was to greatly upset the NYPD. After he notified his contacts within the NYPD that he was "quitting," Ali left the United States to attend the 2010 Olympics in Vancouver. When he returned, the United States would not honor his green card.

"They told me my green card doesn't exist, that it never existed," he said.

He was placed in an immigration holding cell and was scheduled for a January 2011 hearing that threatened to send him back to Egypt.

Ali was released from incarceration after a few months due to health concerns; he suffered from epilepsy. As a condition of his release, he was required to wear an ankle bracelet that restricted his movements mostly to New York City.

Ali wanted help from Christian Action Network, somehow, someway.

I was soon thrown into a tumultuous and suspicious series of meetings, phone calls and e-mail correspondences that had me questioning who was really who, and who was calling the shots. Underlying all this confusion was a deep sense of danger that all the players, including myself, could be at risk.

At first, it seemed evident from talking with Ali that his primary objective was to prove to the immigration judge that he was a former undercover agent for the NYPD. Ali said the NYPD was refusing to cooperate, making it impossible to subpoena Detective Calla to the trial to prove he had been an undercover agent. Therefore, Ali began asking a lot of questions about my relationship with Detective David Calla: Did you have a work address for him? What e-mails did he send you? What did you send to him? Would you testify that Detective Calla said the NYPD had an undercover agent working inside Muslims of the Americas?

Ali's questions to me began to focus so much on Detective Calla that I began to suspect that Ali might be a front man for an NYPD investigation on the detective and that our entire meeting was a smoke-screen. Perhaps the police department thought Detective Calla was giving me unauthorized information about MOA and they wanted him investigated. The NYPD knew I was getting confidential information about Muslims of the Americas from somewhere. It is a fact that incriminating videos and police reports were in my possession. Maybe the NYPD thought I was getting them from Detective Calla (I wasn't). Then again, maybe it was MOA trying to get me to divulge as much information as possible about Detective Calla so they could put him in harm's way. I could not be sure whom to trust.

Either way, I needed to talk to Detective Calla.

I spoke to Detective Calla on the phone shortly after my conversation with Ali. I told him someone (though I would not say who) was asking a lot of questions about our informal relationship. I said I wanted to meet with him, privately, to discuss the matter.

His first question mirrored my own concerns. "Is this MOA or NYPD" who's asking questions about him? He sounded worried. Very worried.

I told him I didn't know. Perhaps it was neither, perhaps it was both, although I did not elaborate. Maybe it wasn't MOA. Maybe it wasn't the NYPD. Maybe Ali was actually telling the truth—that he was an uncover agent who needed proof that he worked for the NYPD to avoid deportation. But I didn't want to discuss it over the phone, so I set up a time to meet Detective Calla in New York City the following Saturday.

Within a few days of our scheduled meeting, Detective Calla called me.

"Is this a young Egyptian man you're talking to who's facing deportation?" he asked.

"Yes, it is," I acknowledged.

"Does he know me by a name that begins with a 'B' and ends with an 'I'?"

"Yes," I said. "He knows you as Detective Bavasi."

"He used to work for me," Detective Calla admitted. "Is he trying to threaten me and my family?"

"Not at all," I assured him. "It seems he wants to locate you. He wants you to testify at his upcoming deportation hearing. He says he needs proof that he was an undercover agent."

"Ali is headed back to Egypt. He's going to be deported," Detective Calla said, noticeably angry. "If he keeps asking questions about me, he'll be put back in jail. The NYPD is going to see if this is a threat against me, my wife and my children. We're going to do a threat assessment on him. So you might get a call from our threat assessment department. And if he keeps asking questions about me, he'll find himself deported even faster."

This was an enlightening call. Very enlightening. Detective Calla had admitted that Ali worked for the NYPD. He also verified Ali's claim that he was known to him as Detective Bavasi. He confirmed that Ali was a young Egyptian man who was facing deportation. Furthermore, he expressed a fear of Ali—as if Ali might have turned coat and could now be working directly for MOA, thereby presenting a threat to him, his wife and children.

I never did get a call from any NYPD "threat assessment" division asking about Ali. And I never got the feeling that Ali presented a threat to Detective Calla in any questions he was asking me.

For his part, Ali only had nice and complimentary things to say about the detective.

"You know, I love the guy," Ali said of Detective Calla, refusing to believe he'd had anything to do with his arrest or deportation hearing. "I think it's coming from people higher up."

Trained Fighter

Ali, who is in his early thirties, looks every part of being a professional boxer and martial arts expert. His arms, legs and abdomen are so superbly sculpted that they resemble a Greek statue. His dark eyebrows accentuate a clean shaven head that looks both menacing and oddly shaped, as if molded for combat. A deep scar marks the bridge of his nose, slicing just below his black eyes. Otherwise, his dark-skinned facial features are free of additional markings frequently pronounced among other fighters. He's not a tall man, perhaps standing only slightly more than five-and-a-half feet. But his lack of stature is eclipsed by a complex personality that can appear gentle, stern, light-hearted and foreboding—all at the same instant. His broad smile is disarming. His boxing glare is fearless. He could easily be two people at once, which is exactly what he claims to have been for the past eight years: a hard-line member of an Islamic terrorist organization and an undercover informant who is also the gentle father of two small children.

When Ali entered the United States to train at the U.S. Olympic Training Center in Colorado Springs, it didn't take him long to run into members of Muslims of the Americas, though he was clueless of the organization's history, reputation or Islamic beliefs. In fact, though he is a Muslim himself, he did not share their strict adherence to Islamic fundamentalist beliefs.

"I knew some of the MOA guys before going to jail the second time. I befriended them," Ali said. "I would go to prayer with them on Fridays and we hung out sometimes. I was about 18 or 19 years old."

But their strict lifestyle and adherence to Sharia law differed from his own Islamic beliefs.

"I went to clubs. I went to parties. I had girlfriends. They didn't."

But the young MOA members liked him, despite what they saw as unorthodox Islamic views.

"I knew the martial arts," he said, "which they liked. I could teach them Arabic. I could teach them how to read the Quran. It wasn't anything formal, just hanging out.

"But at the time," he added, "I was not a member of MOA."

Ali's membership in the MOA didn't happen until after he was placed in jail a second time, on federal charges of entering the United States illegally. Ali won his first trial at the state level in Colorado. His attorney made the claim that Ali used a fake passport to enter the United States not just to further his judo training, but also to earn money to send back to Egypt to help with his ailing mother's medical bills.

His mother died three months after Ali was in a Colorado jail. "My girlfriend went to Egypt, got my mother's death certificate and medical records," he remembers. "And my attorney presented these records to the court, including the money I sent to Egypt."

Ali's attorney argued that his client had to make a "choice of evil" decision in using a fake passport. Under this argument, Ali claimed he committed a crime of forgery in hopes of keeping his mother alive by paying her medical expenses. A "choice of evil" defense, though not permitted in every state, is permitted by Colorado law (CRS 18-1-708). It allows a criminal defendant to argue that between two choices of evil, the defendant chose an action presenting the least amount of duress.

The jury found Ali not guilty. But the U.S. Attorney's Office objected to the jury's verdict and decided to prosecute Ali under federal law. "They charged me with the exact same thing," he said, still miffed that after these many years in the United States he could be charged twice for the same crime.

Back in jail a second time, Ali learned that the federal government did not recognize the "choice of evil" defense. His lawyer was going to need a new legal strategy. Suddenly, Ali's outlook for getting out of jail and remaining in the United States looked dim.

NYPD To The Rescue

Little did he know the NYPD was about to come to his rescue.

Ever since 1990, when Jamaat Al Fuqra was first known to have an Islamic terrorist camp in Buena Vista, Colorado, the NYPD has kept a close eye on the organization, including the movements and activities of its members in Colorado Springs. The NYPD knew that members of the organization were meeting with a man named Ali Aziz and that they were being drawn in by his Egyptian background, his knowledge of the Arabic language and his reputation as an Olympic judo expert.

Two New York detectives met Ali in jail. Ali remembered them as Joel and Ron. They offered him a job as a confidential informant under several conditions, one being that he would take a lie detector test stating he had no plans to harm America. After passing the test, Ali then had to agree to a deal where he would plead guilty to the misuse of a subpoena, a low-grade felony. The plea deal was meant to satisfy the U.S. Attorney General, who wanted Ali prosecuted and deported. Ali's confession meant he would be deported back to Egypt, though without serving any additional jail time. But it also meant the NYPD could then bring him back into the United States at a later time.

The bottom line: Ali would only be allowed to return to the United States if he agreed to become a confidential informant for the NYPD. Otherwise, he would be denied re-entry. They had the upper hand.

"They deported me so they could bring me back in and have control over me," Ali said.

Though the "deal" gave the NYPD complete control over Ali, there were some perks to becoming the department's undercover agent.

Besides being provided a green card, giving him permanent U.S. residence status, Ali would be paid money—lots of money—for becoming a spy inside the MOA organization. He earned nearly $250,000 a year.

"I was paid in cash," Ali said. "Sometimes every month. Sometimes once every three months. I had to sign a sheet of paper for the cash. Originally, I deposited the money in Wachovia, but later on in Chase."

His operation was funded through a corporation called *STK Enterprises.*

Ali kept many boxes of paperwork during his years as a confidential informant. During my three-hour meeting with him, Ali would often pull document after document from a box where the name *STK Enterprises* appeared on receipts, rental bills, airline tickets and even such minor expenses as phone bills. Nowhere, however, did the name NYPD show up on any of the expenses.

"It was a bogus corporation," Ali said. "It was set up by the NYPD."

Included in his boxes were many photos—photos of Ali with members of Muslims of the Americas—pictures of him inside the camps, inside their homes, meeting with leaders of MOA. Friendly meetings. Warm meetings. Meetings that included families and children. Without a doubt, Ali was well known by Muslims of the Americas, and the photos made it almost impossible to dispute that he was very well connected to the terrorist organization.

Ali, I would learn, was not just well connected, but highly placed inside MOA. At the time of his departure as an undercover agent for the NYPD, he was serving as the bodyguard to Barry Adams, the head of MOA operations in North America.

Barry Adams nicknamed Ali "*The Jackal,*" a reference to the international terrorist Carlos the Jackal, who is currently serving a life sentence in France for murder. The nickname should not be taken lightly, especially since it was given to Ali by a Muslim organization claiming to be a peaceful group.

The Jackal

Carlos the Jackal, whose real name is Ilich Ramirez Sanchez, is a Muslim convert and perhaps one of the world's best-known terrorists, second only to the late Osama Bin Laden. Hollywood has scripted many movies about his life and he has been the subject of numerous books and

TV movies—though his Islamic beliefs are rarely discussed.

The Jackal claims to have been responsible for killing more than 1,500 people in the cause of Palestinian liberation, but his prison sentence in 1997 came from the murder of two French policemen and an informant 22 years earlier.

Even though Hollywood and the mainstream media have ignored his Islamic beliefs, the so-called Jackal set the world straight about his Islamic views in 2003 with his book, *Revolutionary Islam*.

In that book, which the Jackal wrote from his jail cell, he praised Osama Bin Laden as a "shining" example of Islam[1] and warned the West: "From now on, terrorism is going to be more or less a daily part of the landscape of your rotting democracies."[2]

After Bin Laden's execution by U.S. forces in May, 2011, the Jackal called him a "martyr." He said the former terrorist leader "will still be remembered in 100 years' time because of what he has done, the example he gave."[3]

For Muslims of the Americas to proudly nickname Ali after Carlos the Jackal, a notorious murderer and terrorist, is, at best, a serious error in judgment. At worse, it is a backhanded endorsement of terrorism.

After being released from his Colorado jail, Ali spent time solidifying his connections to Muslims of the Americas members in Colorado Springs. But the NYPD would have bigger plans for him. They wanted him moved to New York, where Sheikh Gilani boasted his American headquarters.

The NYPD got Ali an apartment in Binghamton, New York, a modest-sized town that Muslims of the Americas claims to be the location of their national headquarters. It is not. "They don't have any offices there," Ali said. "Probably a cell phone."

Instead, their headquarters sits on an 80-acre compound about 40 miles southwest of Binghamton, at a camp buried in the Catskills Mountains in a town called Hancock.

Leader Barry Adams

But Binghamton was close enough to Gilani's American headquarters, and to make matters better for the NYPD, it housed the location of the organization's deputy director of North America, Barry Adams, who had recently been released from prison.

Barry Adams, who has been discussed earlier in this book, was one of four men arrested in 1993 for a plot to blow up an Indian theater and Hindu temple in Toronto. Investigators estimated that the terrorist attack, if successful, would have killed more than 4,500 people.

When arrested, Barry Adams was the passenger in a Buick Skylark being driven by another jihadist, Glen Ford. Police traced the car back to Ford's apartment in New York, where they found two rifles, seven handguns and 2,000 rounds of ammunition—all believed to be in his possession for the upcoming Toronto attack.[4]

It was during the Canadian trial of Barry Adams and Glen Ford that authorities officially linked Muslims of the Americas to Jamaat Al Fuqra.

Ford said in court testimony that Gilani and his leaders in Pakistan convinced the North American group to switch its name from Jamaat Al Fuqra (meaning the Community of the Impoverished) to Muslims of the Americas, because it now had a presence in the United States, South America, Trinidad and Canada.

"They said Al Fuqra was too much like a mystic name," Ford testified. "To identify with areas of work, we said Muslims of the Americas would be appropriate.

"Up to that time, we were kind of tribal," Ford added. "We were all black folks so we were all kind of into a black thing. When these representatives from Pakistan came, it decided to stick."[5]

It was clear early on in America that Barry Adams would run Gilani's North American operations. Sheikh Gilani even married one of Adams' daughters, Naimah, when she was just 17 years old. She now lives in Pakistan. Reportedly, Gilani's black followers in America asked him to marry Adams' daughter to prove he did not discriminate against the races.[6]

Barry Adams ran the North American group even from his jail cell during his 12-year imprisonment in Canada. "Barry Adams ran everything from jail," Ali said. "Canada has contact visits. Leaders from New York would visit him for four or more days."

Ali said that Barry Adams will eventually succeed Gilani upon his death and become the head of Jamaat Al Fuqra.

So it only made sense for the NYPD to place Ali in Binghamton, New York, close to where Barry Adams was living after he was released from jail in 2006.

Ali would become well liked by the future leader of MOA. "I gave him respect because Barry Adams knows how Muslims should respect their leaders. You know, you talk to him with your head down."

But the NYPD wanted Ali to do more than just become respected by Barry Adams and spy on the group. They wanted him to do the unthinkable: They wanted him to help Muslims of the Americas set up overseas operations, to actually help MOA set up their terrorist group in foreign countries such as Saudi Arabia, Egypt, Venezuela and Trinidad. The NYPD, according to Ali, wanted to track MOA operations overseas. And to do that, Ali needed to help MOA travel to these foreign countries and establish a presence.

"MOA wanted to establish a home base in these foreign countries," Ali said.

Because Ali already had a good relationship with MOA leaders before moving to New York, the risky operation had some possibilities. "I have experience," he explained. "My passport says I'm an Egyptian fighter. I'm not the prettiest guy. I speak well. I don't speak the ghetto. I handle myself well. They don't. A lot of these guys have no manners, they have no manners. MOA used me at the beginning because I was a big martial artist. I present myself well. I did things like providing them information about military training. I was involved in a lot of this stuff."

But getting MOA to allow him to be involved in their overseas operations was going to take more than just being a martial arts expert who could handle himself well and behave in public. He had to offer more. And the NYPD had the answer: provide money. Get Ali money to help MOA with their overseas travel expenses.

From his Binghamton, New York, apartment, Ali set up a boxing promotion and management business with the help of the NYPD. That boxing business exists to this day, going by the name of Dominance MMA. It claims to be a management business "devoted to the fighter."

Ali boasts on his web site: "Ali comes from a family of champions. Ali's experience in judo is well documented with a record of 513-33 judo fights."

Dominance boxing is a mixed combat sport that includes judo, jiu jitsu, muay thai and other forms of the martial arts. Ali's web site claims to represent some of the best-known dominance boxers in the country, including the Gracie brothers.

The boxing business would eventually serve many purposes for Ali and the NYPD. But from the beginning, and foremost, it helped explain where Ali was getting all his money to help MOA setup overseas operations.

Establishing Terror Camps

Even though Ali could explain the "source of the money" to MOA leaders, he struggled with the idea that the NYPD wanted him to help MOA set up terrorist operations in foreign countries.

"They (the NYPD) kinda were like we want to start going to other countries, like Venezuela and Egypt. We want you to help establish camps. I was being paid to establish these camps," Ali said.

"The NYPD wanted to follow Muslims of the Americas overseas. They wanted to know their members, their contacts," Ali said. "They wanted to have information about them, what they were doing there, why they wanted to be there."

Furthermore, "they paid for everything," Ali said of the NYPD.

MOA, however, believed Ali was getting the money from his boxing promotion business. The NYPD even helped Ali set up a car business as a cover for his additional income.

"I was fighting and I sold cars on the side. The cars were just to maintain my cover. They told me go start a car dealership. They told me to start fighting in fights, you know? I'd make a minimum $30,000 in the fights," Ali said.

Ali provided MOA with more than just money for its overseas traveling to set up camps; he also helped them with their travel documents.

"I had to get immigration documents for MOA members to travel to these countries. About 15 went to Egypt. I got their visas. I would give the NYPD a copy of their passports and addresses. I would let the NYPD know who is going and who is coming. Everything was under their supervision."

The NYPD, Ali said, helped set up camps in Saudi Arabia, Egypt, Trinidad and Venezuela. During those trips, Ali would send "everything" back to Detective Calla, including secret recordings and photos.

The most successful overseas operation the NYPD helped set up for Muslims of the Americas was in Venezuela. Yet, ironically, the project to get MOA into Venezuela served two purposes which seemed to compete against each other.

MOA wanted to set up a presence in Venezuela, Ali explained, because they believed it was a country where American authorities could never penetrate. MOA could insulate itself from the FBI, CIA or any other U.S. government agency.

"The CIA, if they get caught there, they would be dead," Ali claimed.

The NYPD wanted to help Muslims of the Americas set up a presence in Venezuela for precisely the same reason. If they couldn't get into Venezuela through conventional means, then perhaps the NYPD could ride the backs of a radical, Islamic organization into the country.

To this day, MOA members travel back and forth from Venezuela, including "some important figures in MOA," Ali said.

"There's a very big figure in MOA right now living in Venezuela," Ali said, though he would not elaborate on who the individual was. "(Sheikh) Gilani travels back and forth to Venezuela and he might move to Venezuela."

"The United States has no relationship with Venezuela," Ali added. "You have to understand; Chavez loves Muslims. All the Muslim communities in Venezuela follow Chavez. One of his speeches I attended started with him reciting the Quran before his presentation."

Being of foreign descent gave Ali a natural advantage when operating in Venezuela.

"To them, I'm the Egyptian guy. I speak Arabic. I can get an apartment in Venezuela. I can get a car. I can establish a business. I don't have to say I'm from America. I can just be Ali, understand?

"For example, the CIA was at a mosque one time and the guys at the mosque very much picked them out," said Ali. "They said, 'You're an American. We can't let you through.' People in Venezuela are very (phobic) about Americans. If you're an American, then you work for the CIA. You do. I'm serious about this."

'The Purpose Is To Wage War'

In 2010, an article was published in the *Journal of Counterterrorism and Homeland Security International* that verified Ali's claim that Jamaat Al Fuqra now has a presence in Venezuela. The article states that

Venezuela and Iran have agreed to establish "terrorist training camps" in nearly a half-dozen Venezuelan states.

The following statement seems to give clarity and credence to Ali's claim:

"Terrorist groups such as Al-Qaeda, Hamas, Hezbollah, Jammat Al Fuqra, members of the major drug cartels and gangs, especially MS-13, have been observed training in these camps," the counterterrorism article states.

The article then alarmingly states:

"The purpose of this cooperation is to wage war within the U.S."[7]

After Ali helped set up the Jamaat Al Fuqra camp in Venezuela, he was then asked by the NYPD to go to Egypt to help MOA establish a presence there. He complied, but with great reluctance.

"I told these guys: 'Listen, you want me to go to Egypt? It's my home country. Venezuela, I got no problem. This is my job. I love my job.' I loved it. They told me just go, see what they do."

But the NYPD needed more from Ali than just going, monitoring and reporting. They needed his help getting visas for MOA members.

"They said the whole thing is when you go, you have to help us. We need you to help us get immigration documents. Some countries are hard to get immigration documents. I pulled a lot of strings in Egypt. And my name was very much on everything. I had to use the help of my brother. He's full Egyptian. They put my family in a dangerous situation. But they said, 'Don't worry about it, you're good.' I said 'ok.'"

But now that Ali is under the threat of being deported back to Egypt, things aren't "ok."

"Do you know what are they gonna do to me?" Ali said, speaking of Egyptian authorities if he is deported. "They are going to mistreat me. They are going to drown me. They are going to waterboard me. And then they'll say I was working for Muslims of the Americas. They have the information about 10 people that I brought to Egypt right now. That's what will happen. I will be charged with espionage or as double agent."

When I interviewed Ali, it was just months prior to the overthrow of Egyptian president and military commander Hosni Mubarak, whose dictatorship presented Ali with his greatest threat. With no clear leadership or government in Egypt at the time of this writing, Ali's deportation hearing has been delayed and his future legal status is unknown to me or our organization.

Ali was viewed by MOA as one of its most powerful members, not only serving as the perceived bodyguard to the leader of the group's North American operations, Barry Adams, but also able to fund travel expenses for overseas operations, obtain visas and immigration papers for its members and help the organization with military training and the martial arts.

"I was the guy that traveled for MOA," Ali said. "I established jamaats (compounds). I could set up jamaats overseas."

No wonder Barry Adams thought of Ali as *The Jackal*.

"I was Barry's right-hand man. Some of the MOA members thought I was Barry's bodyguard. I just viewed myself as his companion. I traveled to Virginia and South Carolina with him. I helped settle disputes at the various camps. Barry would visit me. He would bring his wife and kids. He loved me. He said he loved me very much.

"But at the same time," Ali said unabashedly, "I was getting all the information I could during that time with him and giving it to the NYPD."

"I saw a 50-year-old woman tied to a tree and getting beaten ... This is what I think is the biggest disgrace: The abuse. The only thing is, nobody on the camps says anything. Of course they're afraid ... It's Gilani's law."

Ali Aziz, who lived among Muslims of the Americas for eight years.

CHAPTER 13

Modern Warrior Slaves

I REMEMBER SITTING IN A NEW YORK APARTMENT COMPLEX TALKing with an undercover agent with the New York Police Department. The young man said something to me which ignited a vivid memory ... and sent a chill through me.

The memory that came back was of a day in August of 2007—during the height of our film production on Muslims of the Americas (MOA) —when I saw a news article with a connection to my home town of Lynchburg, Virginia.

"Drugs Found Before They Reached Lynchburg," the headline read.

The article explained that Maryland police had intercepted a shipment of drugs headed to Lynchburg and arrested four people, all with ties to the Lynchburg area." The names of those arrested were Mustafa Abdussamad (21), Hussan Rahman (21), Munir Abdulsalaam (24), all from Lynchburg and a 19-year-old girlfriend of one of the suspects, Adrienne Janay Stewart, from nearby Amherst.

The suspects were pulled over on Interstate 95 near Baltimore for speeding. They were on a return trip to Lynchburg after buying drugs in Philadelphia. Inside their vehicle police found two pounds of marijuana and 400 units of heroin, all packaged for sale.

The story was simple enough, so simple that no one would be able to connect any dots between these drug runners and Muslims of the Americas (MOA)—certainly not from reading the news story. But I immediately made that connection and understood its significance. I learned that although all three men once lived inside the MOA compound in Red House, Virginia, they were residents of the city of Lynchburg at the time of their arrests.

It is important to understand that this is typical of how MOA handles its criminal activities. Ever since the 1992 raid on their Buena Vista, Colorado,[1] compound, MOA leaders rarely have their criminal elements living inside their camps committing illegal activities. They move these criminals "off campus" to avoid having their entire camp searched, raided or shut down due to the arrest of one or more of their members.

The strategy is simple. It works to MOA's advantage to have their criminal elements move off campus to avoid the intrusion of law enforcement officials, and it also allows MOA leaders to claim that these individuals are "former members" of their group who were actually "kicked off" their villages because of bad behavior.

In other words, if you want to commit crimes for Sheikh Gilani, the leader of MOA, you also better be willing to be thrown under the bus if you get caught. It's actually a brilliant strategy, which most in law enforcement either have not figured out or don't want to figure out. MOA knows that it is to their advantage to move their criminal elements "off campus" before they begin commissioning crimes.

This story of running drugs from Philadelphia to Lynchburg is no different. The three Muslim men (whose parents still lived in the Red House compound at the time of their arrests) were moved "off campus" in case they were ever arrested.

Did Maryland officials know who they had in custody? It was doubtful. I visited the Lynchburg Police Department to see if they had any intention of notifying the Maryland prosecutor that these young men were members of MOA with connections to Gilani's compound in Red House, Virginia. This was an opportunity, I believed, for law enforcement to connect the dots between the drug supplier, the drug purchaser and the drug money going back to Sheikh Gilani's terrorist organization in Pakistan. But connecting these dots would require cooperation among several state and county law enforcement agencies, including federal law enforcement.

But the Lynchburg police told me they would not get involved in the case. Their response could best be described as prosecutorial indifference. The arrests were not made in their jurisdiction and the Red House compound did not sit in their county. It mattered not that three of the people arrested in Baltimore lived in their city of Lynchburg.

I decided to call the Baltimore County prosecutor on my own. I spoke to Frank Meyer, the assistant state attorney. He had never heard of

Jamaat Al Fuqra nor Muslims of the Americas, but he was very interested in any possible terror connections to the illegal drugs that were confiscated in the arrests. He invited me to Baltimore to tell him more.

When I arrived at his office, I thought it was just going to be a meeting between myself and the prosecutor. I was surprised, however, to see a conference room full of detectives, investigators and members of the FBI Joint Terrorism Task Force. For the next hour, I explained the inner workings of Jamaat Al Fuqra, its criminal past in the United States, its connections to terrorist activity and how the organization commits fraud, runs scams and sells drugs to funnel money back to Pakistan.

When I finished making my summary against Muslims of the Americas, I made a suggestion to the prosecutors and investigators sitting around the conference table. I suggested that rather than focus solely on who sold the drugs to the young Muslim men, why not offer them a plea deal to disclose where the profits from the illegal drugs sales would be headed. By pursuing where the money was going, law enforcement had a unique opportunity to crack down on, if not shut down, the Red House compound and possibly implicate members in other Gilani compounds.

I'll probably never know whether my advice was taken or simply discarded as too much investigative work. More than likely, the latter.

It is worth noting, however, that only one of the men arrested, Mustafa Abdussamad, served any jail time at all, receiving a 10-year sentence with five years suspended. Munir Abdulsalaam received a 10-year sentence, all suspended. The shocker, however, was the sentencing of Hassan Rahman. He received a 20-year prison sentence with all 20 years suspended. The suspension of a 20-year prison sentence would indicate he made a sizeable plea deal for himself and that whoever he "rolled over" on was no small potato.

Several years later, as I sat in a New York apartment complex interviewing this young NYPD informant—Ali Aziz, a Muslim man who had lived under cover with MOA for eight years and who knew about the "Virginia connection"—the memory of my meeting with Baltimore officials came flooding back. Law enforcement had clearly declined to pursue this connection to MOA. Yet years later Ali would confirm this important point:

"The drug money (from deals like the one involving the Virginia MOA members) goes back to (Sheikh) Gilani."

'I Loved My Job'

When I interviewed Ali with two members of my staff, we met in a conference area on the first floor of his high-end apartment complex. He lived there with his wife and small daughter. Within a year, Ali would become a father again, this time to a son.

At times, as Ali discussed his role as an undercover agent for the NYPD, he seemed conflicted.

"You know what? I really loved it," he said, allowing a broad, almost Cheshire-cat smile to cross his face. "I did love it. I really did. It's exciting. It really is."

But he also appeared somber about his role of playing spy inside an Islamic terrorist network and the dangers it may pose to his family. "I'm not a James Bond," he said. "I'm just a regular guy. I'm a regular guy trying to raise my daughter. That's what I want to do."

But he's not a "regular" guy. Not by any definition. Forget "regular" —the NYPD did not want "regular." They wanted somebody who was *irregular*, somebody they could regulate, somebody they could control, as when they asked Ali to move out of his apartment building in Binghamton, New York, and move directly onto Gilani's 80-acre headquarters in Hancock, New York.

Both the NYPD and Muslims of the Americas wanted to see Ali relocate to Hancock. The move seemed to please everyone—except Ali.

"It wasn't like we all hung out," he said of himself and the other members of MOA after he made the move. "They knew me. They wanted me to talk to them. I was *the guy* they had heard about. After that, I did a lot of traveling. I traveled to settle disputes like, you know, we have a problem ... money, transactions."

Ali would live on the Hancock compound for two years. He had a house there, which was nothing but a dump when he first moved into it. It would cost him thousands of dollars to remodel it into something livable.

"This is what the NYPD[2] had wanted for the past 20 years," Ali said of his move to Hancock. "They wanted someone living inside the Hancock camp who's an undercover agent."

On the other hand, MOA leaders also wanted Ali to move to Hancock so he could marry into the "family." For MOA, marriages are a way of cementing relationships, much in the way Sheikh Gilani was asked to marry the daughter of Barry Adams to cement his loyalty to the black race.

"They were telling me I was supposed to be married and having children," he said of the MOA leadership.

And not just that he *should* marry, but *whom* he should marry.

"They (the NYPD) wanted me to marry this girl whose brother is a big, big leader in MOA," Ali said. "They wanted me to marry this girl. I told them, 'I can't marry this girl. It's against my morals. I can't do this.' But they left me with no choice. They said, 'You can help her because she is depressed.' I let them convince me."

The marriage would be an "Islamic wedding," meaning an illegal marriage—no license, no marriage certificate, no pesky state records. Ali thought the NYPD would be on his side. Surely his "handlers" would understand the dilemma he was in—being forced into an illegal marriage. Perhaps the NYPD would also realize the problem of living on one of Gilani's compounds and being under the direct control of MOA.

"I told the NYPD my predicament, but to my surprise, they agreed with MOA," Ali said. "They put pressure on me to marry her. They said, 'Hey buddy, this is the name of the game. If you don't marry with them, they won't need you anymore, and then we won't need you anymore, and we will send you back to Egypt.'"

Because of the threat, Ali started keeping records of his dealings with the NYPD. "This is when I started keeping stuff. I have five boxes full," Ali said, pointing to one of those boxes sitting on the floor in front of him. "They tell me, 'You have to choose; you wanna live in this country and live here? Or do you wanna go back to Egypt?'"

Ali opted for living here, even if it meant living in Hancock and agreeing to marry one of the leader's daughters ... illegally.

I have visited the outside of the Hancock compound a couple times and flown over it once. It's typical of virtually every other MOA camp. It's in a heavily wooded area off the beaten path, with mostly battered trailers and homes and a couple of newly constructed buildings thrown into the mix. It has dirt roads lined with old cars, new cars and junk cars. Wooded debris, discarded scrapings and demolished buildings can be seen throughout the area, giving it an unsightly appearance from above. It has its own graveyard, similar to those found on other camps. And the property has a couple of small lakes, which have been used as "open areas" to shoot their weapons across. Not surprisingly, Hancock also has a guard shack to intercept unwanted visitors.

By all accounts, Hancock is the camp that houses the leaders of MOA and makes decisions for the rest of the camps throughout the United States.

A Bittersweet Marriage

Ali's marriage to a girl he hardly knew could best be described as bittersweet. The NYPD was happy. MOA was happy. And the girl was happy. To make this bitter pill easier for Ali to swallow, however, the NYPD paid for the honeymoon.

"They gave me the money," he said. "They bought me a honeymoon. Yeah, they paid for my honeymoon."

Perhaps it was the least they could do after forcing him into a loveless, illegal wedding to a 19-year-old girl whose father is one of the leaders of a known terrorist organization. But there was no sex on the honeymoon. And there wouldn't be any for months to come. Ali did not love the girl and he didn't want to get her pregnant. Birth control, however, was not an option.

"MOA has these rules," Ali said. "You're not allowed to take birth-control pills. Not allowed to use condoms. This is from Gilani. It is forbidden."

Ali confirmed what our research had already shown: That the MOA's policy was to encourage members to collect as much public assistance as possible, and the more children they had the more assistance they received, much of which was returned to Sheikh Gilani in Pakistan.

Yet Ali took his marital obligations seriously. He said he felt bad for his MOA wife.

"The girl didn't know how to write or read, so I started helping her. She went to school. I took her on trips; to new places. Afterwards, I really started to like her, but I wasn't sure if it was love."

But Ali's reluctance to touch her was upsetting his new wife. "She would ask me, 'What's wrong?' It was a big problem, being married to someone you don't even touch," he said. "I felt really, really guilty. I feel guilty to this day.

"The house we were living in was a shared trailer," he said, meaning other Muslim families were living with him. "It was disgusting. It was crazy. But I fixed it up real nice. I spent almost 35 thousand dollars."

Eventually he did "touch" his wife and she became pregnant, giving birth to a boy in 2006. The child made everyone happy—the girl, MOA, even the NYPD. "The NYPD was so happy," Ali said. "As soon as I married this girl and had a child, I could be more trusted in MOA ... But because of who her brother was, I got access to everything. I get access to meetings, everything!

"But this was a thing I was forced to do," Ali continued, suddenly sounding defensive. Perhaps it was because he understood that an innocent child had to be born and a young girl had to be wed just for the benefit of others, so that the NYPD could have their "inside" man and MOA could have someone they trust.

Even after taking a solemn moment to reflect back on his former wife and young son, both of whom still live on the Hancock camp, Ali concluded, "I had no other choice."

"She still loves me," he said, clearly wrestling with some residual emotions he has for her. "She tells everyone I'm the best thing that ever happened to her. But I could not lie to her anymore. She's not my wife anymore. We got divorced."

What began as an "Islamic wedding" ended as an "Islamic divorce." No lawyers. No courts. No pesky state records. It's as if the marriage never happened.

"My life story is crazy," he said.

The divorce did cause some minor problems in Ali's relationship with MOA. But internal differences and fighting between MOA leaders seemed to solve the crisis.

"The whole thing is, her father hated Barry Adams," Ali said of his father-in-law's relationship with the leader of MOA in North America. "Her father hated me because I was hanging out with Barry Adams all the time. He didn't think Barry Adams should be in charge of MOA. And her father started a lot of problems between me and my wife. And when I started traveling to all those countries like Venezuela, stuff like that, he was not happy with that. The problem came from her family, not from me."

Ali was able to maintain a comfortable and close relationship with Barry Adams. But the internal power struggles of MOA leaders, and those who disagree with Barry Adams' leadership, gave Ali an inside glimpse into the abnormal Muslim beliefs of Sheikh Gilani and his followers.

"They cannot say anything bad about Barry Adams because they think Gilani will turn them into a monkey," he said.

Really? A monkey? When asked if he really thought MOA followers believe that, Ali said, "Yeah, of course." Gilani's assertion that he can turn his followers into monkeys (or worse) comes from his own odd interpretation of Surah 5:60 in the Quran.

Gilani writes: "Should not I tell you about the worse people before Allah whom were cursed and they earned His wrath and whom He turned them into monkeys and swine and worshippers of Satan? These are the worst people who have gone astray from the straight path."[3]

Most Muslim scholars apply this verse only to Christians and Jews, but Gilani applies it more broadly, to Muslims, as well.

More recently, Gilani has claimed he also has the power to turn the dead into the living. "Sheikh Gilani has revived brain-dead patients," Gilani's lieutenants boasted about their leader in 2009. And he has been able to transfer these medical miracles to some of his followers. "And for the last 25 years (Gilani) has trained people who can heal and cure and are doing so on the hospital level."[4]

The Omnipresent Sheikh

Ali knows only too well how strong a hold Gilani's mysticism has over his American followers. Gilani's mysticism is derived from his Sufi beliefs. He proudly boasts that he is head of the Qadri order of Sufis, which maintains that its leaders have the power to be everywhere and anywhere and have the ability to be in the hearts and minds of their followers.

A famous story about one of Gilani's early predecessors—Sheikh Abdul Gilani, who lived from 1077 to 1166—explains why the current-day Sheikh Gilani is able to control his followers with such a tight grip. Many centuries ago, Abdul Gilani gave his disciples an order to slaughter a chicken in a place where no one could see them commit the butchery. A few hours later, the story goes, all of them returned to show Gilani their butchered chickens, except one disciple. It wasn't until the next afternoon that the missing disciple came back, with his chicken still in his hand and still alive. The disciple explained that he could not slaughter the chicken because the sheikh commanded his followers that no one else could witness the butchery.

"I tried all day yesterday," he told the sheikh, "and all night and all morning today to find a place where God is not present, where the prophet is not present, and where you are not present, and I could not find such a place. How could I slaughter the chicken?" Sheikh Abdul Gilani praised his disciple while gently criticizing the others for forgetting that he, too (along with Allah and the prophet Mohammed) can be found everywhere.

"Some of you took the order literally," the sheikh told his disciples about slaughtering the chickens. "And you did not keep in your heart that I am with my disciples, wherever they may be. But your brother here knows that I am in his heart 24 hours and that I never leave him. His only desire was to obey my order and to keep my respect, not seeking to understand the reason for the order or to try to discover its purpose."[5]

This story is illustrative of its modern counterpart, providing a glimpse into the mindset of the Qadri order and its rule over its disciples by the Gilani family line. Ali confirms that believers today believe Gilani is "wherever" his disciples may be. He is in the heart of his disciples 24 hours a day. Today's Sheikh Gilani will never leave his disciples; his only desire is that his disciples obey his orders and keep his respect, "not seeking to understand the reason for the order" or even trying "to discover its purpose."

In other words, MOA members are to follow Gilani's orders blindly and without questioning.

The patriarchal Gilani from long ago also instructed his followers that their daily life should be "governed by Muslim law." The "peak" of Muslim law, he said, "is jihad," and the purpose of jihad is "to eliminate oppression of Muslims by non-Muslims and to establish Islamic justice."

Islamic Justice Today

Today, Sheikh Mubarik Gilani, the current leader of Muslims of the Americas, couldn't agree more with his ancestor leader of the Qadri order about eliminating the "oppression" of Muslims. In his Soldiers of Allah video, a paramilitary training tape made for his followers, Sheikh Gilani says: "For the past 10 years we are helping Muslims all over the world, wherever they are oppressed ... We have prepared them to defend themselves and given them highly specialized, you know, training in guerilla warfare."

Almost mirroring his legendary ancestor's defense of oppressed Muslims, Sheikh Gilani says on film, "I present before you a documentary film showing you in helping and training oppressed Muslims."

What's more, Gilani's followers believe it is possible for their leader to live forever, a belief supported by Gilani's lieutenants, who often write, "May our murshid (teacher) live forever."

In my interview with Ali, he said MOA followers treat Gilani as if he is a sort of god, and some of the stories surrounding Gilani bear this out. In 2011, for instance, Sheikh Gilani was reportedly sick to the point of death. Rumors speculated that he was dying of asthma. Some speculated that he was poisoned. But according to Gilani's lieutenants, he was never really sick at all. The lieutenant sent a letter to MOA members in the United States assuring them of their teacher's good health.

"He (Gilani) would like to reassure all that firstly they should never panic because he's alright and he is not from this world," the lieutenant wrote, adding that Gilani was not sick; he was just temporarily leaving his body and traveling to a higher realm in order to visit others. "He leaves his body at times and at night breathes in the name of Almighty Allah ... At this time everything malfunctions—causing lungs to collapse—and heart conditions change. Something then becomes wrong with his body at this time (but) he is able to visit many. When he comes out of his body, many things transpire."

Even Gilani, in direct words to his followers, has declared: "I'm not an ordinary person."

Ali is disturbed that Gilani's followers not only treat him as if he is a god, but actually believe it. "The way they treat Gilani is forbidden in Islam," Ali said. "I don't believe any of this stuff from this guy in Pakistan. He's crazy. They treat Gilani like he is a god. You understand? They have his picture all over their houses. I'll tell you what, I love my religion. I think Islam is a great religion. But the way he preaches Islam makes everybody think we're all crazy."

For some in the MOA camps, they've never known any other life, said Ali. Their schooling, where there is schooling, is laughable, possibly even criminal. In the York, South Carolina, MOA compound children are taught in a storage shed. Local authorities are fearful of even discussing how these children are taught and what they are being taught. Ali's wife at Hancock could barely read when he met her.

"They have school on the Hancock compound," Ali said. "But a lot of the kids don't go to school; 90 percent of them can barely read or write. It's sad. It's sad to see this in America."

Four Generations

All the children really know, Ali said, is what Gilani and their leaders tell them. "It's four generations," Ali said. "In MOA there are four generations. You are born into this, you have to believe in this. You can't be Christian; you have to be a Muslim. Some of these people grow up there, and they don't know anything else but this."

The most vulnerable and emotionally abused in the camps are women. "They are insecure," Ali said of the women. "They don't know anything. They don't know about the outside world. They depend on everything from a man."

Many of the women are forced into polygamous marriages at very early ages, marriages that take place inside the camps. Ali calls them "silent" weddings. Though such "silent" weddings are standard throughout all the villages, not all marriages are illegal.

"Maybe they have one of them get married at city hall," Ali said, "to get some food stamps and a lot of other things. A lot of them use public services like crazy. Food stamps. Everybody's on food stamps."

More than 90 percent of the women are on state benefits, Ali claims, with a portion of this money going back to Sheikh Gilani in Pakistan. "They have so many kids," he said of the women. "Eight kids. Nine kids. They have to raise them and they don't have a lot."

Not a lot of money. Not a lot of housing. But a lot of kids. That's a woman's fate in the camps.

"Sometimes two families live in the same trailer," adds Ali. "Sometimes three families live in one trailer. It's real. This is real. Sometimes two wives live in the same house and have different kids."

Because of their seclusion, lack of education, forced marriages, fear of beatings, dependency on men and their religious slavery to Sheikh Gilani and his male lieutenants, women in the camps are stripped of any independent desire to flee.

"After four generations," Ali said, "they are living in their comfort zone."

Brutal Discipline

Discipline in the camps is ruthless and is executed for both punishment reasons and to intimidate its followers from ever leaving.

"This is one thing I want you to really believe," Ali told me in one of his most distressed moments during the interview. "I really believe, from the bottom of my heart, I want to help the woman and children, of course. It's ... if somebody breaks a command, you could be tied to a tree and hit with sticks. This is crazy."

Members are beaten for such violations as cursing, disobedience to the leaders, watching programs on TV they're not supposed to watch.

"Sometimes they do a crime," Ali said, explaining that a "crime" is doing something forbidden by Sheikh Gilani. "Sometimes they do a crime like that and they lash you. I gave the NYPD some tapes of evidence of kids getting beat, women tied to trees, stuff like that. That put me in a bad situation because I exposed these abuses."

Age and gender are not factors in these horrific beatings.

"I saw a 50-year-old woman tied to a tree and getting beaten, and Hussein Adams (Barry Adams' son) is right there. That's one of the things, honestly, this is what I think," Ali said, sounding clearly flustered. "This is what I think is the biggest disgrace, the abuse. The only thing is, nobody on the camps says anything. Of course they're afraid."

Men, too, live under the wrath of these camp beatings.

"Some of the men get caught in fornication or lying to an authority," Ali said. "It happens throughout Gilani's camps. Yeah, it is the law. It's Gilani's law."

Most men want to remain in the camps as obedient followers of Gilani. Those who want to leave are fearful of reprisals and the loss of their children.

"Some people are there because they're scared," Ali said. "They don't know what to do. They have their children there. They're scared of the wrath of Gilani. They think, you know, they're afraid they will get punished. They are so controlled, so brainwashed. It's crazy."

MOA leaders not only want to brainwash their followers, but they also want to brainwash law enforcement. The Hancock compound routinely invites law enforcement, including the local FBI, to picnics on their property—an invitation that can be seen repeated at other MOA camps.

"They bull**** them," Ali said of MOA leaders when hosting picnics for law enforcement. "They bull**** them. MOA puts up an American flag when they come to the camp. After that, they take the America flag down and put their flag back up.

"Slick," he said of the MOA.

Ali berates the local FBI agents and the New York State Police who visit the Hancock camp. "Of course, you have to understand, these guys don't know," Ali said of the local FBI agents and State Police officials from Albany and Binghamton. "There are other FBI agents in the know. The NYPD is in the know. But they don't share their information with these guys.

"They come. They hang out," Ali said of local law enforcement. "They eat food. They get photos taken with the leaders and kids. They're not really investigating. These people aren't investigating them at all. Not these people."

When asked why MOA would want to be so friendly with local law enforcement, Ali responded: "And that puzzles you? What do they say? Keep your friends close and your enemies closer."

Although lots of children can be seen in the photo-ops with law enforcement in a picture I showed him, Ali said, "This is nothing. Over half the kids are hiding in the back when they come to visit. MOA leaders tell them, 'You go hide in the back. Don't come out.' It's about three times more kids than what is in that picture. I was there."

Ali said that children on the Hancock compound learn at an early age that it's OK to commit crimes against non-Muslims and to engage in scams.

"A lot of them do welfare fraud. They do all kind of scams. All kind of scams," Ali added with emphasis.

"MOA does not want to lose out on opportunities of a crime being committed. They might have a guy sell a $10 drug or do a pickpocket. Maybe they have someone else, like in Philadelphia and Virginia, go sell a kilo of drugs.

"The drug money goes back to Gilani," Ali emphasizes.

Money Flow To Pakistan

All of the crimes committed by MOA members, on or off the compound, are approved by MOA leaders, Ali said, with much of that revenue going back to Gilani. "Everybody on the compound is obligated to give a percentage of their income to Gilani," Ali told me.

"They always say he's poor," Ali said of Gilani. "We're told he doesn't have this, and doesn't have that. But I've seen pictures of his houses, his cars, his Mercedes. And all these people in America are sending him checks." Ali couldn't help but laugh at the absurdity of it all.

Crimes committed by MOA members go beyond financial, drug running and thievery, Ali said. "A lot of the children that grow up there become drug dealers. Some become murderers.

"I would get in trouble if I told you everything I was providing to the NYPD. It would violate my immunity," Ali said. "So I'm not going to say what kind of crimes. I was providing information to the NYPD about people who committed some very serious crimes. I'm talking about ..." he deliberately stopped to search for new words. "What is the worse crime you can commit?"

"Murder?" I asked.

"I gave evidence of serious crimes to the NYPD," is all Ali would say. "I have evidence. I give them some very, very serious crimes. I tell them somebody did this and this and this. You know, bad people. And people got hurt very badly.

"And guess what?" Ali asked rhetorically. "The crimes haven't been solved. The NYPD can solve these crimes. They could solve them. They have the evidence."

But for the NYPD to solve these "serious crimes," it would probably mean disclosing Ali's true identity. "I guess they did not want to blow my cover," Ali said.

He added that MOA no longer does "mass military training" among its members.

"It's like a formed military squad," he explained. "It's certain groups. Certain individuals. Certain names. Certain guys. It is a very, very select group they have. It's a lot of people. But it's not like they train every day. It's various people training in different positions."

Special training is available for the most trusted members of MOA.

"There's a twist," Ali said. "The people who have helped Gilani, he will train them in Pakistan and they will go back to their own countries. The person who is providing the training answers the question; it's the big boss."

He said the FBI knows this, and the NYPD has a lot of evidence— enough to shut down the camps.

"Listen, listen," he said. "The FBI knows about the training. So does the NYPD. They have tapes. They have videos. They have the audio. They have a lot. They have everything—enough evidence they can close these camps."

Though some private investigators have reported that the Hancock compound has tunnels where weapons are stashed, Ali denied that such tunnels exist.

"There are no tunnels. No tunnels. No tunnels." It was a point Ali to want to make clear. But he quickly added, "but there are a whole lot of guns."

Some of those guns violate federal law, Ali said. "I bought guns from MOA to give to the NYPD. The NYPD wanted them," he said. "I purchased guns that violated federal law."

Asked why the NYPD wanted him to purchase the illegal guns, he replied, "Just to see them. To build a case, I guess." But did they ever build one? "Of course not," Ali lamented. "But they could at this point, with all the information and evidence I gave them."

MOA's military squad has been shown in a variety of training tapes, Ali made sure to point out, including the "Soldiers of Allah" tape which our organization obtained and exposed in our film.

"The 'Soldiers of Allah' video is old," Ali said, "but the film has carried on. All of them, everyone, has seen 'Soldiers of Allah.'"

But there are other military training videos. "There's a lot ... a lot," Ali emphasized. "I gave Detective Calla some very serious tapes about training in Pakistan."

At one point, Ali said he was part of the military training, claiming he helped teach them to fight.

"Yeah," he said. "I was a part of it. I went to Virginia for training. I was there. The NYPD knows." But the training didn't take place at the Red House, Virginia, compound where MOA has a large presence in a heavily wooded area.

"We took classes with some guy in Virginia," Ali said, refusing to reveal any further details.

When The Time Is Right

The purpose of the military training is to be ready to fight for Sheikh Gilani when the time is right.

"That's what they've always said," Ali said of the MOA leaders. "The ultimate purpose is to be ready when the time is right.

"I'm actually gonna give you something about MOA and their belief. It's more religious than anybody knows. It's a part in Islam. Islam is a part of certain things. Certain things will happen, you understand? Some Muslims believe in it. Some Muslims don't believe in it."

With this mixture of tension, mystery and insight, Ali asked me a question.

"Did you ever hear about the Mahdi? Do you know the Mahdi?"[6]

I had heard about this religious figure in Islam before, I told him. For most Muslims, the Mahdi is believed to be the coming "savior" of the world.

"The Mahdi and Jesus will fight the antichrist together," he said. "This is what I believe. This is what they believe. The Mahdi and Jesus Christ will fight the antichrist together."

The Mahdi is alive and well, according to Sheikh Gilani. The MOA leader made the claim in a 2009 article in the *Islamic Post*, an internal publication of Muslims of the Americas. In that article, Sheikh Gilani revealed to his followers that he has personally met the Mahdi and that this Islamic figure would soon be revealed to the world. This coming revelation would not take decades, he said, but just a matter of years.

The appearance of the Mahdi is the final chapter in Gilani's teachings to his followers that they are the one "chosen group," among 73 Muslim groups, which Muhammad predicted would be saved during the end times. This is an important teaching among Gilani's followers, because out of 73 Muslim groups, "only one group is worthy," confirms Ali. "Gilani tells them that they are the one group."

The message to MOA members was abundantly clear in the *Islamic Post* article: They are the chosen group of Muslims who must now be ready to help the Mahdi fight the antichrist.

"The tide is about to turn," Gilani told his followers in the article. "The world will change forever, and for good. The end time has started."

Ali was so concerned when he saw this article that he reported it right away to his contacts in the NYPD. He views the statements and predictions by Gilani as a deliberate attempt to exercise control over his American followers from Pakistan.

"This is how you control someone over here by someone they have never even seen," Ali said. "You got all these young kids here. You walk up to them and ask them, 'What do you want to do?' 'I want to fight for Gilani.' That's what they want. It's not good."

At times, it was clear that Ali struggled to decide how much information to disclose to me. This point of the interview seemed to present his biggest challenge.

"I can't really let you know everything I know right now," Ali told me. "But I'll tell you something. After I picked up the *Islamic Post* and saw Gilani's article on having met the Mahdi, I called Detective Calla (of the NYPD) and I said, 'I have to see you.' He said, 'What's going on?' I said, 'I have to see you. This is the sign they all have been waiting for.'"

By the time Ali had this meeting with David Calla and other detectives of the NYPD, he felt his relationship with them was more than just an "informant." He was someone they could trust.

"I wasn't just an informant anymore," he said. "I was a guy sitting on the board with them. I was a guy going to dinner, having lunch with them. I was the guy they were asking to help make a decision. You understand? I earned their trust."

Ali met the detectives. He told them his fears and concerns. This was big. This was the final stage before Armageddon. First the Mahdi, then Armageddon. This is what Gilani was telling his people.

"The end time has started," Gilani told his followers in the newspaper article. "Soon after the physical appearance of Hazrat Imam Mahdi, Jesus, son of Mary, will come down from the heavens and land at Masjid Aqsa in Jerusalem. The much anticipated Armageddon will later on take place."

The Mahdi? Armageddon? The message that Gilani was sending is clear: He was preparing his people to get ready for the end times.

"This Mahdi thing is scary," Ali said. "It's very scary because I know the rest of the story. When Gilani comes out and said he knows the Mahdi in the newspaper ... I was shocked."

Ali was hoping the NYPD would act against the group, perhaps shut them down with the information and evidence he had already provided police.

"You have to understand this," Ali said, expressing his extremely urgent views. "These kids, all they been living for their whole lives is they want to fight a holy war. These are kids. They start at age 17 in the compound and they become a gangster, they wanna become gangsters for what they think is a holy war."

Why wait any longer to shut them down? Ali questions.

"The government has enough stuff to put the MOA away by the end of the year," he states emphatically.

But the NYPD has not shut them down. "I got the feeling that I think the government is scared."

By the time the NYPD does act, it will be probably be too late.

"Let me tell you something," Ali said. "If Gilani tomorrow told everyone, set yourself on fire, everybody would burn themselves. This has been going on for 30 years. And people praise him. They give him money. They kiss his feet. It's crazy. These people are slaves. I call them the Modern Warrior Slaves. That's what I call them.

"It's very simple," Ali warns. "MOA is asleep. They are asleep. They are a bomb. Here is the scariest part of MOA. Anything can happen with MOA at any time."

Ali also warned me, and Christian Action Network, about our efforts to continue exposing this terrorist group.

'You Are In Danger'

"You are in danger," he said. "You have to understand, these people are not the nicest people. They have to do what they got to do. I know this for sure. They will do whatever. They have tried to kill their own people."

Ali's own future, at the time of this writing, was uncertain. We may never learn the final outcome of his immigration status or whether he was deported back to Egypt.

"The NYPD thought I would give up and get deported to Egypt and die there. They never thought I would fight," he said.

"I want to raise my daughter," Ali said. "I already have a son, and I know, it's gonna be so unfair for him because he still lives on the compound."

"I would give ... I would do anything not to lose my family," Ali said somberly. "What are they trying to do? What they are trying to take from me is my family. They are trying to take away my freedom. I have to give everything. They don't really care about me."

To save his family, to hopefully win his immigration status, Ali hoped it would help by getting his story out. "If this is going to come out, it's going to come out," Ali said.

"One day I want to take my son and apologize to him. I hope he forgives me. But right now, I am going to have to focus on what happens to my family."

"Pakistan is the most dangerous country in the world today. All of the nightmares of the 21st century come together in Pakistan: nuclear proliferation, drug smuggling, military dictatorship and above all, international terrorism."[1]

K. Alan Kronstadt, commenting on Pakistan-U.S. Relations in 2009.

CHAPTER 14

No Official Comment

SEVERAL YEARS AGO I TRAVELED TO COMMERCE, GEORGIA, where a Muslims of the Americas (MOA) compound is located. In my possession was a video showing MOA members training for jihad[2]. It clearly and unmistakably proved that, despite all the protests from its members and leaders, MOA was in the business of creating guerilla warriors from among America's citizenry, training them to strike within the United States.

My objective was to travel onto the Commerce compound and show the video to its members. I wanted to see their reactions, and I wanted to know once and for all: Do they approve of this guerilla-training activity? Will they renounce it or continue to deny its existence?

Before making the risky and dangerous trip onto the Commerce compound, I stopped at the local police department and asked for an escort. I showed them the film, explained the potential danger and asked for their protection.

Their answer was an unequivocal "no." No police officers would accompany us, nor would they guarantee our safety or provide any security for us. If we entered the camp, they told us, we did so at our own risk. Because of the potential danger, and knowing that the police would not protect us if we ran into any trouble, we had no choice but to turn around and head back home.

This response by law enforcement in Commerce, Georgia, was dispiriting and disappointing, but not all that surprising—because I know law enforcement at all of its levels is ill equipped to prevent crimes, only to punish them once committed. This difference between the perception that we have of law enforcement and the reality is not a subtle one. Although the local police cars we witness patrolling the streets may often display the soothing slogan, "to protect and serve," law enforcement's primary goal is to prosecute once a crime has taken place—not necessarily to prevent it.

This attitude explains why, since the September 11, 2001, attacks, Americans have been forced to undergo increasingly burdensome airport screenings, restrictions, nude body scans and gropings, indignities involving children and the elderly, curtailment of traditional American freedoms—yet without any real success in stopping homegrown terrorism or in addressing the underlying goals of homegrown jihadists.

They still want to kill us ... and they are succeeding. All of these new restrictions are the result of our lukewarm war against radical Islam, yet more and more American citizens are becoming radicalized in secret enclaves and within American mosques.

This attitude is also evident in law enforcement's lack of preventive action against MOA in particular, despite knowing the absolute truth about its makeup and long-term goals.

An FBI agent who spoke with one of our staff members a few years ago thinks he has another important explanation for the lack of action on MOA. In one word, the reason law enforcement turns a blind eye to the simmering danger posed by MOA is "Pakistan."

This FBI agent admitted, "We know all about their activities." He also confirmed that the FBI has traced money from the camps—some of it obtained through welfare scams and drug sales—overseas to London. "When we wanted to trace it from London," said the agent, "we were stopped. (The U.S. government) has no interest in pursuing it because Pakistan is an important ally, and we don't want to do anything to jeopardize it."

An Assassination in Pakistan

Pakistan's former Prime Minister, the impressively photogenic Benazir Bhutto, appeared to have it all. Oxford educated, with an aristocratic demeanor and accented voice evocative of her British connections, she cut an exotic figure with her de rigueur flowing head scarf, kohl-outlined eyes and red-painted lips.

On the afternoon of December 27, 2007, Bhutto—running once again for the post of Prime Minister after several years of self-imposed exile from Pakistan—made the fatal mistake of standing up through the sunroof of her bullet-proof car to wave to her cheering supporters. She had just finished a speech in the city of Rawalpindi to advance her candidacy; she wanted to oust the corrupt Musharraf military regime, bring democracy to Pakistan, and rein in the militant Islamic forces which despised her for her friendship with the United States and pro-Western ways. Despite credible threats that her life was in danger, and having already survived one assassination attempt just a few weeks earlier, Bhutto was riding high from her speech.

She slipped into her waiting bullet-proof car, which was also equipped with tinted windows for extra security. A photograph of the moment just prior to the attack showed that she took the time to pull out a hand mirror and apply some of her trademark red lipstick. As the car began to pull away, Bhutto, in a triumphant mood, stood up through the sunroof of her car to smile and wave to her supporters. Within 30 seconds bullets ripped through the air and she was fatally wounded. She died less than two hours later on a hospital operating table.

When the chaos died down, it was learned that a suicide bomber had fired shots at her, then detonated a bomb next to her vehicle. At least 20 people, including Bhutto, died in the attack. Although no autopsy was performed on her body, it was later certified that Bhutto died of head trauma, either directly from bullet fire or from the blast impact that slammed her head into the sunroof. President Pervez Musharraf, Muslim extremists or the ISI (Pakistan's intelligence agency)—or a combination of all three—may have been involved in the attack, according to speculation.

In the immediate aftermath, however, Al Qaeda took credit for the assassination, bragging: "We terminated the most precious American asset." But Al Qaeda's assessment was incorrect—because America's most precious asset at the time was not Benazir Bhutto, even though her pro-America sympathies and anti-terror hardline stance had won her many friends in the United States. America's greatest asset, some would call "puppet," was then President Pervez Musharraf. It was he, often known as a remarkably adept "double dealer," who was of highest value to the American government and its need to slip in and out of the Pakistani border with Afghanistan unfettered.

Musharraf appeared to have delivered little to the Americans in terms of anti-terrorism, but appearances were often deceiving. In the post 9-11 environment, Musharraf offered up some of the biggest names in the terror world, including Khalid Sheikh Mohammed. Even while the Musharraf regime appeared to protect other high-ranking terrorists like Osama Bin Laden, he continued to open up pathways through the tribal regions to allow a flow of U.S. supplies to U.S. troops, and Musharraf also permitted drone attacks that led to the deaths of hundreds of Al Qaeda militants over the years. Yes, he was embroiled in corruption, violence, two-timing and underhanded political maneuvering, but Musharraf earned his billions in U.S. taxpayer aid by allowing the U.S. government to have its way at critical times.

Musharraf embodied the perfect blend of self-interest, corruption and American sympathy to make himself of greater use to the United States than a purist like Benazir Bhutto. Just as the wives of King Henry VIII soon caught on that it wasn't safe to get too close to the infamous monarch and that it might be less perilous to cultivate other friends, as well, Musharraf and other Pakistani leaders have learned that if they cooperate too much with either the United States or the Islamic militants, there will be hell to pay. The best road is the one in the middle.

WikiLeaks

In May of 2011, a shocking new tidbit was revealed by WikiLeaks. The news made few headlines, but it confirmed what had long been suspected: That the Bush Administration consciously made the choice of Musharraf over Bhutto—knowing that while Bhutto was more pro-democracy, she was less inclined to be manipulated. The WikiLeaks report reveals that the U.S. embassy in Islamabad refused to provide security to Bhutto in the weeks prior to her assassination, despite personal requests to members of Congress.[3] Bush officials, WikiLeaks revealed, while in no way seeking Bhutto's assassination, nevertheless allowed the circumstances for it to ripen by failing to step in and protect her. In the aftermath, Musharraf—a prime Bhutto rival—was arrested for complicity in the assassination, although charges were ultimately dropped.

According to WikiLeaks, Bhutto handed over a written request to U.S. Ambassador Anne Patterson two months before she was killed, asking her for enhanced security because she feared for her life. "The cables reveal that the U.S. chose to look the other way, suggesting that (Bhutto) should work constructively with General Pervez Musharraf's government, the same organization that (she) insisted was out to kill her."[4]

As if it wasn't obvious enough that Washington—under not just the Bush Administration, but previous and subsequent ones, as well—was willing to tolerate quite a lot from this rogue nation and its corrupt leaders in exchange for its own militaristic needs along the Afghan border, news was revealed in July of 2011 that Pakistan had been funneling millions of dollars annually in successful and secret efforts to influence Congress, the White House and the Justice Department.[5] This was accomplished through a Pakistani spy network which feigned representation of a D.C.-based agency that lobbied for Pakistani issues.

Appearances Matter

Perhaps nothing exemplifies the frequently strained and inexplicable relationship between the U.S. and Pakistan more than the assassination of Benazir Bhutto and America's failure to protect her from our own sworn enemies. This brutal event in Pakistan's recent history is also a telling example of why terrorist groups like Pakistan-bred

Jamaat Al Fuqra, which operates unimpeded in camps throughout the United States under the front name of Muslims of the Americas, are allowed to carry on their terror training and fomentation of anti-American sentiment for generations here without any real opposition from law enforcement in the United States. In short, the U.S. government needs Pakistan, so let's not rock the boat by creating the appearance that we are harassing Muslims in America—even if they are, in reality, terrorists in training.

Other questionable connections between Pakistan and the U.S. government have also been uncovered. Reports have surfaced that Pakistani terrorist leaders have worked with the U.S., along with their Pakistani protectors like Musharraf, to ensure that U.S. supply ships in the Arabian Sea are protected from attack, that the U.S. embassy in Islamabad is not targeted for terrorist attack, and that reasonable port fees are assessed for U.S. ships in Dubai. These terrorist networks also ensure that the land route from Karachi to Afghanistan allows U.S and other goods to move into the landlocked country unimpeded. In exchange, reports claim, the CIA has "looked the other way" on the terrorists' involvement in currency and driver's license counterfeiting, the heroin trade, counterfeit CDs, protection rackets, extortion, hawala loans[6], Pakistani and Indian passport forgery, nuclear black marketing, murder for hire, and hashish trafficking, the latter encompassing a criminal network stretching around the world and employing thousands of people.[7]

In July 2011, it was not all that surprising when additional reports surfaced that terrorists in the region of Pakistan and Afghanistan had been receiving millions of dollars of American money to fund their crimes against us, taxpayer money intended to be used as legitimate aid to our allies that was being diverted and handed over to our enemies.

Yet none of this satisfactorily answers the question: Why won't law enforcement shut down terror training camps in America? It could also be posed this way: Is it really that surprising that the same group connected to the kidnapping and beheading of *Wall Street Journal* reporter Daniel Pearl in 2002, Jamaat Al Fuqra—which has known connections to terrorism within the United States and has been quietly ignored by law enforcement in both Pakistan and the United States—is allowed to operate freely here under the thinly veiled guise of a poor, black, separatist Muslim group? If they could not, or would not, prosecute Al Fuqra/MOA and its leaders for involvement in the horrific Daniel Pearl case, which should have been a slam dunk, why would they move to shut down their camps on American soil which claim the protection of religious freedom?

Simply put, law enforcement agencies had their chance in 2002 to shut down terror training camps in America after the Daniel Pearl connection hit the news—and at several other checkpoints along the way—and they chose to take a pass.

Though clearly law enforcement officials—including local, regional, state and FBI—know about the dangers of Al Fuqra and have, on several occasions over the years, prosecuted its members in the U.S.—the simmering danger that lies over the horizon is not addressed. Why? As many have theorized, our quirky relationship with Pakistan, which has in recent months reached a new boiling point, may be the real reason why terrorists in training in the United States are allowed to soldier on with impunity—until, of course, they actually strike out.

It is generally understood that our need to have leaders in place in Pakistan who will do our bidding, allowing us to travel across their porous borders to ship supplies to troops in Afghanistan and fight terrorist enclaves in the tribal regions—even if these leaders betray us, and cost us billions of dollars every year in aid that often ends up being leveled against us in the form of bullets and suicide bombs—is the reason for turning a blind eye to terror groups in the United States like Jamaat Al Fuqra. Call it quid pro quo, or tit for tat, it boils down to the same thing: Many believe the United States simply looks the other way on the issue of terrorist training in American in exchange for favors in Pakistan.

In a meeting with an FBI agent who worked in the Virginia region near the notorious Red House MOA camp which once gave refuge to the Beltway Snipers and other dangerous terrorists, I asked why the FBI—with its vast storehouse of evidence against Al Fuqra and MOA—didn't shut down the camps. The answer was simple and direct: "Pakistan."

Many, however, would argue it's not a good enough reason given the abundance of evidence against Al Fuqra/MOA. There may be a number of other reasons at play that prevent law enforcement from acting on the many warnings that Al Fuqra/MOA is a bomb waiting to go off. Is Pakistan's tenuous relationship with the United States really the reason that law enforcement won't do something about this threat simmering in rural enclaves throughout America, a stewpot that is merely waiting, as one of its undercover members asserts, one word from its leader in Pakistan to strike at us? Or are other forces at work?

The Politics of Denial

This refusal to act in the face of obvious danger—akin to the "kicking the can down the road" philosophy—is what investigator Susan Fenger simply calls "politics." It is the nature of the political beast that emanates from Washington, D.C., that she believes is driving law enforcement to ignore the threat.

Whether or not "politics" as defined by Fenger encompasses the political hot potato of Pakistan remains to be seen. But Fenger knows what she's talking about. Among investigators at all levels, Fenger has prosecuted more members of Al Fuqra and uncovered more details about their operation in the United States than anyone else. Yet ironically, she was approached by FBI members in 1991 who were already investigating Al Fuqra and its front group, Muslims of the Americas. When Fenger was contacted and told there were terrorists in Colorado, she, like everyone else, was shocked.

An employee of the Colorado Department of Labor, Fenger was a forensics and white-collar-crime expert. After learning that the FBI suspected members of a Colorado MOA camp of scamming the state's welfare system in order to defraud the system of money to fund terrorist activities, Fenger spent the next two years building cases against its members by cross-referencing welfare and worker's compensation claims. At one point, she was called into then-Governor Roy Roymer's office along with other investigators, including the FBI, and was told by the FBI: "We're pulling out; we've gotten word from Washington that we're not going to get involved in this."

Gov. Romer pointedly turned to Fenger and said, "I don't want terrorists here in Colorado, so, what are you going to do about it?"

Fenger offered to take over the probe and got the go-ahead from the governor. After an exhaustive financial fraud investigation (detailed elsewhere in this book), Fenger obtained grand jury indictments, then led a raid on the Colorado MOA camp, where arrests were made. In all, Fenger's investigation led to numerous arrests across the nation, all with the FBI standing on the sidelines.

Fenger also learned that the CIA and FBI were both separately investigating MOA and its Al Fuqra connections[8] but were told to back off by the Clinton Administration, which had just taken the reins in Washington. "They also weren't going along with this business about terrorism here on U.S. soil," said Fenger, a view that many investigators shared. Even she had trouble believing it at first, she admits. "If you go back and look at the Clinton Administration, they were giving a signal to the CIA and the FBI that they didn't want them working together ... It's what I was gathering ... I put two and two together and got four ... that's why I say it was politics that prevented the federal government from taking action."

As late as 2007, Fenger said, "Our government would love to get (Sheikh) Gilani. He was part of the (Pakistani) ISI, which is like the CIA in Pakistan, and he really is manipulative and knows how to handle people."

Furthermore, she knows, "from firsthand knowledge ... that the FBI is still looking into the group."

This startling revelation came seven years after the federal government, in cooperation with the government of Pakistan, released a statement saying that Sheikh Gilani had no involvement in the kidnapping and murder of Daniel Pearl. As pointed out earlier, Gilani was arrested in Pakistan in 2002 in connection with Pearl's death but inexplicably let go. The contradiction between what the U.S. government says about Gilani and his jihadist organization (that they pose no danger), and the fact that federal agencies are still investigating the group, is maddening.

Also maddening is the fact that Al Fuqra/MOA had been listed on the State Department's list of terrorist groups but was removed in the year 2000 after what appeared to be a period of inactivity. This official attitude of our government conflicts with what Fenger knows to be true—that the FBI is continuing to investigate the group—and from our own undercover source who confirms that Al Fuqra/MOA has never stopped training for terrorism. In other words, they may be considered by law enforcement as sleeper cells at worst, but even that explanation doesn't wash because they're not really sleeping. In 2010 the *Journal of Counterterrorism and Homeland Security International* published an item confirming that Al Fuqra had been "spotted" training in Venezuela. "Terrorist groups such as Al-Qaeda, Hamas, Hezbollah, Jammat Al Fuqra, members of the major drug cartels and gangs, especially MS-13, have been observed training in these camps," the report states.[9]

What's more, the group known as Jaish e-Muhammad, an Al Qaeda terrorist group from which Al Fuqra splintered, and therefore a sister organization, is still on the State Department's watch list. In fact, Al Fuqra fraternizes and cooperates with the majority of groups still listed as official terrorist organizations. There is no logical reason to remove Al Fuqra from the State Department list, while keeping on many of its crony organizations. The only difference between Al Fuqra and these other groups is the presence of Al Fuqra's front group, Muslims of the Americas, which maintains dozens of compounds in America populated with poor, mostly black American citizens. If law enforcement shuts them down because of their terrorist connections, they run the risk of being labeled racist and anti-Muslim. Public pressure would be relentless.

In fact, that has already happened in several cases. Susan Fenger came up squarely against public pressure to leave the Muslims in Colorado alone after she led a raid on the Colorado compound. Newspaper accounts of the raid and subsequent arrests "made it look like we were after this poor group of Muslims who had left the city in quiet and peace—away from the city life to raise their own animals, raise their children and were peaceful people," she said. "And all the newspapers were giving the governor and attorney general, vis-a-viz me, a bad name."[10]

Fenger ran into another brick wall when her investigation showed that a Pennsylvania MOA compound was also involved in the white-collar crimes, to the tune of stealing $153,000 from worker's compensation there. The Pennsylvania Department of Labor "would not do anything with the case," Fenger recalls. "They sent it to the state auditors, and they said, 'What, terrorists? We're not going to get involved,' so they sent it to the state police. The state police didn't know how to put a case together for white-collar crime, to do the sort of things I had done. They didn't do anything."[11]

Today, Fenger's investigation is still the gold standard when it comes to evidence against Al Fuqra/MOA. But Fenger herself has quietly disappeared. The last I heard of her, she had a $50,000 bounty on her head, placed there by Sheikh Gilani as retribution for the prosecutions in Colorado.

Do No Harm and Sound No Alarm

Law enforcement at all levels—local through federal—has had Al Fuqra and its front group, Muslims of the Americas, on its radar since around 1980 when the founder of both groups, Sheikh Mubarik Ali Gilani, was stirring up trouble in Brooklyn's Muslim community. Following the first World Trade Center bombing in 1993, in which Al Fuqra played a role, Gilani fled the country and has not had a public presence in the United States since.

One sighting, however, was noted by a real estate agent in Colorado, who recalls that Gilani—"a big, overweight fella ... who smelled very bad"—personally purchased a property close to the MOA compound he had founded, but then quickly resold it.[12]

Although Gilani was planting jihadist communes throughout the United States during the 1980s and 1990s, his name registered twice in big ways following two pivotal events—the 1989 discovery in Colorado of a storage locker that was filled with incriminating evidence of terrorist activity related to Al Fuqra (which ultimately prompted Fenger's investigation and raid of the compound), and in 2002 when he was arrested in Pakistan following the kidnapping of Daniel Pearl.

In both cases, however, the official law enforcement response was to downplay the threat from Gilani and his jihadist structure and to protect the religious rights of his followers. Despite several arrests over the years of MOA members in connection with welfare scams, bombings, drug and weapons violations and even murder, law enforcement has taken a hands-off approach toward this group unless its members flagrantly disobey the law.

Shockingly, members of the FBI and local police and sheriff's offices have taken such pains to appear conciliatory to MOA enclaves that they can frequently be found picnicking with them or engaging in "interfaith" gatherings, ostensibly designed to display unity to the surrounding communities and, of course, to a media that laps it up.

In one ludicrous example of this outreach, the FBI and New York State Police presented special awards to the Muslim Scouts of America from the Hancock, New York, headquarters of MOA. Fenger proved in her Colorado investigation that the word "scouts" as used by MOA is a code word for "jihadist soldiers." And, of course, Fenger also proved that the FBI has known this for years.

Just like Obi-Wan Kenobi waved on the storm troopers in Star Wars, telling them "there's nothing to see here," the FBI and other law enforcement agencies keep telling the public "there's no terrorism here" until the public believes it.

"Political correctness" plays into this "sound no alarm" theory of why law enforcement ignores the Al Fuqra/MOA threat. In the wake of the Beltway Sniper attacks in 2002 in the Baltimore and Washington, D.C., region, the Council on American Islamic Relations (CAIR), a Muslim Brotherhood-founded organization and close ally of MOA, pulled out all the stops to suppress media reports that identified the snipers as Muslim extremists. Of course, not only were they Muslim extremists, they were also connected to Jamaat Al Fuqra and followers of Sheikh Gilani. So successful, however, was CAIR's campaign to label any mention of the Muslim connections as an anti-Muslim witch hunt, that to this day most Americans believe the snipers were lone gunmen disgruntled with their lots in life.

Even President Bush played to this mindset, with tragic consequences, stating repeatedly that the Muslim religion is a peaceful one merely hijacked by a few radicals. In the years since he made that statement, hundreds of thousands of people have been slaughtered around the world in the name of "the religion of peace." It was, in fact, frequently painful to watch Bush grope for new words of praise for Muslims in the aftermath of 9-11, while on the nightly news Muslims around the world—including American Muslims—danced in the streets, howling with delight like it was the Fourth of July, in celebration of the World Trade Center carnage.

The Water Supply Police

Perhaps one of the most extreme examples of this P.C.-infused "sound no alarm and do no harm" mentality was seen in the early 1990s when an investigation into the New York headquarters of MOA was shut down and the investigators fired and demonized when it was learned they were surveilling the compound.

The Bureau of Water Supply Police, a unit within the federal Department of Environmental Protection, was the "culprit." After investigating a series of complaints—that there was gunfire and military drilling at the camp, that a serious fire there had not been investigated, that there may be irregularities with residents' drivers' licenses, building code violations, and more—the Water Supply Police began to have concerns that a nearby water reservoir might be in danger of contamination. This fear was so eminently reasonable, given the terrorist connections of the MOA camp, its founders and some members, and also considering other undercover information that would subsequently be supplied from within the camp, that it deserved investigating. Yet the final searing determination was that the investigation had been conducted "solely because of the fact that the community is made up of black individuals."[13]

Yet such an investigation was not unusual, a fact the investigators stressed during the subsequent probe of the investigation itself. The DEP's Water Supply Police had, in previous years, properly investigated the radical Weatherman group and threats that they had "the will" to contaminate a nearby water source.

One investigator, who recovered spent shell casings on the MOA compound in New York, defended his inquiry. "In order to contaminate the reservoirs you must have the will to do so. This stuff (the shell casings) tells me they had the will."[14]

In the end, the prevailing atmosphere of political correctness prevented the investigators from continuing. What they suspected, but could not prove, was what another law enforcement agency would soon learn with the aid of an undercover agent embedded within Muslims of the Americas: That the compound was, indeed, a terror training facility with jihadist tentacles stretching around the world.

The hypocrisy of one law enforcement agency shutting down the investigation of another, while yet a third agency is investigating and confirming the very same terrorist activity, is staggering.

Land of the Free

One argument frequently used by law enforcement to explain why they don't shut down MOA camps is that this is America—and unless members of MOA flagrantly violate the law, they have a right to believe whatever they want.

But what if their belief system advocates illegal activity? Treason and sedition are still crimes in America. Article 3 of the U.S. Constitution defines treason as "waging war" against the United States or providing "aid or comfort" to America's enemies. Furthermore, Title 18 of the U.S. Code states that "whoever knowingly or willfully advocates, abets, advises or teaches the duty, necessity, desirability or propriety of overthrowing or destroying the government of the United States or the government of any State, Territory, District or Possession thereof, or the government of any political subdivision therein, by force or violence, or by the assassination of any officer of any such government" is guilty of sedition.

Under these laws, the Ku Klux Klan was banned in the 1920s because it advocated a violent overthrow of the existing society, yet anti-treason laws are today widely ignored. The reason is obvious: The cloak of the First Amendment rights to religion and free speech is now deemed to supersede the government's right to prosecute those who seek harm to the nation. This shift has occurred not necessarily through legal precedent, but through a shift in public opinion.

Many, in fact, would argue that Islam in the United States is an illegal religion because it advocates the murder of those who don't follow it and commands its followers to kill critics of Islam—critics who are practicing the constitutionally protected right of freedom of speech. Yet not since 1952 has an American citizen actually been convicted of treason, despite a parade of anti-American jihadists who have vowed to topple the United States. In 2006, a California man who joined Al Qaeda was charged with treason. The man, Adam Gadahn, is currently a fugitive believed to be living in—where else—Pakistan. As late as June, 2011, Gadahn was still appearing in Al Qaeda videos spewing jihadist rhetoric. In his last video he called on all American Muslims to buy weapons from gun shows and carry out random, lone-wolf attacks. "America is absolutely awash with easily obtainable fire-arms," Gadahn exhorts listeners. His message is eerily similar to that of Sheikh Mubarik Gilani, who, in a guerilla training videotape, called on his American followers to "act like you are a friend, then kill him."

What is the difference between Gadahn's crimes—threatening the United States—and the statements made by Sheikh Gilani and his followers? If Gilani founded Muslims of the Americas with the purpose of "purifying Islam through violence," why is that not treasonous, while Gadahn's threats are worthy of charges? The most obvious difference between the two is that Gadahn is no longer living in the United States and can't really be prosecuted on the treason charges. Thousands of MOA members, most of them poor blacks, are living on American soil without any interference from law enforcement, quietly—for now—following the seditious dictates of their jihadist leader in Pakistan. The other difference between Gilani and Gadahn is that Gilani, out of one side of his mouth, professes to be peaceful and encourages non-violence among his American followers. His secret messages to his followers, though, many of which have been intercepted, are clear-cut exhortations to violence.

There is another specter that haunts the American landscape: the Japanese internment camps. In the land of the free, it is no longer considered a sign of patriotism and self-preservation to close down and shut away those who give the appearance of being dangerous. The danger must be much more evident than mere appearances. As we have already established, law enforcement generally waits until the crime is committed before acting.

Law enforcement agents we have spoken with at all levels merely throw up their hands in frustration over the MOA/Al Fuqra threat. What are we supposed to do about it? they ask. This is America. Sheriff Bruce Bryant of York County, South Carolina—where a 36-acre MOA compound is located, and which has hosted an array of notorious characters in the jihadist world—has stated publicly that he has concerns about the camp but can't do a thing about it.

"The Constitution protects them and their right to be there," he stated. Even though their camp is located near the Catawba Nuclear Station and he has investigated numerous complaints of gunfire and military drilling, "somebody," he pleads, "tell me how to shut them down?"[15]

Big Fish to Fry

Another theory used to explain why law enforcement won't shut down Al Fuqra/MOA terror training camps is that they're waiting for the big bust. This argument makes some sense, because we know that law enforcement has undercover agents embedded in MOA—sometimes with the assignment to spy on each other to make sure the undercover information is accurate—and that they know illegal activity is ongoing there. As one undercover agent told me: "They (law enforcement) have enough information to shut down the camps."

Just the confirmation that spies are being used to report on MOA activity, and that some big arrests, detailed in other chapters, have resulted presumably from this intelligence, is proof that law enforcement is watching this activity with great care. From time to time a compound member is arrested, sometimes on a serious charge, but there is no denying that the incidence of criminal activity attributed to them has been on the wane. One former member who lived in the York, South Carolina, MOA compound told a neighbor that they have been instructed—by Sheikh Gilani himself—to quietly move out of the camp and blend in with the surrounding neighborhoods. This has obviously occurred, as camp residency numbers dwindle in compounds across the nation. Some are even reported to have shut down and their members scattered.

This trend, however, is cause for great concern when cross-referenced with what an undercover agent told me about the group's secret formation of an "army" of jihadists, an army created from members across the nation who are ready to be called up at "one word" from their leader.

Law enforcement may be monitoring activity in these camps around the nation, waiting to catch the big fish at the top of the food chain, but this strategy is a dangerous one given the group's ability and desire to remain under the radar in order to plot a large-scale attack.

Despite all these attempts to explain why law enforcement won't shut down the Muslims of the Americas camps, despite a wealth of evidence against them that they are training for terror and stirring up jihadist sentiment, none of these explanations individually—nor even all of them at play at once—really makes much sense to the average citizen. The question I have been asked over and over again is, "Why? Why won't they shut them down?" Even Ali Aziz, the young Egyptian man who lived among MOA for eight years as an undercover informant for the New York Police Department, can't adequately answer the question.

When asked, Ali just shrugs. "I think the government is scared," he said. After providing law enforcement with shocking details about terror training, jihadist activity, illegal weapons and drugs, and abuse of its members, Ali assumed that something would be done.

"I was shocked that these camps weren't shut down."

If Ali is correct—that Al Fuqra/MOA has formed an army of jihadists and is preparing to attack within the United States—then we know one thing for sure: Law enforcement will have to respond ... eventually.

"Islam is on trial. And we as Americans are on trial as we deal with it. This is not the American way."[1]

Muslims of the Americas leader Khadijah Ghafur, after the City of Fresno revoked the license of her charter school program.

CHAPTER 15

Dust in Our Eyes

IN 2001 IN DUNLAP, CALIFORNIA, JUST 10 MILES NORTH OF A Muslim compound known as Baladullah, lived a 69-year-old man, Robert Champlin, and his wife Rachel, who had just returned home from grocery shopping. After putting his groceries away, Champlin went outside to feed his four cats located in a tree house. The cats seemed oddly afraid to enter the tree house to get their food. Champlin thought perhaps a wild animal was nearby, spooking the cats.

When Champlin saw some movement in the tree house, he was startled. Again, thinking it was some wild animal, Champlin was surprised to see a thin, African-American man suddenly appear at the door and begin walking down the tree-house steps. Abdullah said he was hurt, and he continued talking and walking toward the older man. Champlin tried to stop Abdullah, insisting he carry on the conversation on the other side of his gated property.

"Are you afraid of me?" Abdullah asked.

"Yes," Champlin said.

As Abdullah headed toward the gate, Champlin went back into his house. But when the young man turned once again toward his home, Champlin went to his bedroom to pick up a pistol. From his living room window he could see the man heading toward his front door.

"I yelled at him to go to the gate, and this time he jumped the gate, ran across the road and jumped a fence into the neighbor's property," Champlin would later tell reporters for the *Fresno Bee*.

At 4:45 p.m., Champlin called the Fresno Sheriff's Department to report the incident. Deputy Erik Telen heard the call and arrived with Deputy Brent Stalker.

Deputy Telen was just a young man himself. The 26-year-old father was raising two little girls along with his pregnant wife. They were expecting their first son in just a couple of months. Telen was described by friends as the perfect model of a family man. His mother-in-law, in fact, lived next door and his own mother lived just across the street.

"He wasn't the rough and tough kind with a send-them-to-hell attitude," the Sheriff's chaplain said of Telen. "He was a very compassionate being."

Telen and Stalker searched the property of Champlin's next-door neighbor for 45 minutes. The Sheriff's Department even dispatched a helicopter to get a bird's-eye view of the area. But Abdullah could not be found.

For most of America, having a sheriff's department perform an hour-long search, including the expense of sending a helicopter, would have seemed excessive—especially since the search could have focused on nothing more than locating a harmless and confused vagrant. Yet the search continued for another 40 minutes.

Just when the effort seemed hopeless, Telen and Stalker noticed a broken window in the home owned by neighbors Robert and Rose Gregory. The Gregorys were not home at the time, and the officers received permission from the couple's daughter to enter the house. As Telen approached the kitchen area from the living room and turned the corner, he was shot several times by Abdullah, who was hiding behind a cast-iron stove.

Telen died immediately, though police did not know this until they pulled Telen's body out of the home.

After shooting Telen, Abdullah began a five-and-a-half-hour standoff with police that involved more than 100 officers, including SWAT teams from the cities of Clovis and Fresno. Police would describe in awe the "hail of gunfire" they faced each time they tried to rescue Telen or apprehend the shooter.

This horrifying standoff with Abdullah put the nearby Baladullah camp on investigators' radar in a big way when they learned that the gunman had been a resident of the neighboring Islamic compound. A quick investigation also proved that the sprawling Islamic ranch was owned by an obscure Muslim group known as Muslims of the Americas (MOA).

'City of God'

The 2002 debacle that unfolded at Baladullah seemed to have it all—murder, fraud, fugitives, lies, deception, shootouts, arrests, scandal and heartbreak. So many were the twists and turns at Baladullah that the story itself could be viewed as nothing more than a shameless soap opera that needed a scorecard and a rewind button to be understood.

In other words, it was a typical MOA criminal operation.

Baladullah, which translates to "city of God" in Arabic, was MOA's largest known compound. It sat about 60 miles east of Fresno in a mountainous area of Tulare County, California. Reports vary on its size, ranging from 440 to 1,800 acres. Still others placed it as low as 300 acres. In its heyday in 2002, Baladullah had about 100 residents who told the media they bought the complex to raise chickens, grow olive trees and lead a secluded life in an effort to save their youth from drugs and crimes.

What else was new? This same spin (other than the olive trees) was heard 10 years earlier, just before Colorado authorities raided the MOA compound in Buena Vista. What began as an investigation into a $335,000 workers' compensation scam turned out to be an investigation into a terrorist group that led to the discovery of illegal weapons, bomb-making devices and documented assassination plots.

Ten years later, however, this same spin played out again, this time in California where, if authorities would have taken a moment to examine the organization's past and looked past their *"we are a peaceful Muslim group who only want to be left alone"* spin, they could have readily seen the tragedy and scam that were coming at them full steam.

But fear intervened, as usual. Fear of attacking a minority religious group. Fear of being cast as racist for questioning the motives of an all-black sect. Fear of being called sexist for attacking its female leader.

Fear

In many ways, fear is the secret weapon of Muslims of the Americas. Its founder, Pakistani cleric Sheikh Mubarik Gilani, also founded a so-called Islamic "university" in Saudi Arabia—now apparently based in the United States—called the "International Quranic Open University" (IQOU). The IQOU is also based on instilling fear into its pupils, who, in turn, are taught to instill fear into their victims.

The purpose of the university, Gilani says in one guerilla-training film, is to witness how "ordinary youth is turned into, you know, very much like tigers and they have gone back with their people and they are training them in the very same, you know, self defense and guerilla warfare."

The strategy of MOA and its sister "university" group for dealing with outsiders has remained consistent over the years and comes straight out of the Quran:

"I will throw fear into the hearts of those who disbelieve." (Quran 8:12-13)

Neighbors fear them. City officials fear them. The media fears them. Even local police fear them. Most of the fear comes from their reputation as bullies, assassins, murderers, fire bombers and their connection to such high-profile terrorist acts as the first World Trade Centers bombing and their mixing of chemical explosives for the "Day of Terror" plot against New York City.

But fear can come in other forms, not just fear of harm. A person can also fear having his reputation blighted, such as being labeled a hatemonger. And this is one of MOA's most successful tactics—to paint authorities and even neighbors as racists, sexists and "Islamophobes" if they dare to point their fingers at the organization's criminal activities. For state authorities not only to fear for their lives, but also to fear being labeled hatemongers, can mean the difference between successfully prosecuting these Islamic camps or spinelessly allowing them to continue in their illegal conduct.

All of these fears were in play as the Baladullah saga unfolded.

Caving In

Early on, the City of Fresno had dust thrown in its eyes. When the Baladullah camp first set up operation, city authorities caved in to fear. Rather than looking deep into the background of this Islamic group and its terrorist past—which was on record for all to see—Fresno city officials threw caution to the wind, deciding it was best to help this all-black minority religious sect and its female leader with its supposed mission of saving children from the corruptive influences of the outside world.

The City of Fresno granted them the right to operate a state charter school, giving them $4,600 per student. And for all their altruistic, if not naive, efforts, MOA played them like an overfed cat with a mouse between its swatting paws.

MOA opened its first charter school in 2000 in the City of Fresno, and another inside a ramshackle home that sat on the Baladullah compound. Within a year, not surprisingly, Baladullah claimed they had nearly a dozen charter schools located around the state, some as far as 200 miles from the city of its original charter. Locating these campuses outside the county was completely legal, but it made it nearly impossible for the city of Fresno to perform on-site inspections with their small staff.

"It became a logistical nightmare for the school district to keep up with them and their expansion," said Mike O'Hare, the president of the Fresno Unified School Board. "We don't have the time and the personnel for it."[2]

It was just the way MOA likes things—difficult, confusing and complex.

Calling their schools GateWay Charter Academy, MOA quickly claimed that their enrollment of 600 students in 2001 was about to dramatically increase to 1,400 students in 2002. The increase in students would mean a jump of state funds to GateWay from $1.3 million a year to $5.5 million annually. GateWay would also claim that they employed 168 teachers, administrators, school staff members and maintenance personnel.

Anyone with basic knowledge of Muslims of the Americas would have their jaws hit the floor in both shock and incredulous laughter at such claims and numbers. The thought that this terrorist group, in just a year's time, could find 1,400 children and 168 employees to fill more than a dozen academies throughout the State of California was simply insane. And when the dust settled and the facts were finally revealed, when the mouse finally escaped from the frenzied swipes of the cat's paws, all these children did not exist—and neither did the employees.

The ultimate undoing of GateWay Charter Academy was brought about through the typical arrogance of MOA officials who think authorities will never shake the dust from their eyes, that they are dimwitted, inept and dreadfully fearful of their bully tactics and accusations of being labeled Islamophobes.

MOA had the audacity (or stupidity) to ask Fresno for an additional $5.5 million when they couldn't even account for the $1.3 million that had been given them the previous year.

On January 16, 2002, the City of Fresno revoked their school charter. One week later, the State Department of Justice assisted in raiding GateWay schools with the help of 65 state and local police officers serving search warrants at sites around the City of Fresno. They took more than 100 boxes of documents and 60 computers.

The reaction of MOA was typical, predictable and tiresome.

"Islam is on trial," said Khadijah Ghafur, the then 51-year-old leader of the MOA camp in Baladullah and head of GateWay Charter Academy. "And we as Americans are on trial as we deal with it. This is not the American way."

It is not as if the City of Fresno didn't know, couldn't have discovered or learned more about this Muslim sect sitting in the Sierra Mountains with their chickens, olive trees and disheveled children before granting them a license to operate a charter school.

A sign leading into the Baladullah camp made it known that it was a campus site for Sheikh Gilani's "International Quranic Open University." And state authorities were well aware of Sheikh Gilani and the differing names of his terrorist operations, whether they were called Jamaat Al Fuqra, Muslims of the Americas, Muhammad Commandos, Soldiers of Allah or International Quranic Open University.

The Baladullah camp, enveloped in barbed wire, had a small air-strip and a target range, as is typical on Gilani's compounds. Neighbors said the entrance was occasionally guarded by young men with guns. Some neighbors complained of the gunfire.

"Gunfire in the afternoon and gunfire late at night," said one neighbor. "Some of it sounds like target practice, and other times it sounds like rapid fire. It makes you question whether or not they've got automatic weapons."[3]

There was absolutely no excuse for California authorities to grant a charter-school license to Gilani's camp in Baladullah, other than they were operating out of fear—fear of being labeled hatemongers or Islamophobes.

Even the Tulare County Sheriff's Department, which had juris-diction over the camp, came to the defense of the Muslim group when the community began voicing concerns about their criminal and ter-rorist past.

Lt. Greg Langford said of the Baladullah camp, "They've been pointed to as terrorists, and they're scared someone is going to hurt them." He said the Sheriff's Department was more afraid *for* the peo-ple of Baladullah than *of* them.[4]

It is astonishing to read how the Sheriff's Department feared its own citizens, as if the native residents were the real potential terrorists and not the group with a proven track record of targeted murder, as-sassinations and fire-bombings. Imagine how the community must have felt when law enforcement began pointing the finger directly at them, as if somehow they were more prone to violence than the Muslim group with a proven murderous past.

The Tulare County Sheriff's Department couldn't fall on its knees fast enough to placate Gilani's militant, criminal and terrorist empire. How utterly embarrassed the Sheriff's Department must have been, or should have been, to eventually learn that this "peaceful" Muslim group had just swindled $1.3 million out of the pockets of the very people whom the Sheriff's Department was accusing of being the real terrorists—the community that paid for their salaries.

The Baladullah camp immediately seized upon the opportunity presented by such ignorant and self-effacing statements from the Tulare County Sheriff's Department by presenting their legal problems as nothing more than a white versus black case of racial discrimination.

"If it was a school run by whites, the school board would have bent over backwards to let them fix up their problems," said one attorney for GateWay, Frank Muna.[5]

Actually, if the City of Fresno had "bent over backwards" and investigated the group, rather than cave in to the fear of being labeled hatemongering Islamophobes, they could have easily seen how the Baladullah camp was connected to terrorism.

The group didn't just pop up out of nowhere. In 1983, the Los Angeles County Sheriff's Department received a call that a couple of prowlers were operating in a residential area of Compton, one of the oldest cities in the county just south of Los Angeles. When police arrived they noticed two men stowing something in their car trunk. What they found was a rifle and a silencer in the trunk and a police scanner inside the car. Police also found documents linking the two men to Sheikh Mubarik Gilani and his Jamaat Al Fuqra terror group.

One of the men on the scene of the police search was Abdullah Baqi, who had been described by law enforcement as the west-coast leader of Jamaat Al Fuqra.[6]

Abdullah Baqi was significant not only because of his leadership inside Gilani's terrorist structure, but also because he was the husband of the woman who would become the leader of the Baladullah compound and head of the scandalous GateWay Charter Academy, Khadijah Ghafur.

Both Baqi and his wife, Khadijah, would remain in Compton and, in 1983, open a branch of Gilani's International Quranic Open

University in a modest home in the area. They would soon have to move, however, when their landlady became shocked to learn they were allowing dozens of other people to live in trailers behind their home.

In 1984 Baqi and Khadijah moved about 100 miles east of Compton to a remote spot in the high desert of the San Bernardino Mountains, called Summit Valley. They bought a 10-acre parcel of land and lived in military-style tents and old trailers. There were at least 20 children on the site. By 1986 they had all mysteriously vanished.[7]

Incriminating Evidence

But when the Baqis left Summit Valley, they also left behind incriminating evidence about their connection to terrorism and Jamaat Al Fuqra. Sheriff's deputies searched the site after they fled and found typewritten notes about the 1983 murder of a Muslim leader in Michigan, as well as photographs of a mosque that had been firebombed.

This earlier Michigan case involved two Fuqra members who lured the leader of a minority Islamic sect out to dinner, only to follow him home where they shot him to death. It is believed that Gilani ordered his murder because he didn't like the brand of Islam being taught at his mosque. The ruse is reminiscent of Gilani's instructions in his guerrilla-warfare training film, "Soldiers of Allah", to "act like a friend and then kill him." The coldhearted nature of the murder—luring this man to dinner, dining with him, engaging in pleasantries and fine food, pretending to be sincere and offering friendship, all the while knowing they were going to follow him home and shoot him to death—should speak volumes about the ruthlessness, deceitfulness and treacherous nature of Gilani and his followers.

After murdering Dr. Mozaffar Ahmad at his home, the two Fuqra members then drove to his mosque in nearby Detroit. They set off a firebomb at the mosque, but both Fuqra members died in the resulting explosion. The gun used to murder Dr. Ahmad was found on one of their bodies. Not only were the typewritten notes of Dr.

Ahmad's murder and photos of the mosque that was firebombed found at the Summit Valley site, but so were photos of Abdullah Baqi with one of Jamaat Al Fuqra's most infamous terrorists, Stephen Paul Paster.

Paster was, and still is, considered by law enforcement to be Jamaat Al Fuqra's explosives expert. In 1983 Paster, who was one of the few white males inside Gilani's terrorist structure, made a dubious name for himself after he firebombed an Oregon hotel owned by an Indian religious leader. Despite his reputation as an explosives expert, Paster blew off most of his hand while planting the pipe bombs.

Paster was arrested, escaped from a hospital, and was then re-arrested on June 26, 1985. He was captured at a Fuqra camp in Buena Vista, Colorado. Hiding fugitives is not unusual for Gilani's Muslims of the Americas compounds. Even the Baladullah camp would ultimately be caught hiding a fugitive or two. Paster would receive a 20-year prison sentence for the bombing, but would only serve a minuscule four years. Paster reportedly moved back to Pakistan, where, U.S. intelligence believes, he has been providing explosives training to visiting MOA members ever since.[8]

After Baqi and his wife, Khadijah, abandoned their Summit Valley camp, leaving behind a wealth of terrorist connections for police to discover, they disappeared for several years. In 1989 they would be found again, this time at a former Baptist youth camp in Central Sierra.

When purchasing the youth camp, Khadijah told the property manager that she wanted to use the site to shelter disadvantaged children and their families; again with the kids, again with the Mother Theresa-like image of saving children, again acting as if she were Islam's white knight for disadvantaged kids.

Soon neighbors began hearing gunshots. Dozens of families were living together in only a few cabins. Authorities cited the Muslim group for violating building and safety codes. By 1993 they had also fallen months behind on their rent. The owner filed for eviction.

Without explanation, and always refusing to answer any reporters' questions about where they suddenly found the money, the group moved again, this time from the Central Sierra camp to the foothills of the Sierra Mountains, where they purchased what would become the Baladullah compound of nearly (by some accounts) 1,800 acres.

An important fact to note is that the property was once part of a 3,400-acre property owned by a drug rehab group known as Synanon. MOA renamed it Baladullah.

Synanon

The connection to Synanon would become an important one. Synanon had been famous from the 1960s through the 80s for many reasons. It had hosted some notable clientele who received treatment for addictions, including musicians and actors. Bob Dylan, though never a client, referred to Synanon in his song *Lenny Bruce*. George Lucas actually used women from Synanon as actors in his film "THX 1138" because they sported shaved heads, a practice imposed by the group's founder. The group had already made its mark on the culture through its association with some well-known iconic figures.

Although Synanon began as a drug rehab program, it turned into a cult responsible for the beatings of former members nearly to death and the issuance of death threats to anyone who tried to expose the brutal nature of their religious sect. In addition, married couples were forced to break up their marriages in order to pair up with new partners, and men were given forced vasectomies. The group had also been charged with attempted murder when it placed a rattlesnake in the mailbox of an attorney who brought a lawsuit against Synanon for abducting his female client.

Synanon eventually abandoned the Badger camp after intense public scrutiny. Before Muslims of the Americas took it over, the Los Angeles Police Department searched the ranch and found a recorded speech by its founder, Charles Dederich, in which he said, "We're not going to mess with the old-time, turn-the-other-cheek religious postures ... our religious posture is: Don't mess with us. You can get killed dead, literally dead ... these are real threats. ... We will make the rules ... I am quite willing to break some lawyer's legs, and next break his wife's legs, and threaten to cut their child's arm off."[9]

Synanon was not an outfit to be messed with. And although long gone from the ranch, it would play an integral role in the drama that would unfold after MOA took over the property.

By the time MOA did move onto the ranch, the site had buildings, a firing range and a small airstrip. It seemed like a perfect place to locate an organization with its own terrorist history. So pleased was MOA with its new site that they hired one of Synanon's former members, Doug Hurt, to be its attorney to represent them in their case against Fresno in their subsequent charter school scam. They even placed Doug Hurt as a board member of GateWay Charter Academy.

To place a past member of Synanon on the MOA school's board—with Synanon connected to criminal acts such as beatings, malicious threats and attempted murder—could hardly be viewed as an effort by Baladullah to flee its own connections to criminal and terrorist activities. But Doug Hurt, not surprisingly, denied that Synanon had any connections to criminal activity, despite evidence of audiotapes, member testimony, arrests and even guilty pleas by two Synanon members of conspiracy to commit murder.

Who better then, despite all the evidence to the contrary, to help the Baladullah camp deny it had any connections to terrorism? Hurt even told a Fresno television station that the organization had no connection to Gilani, despite a sign leading into the groups' Baladullah entrance stating it was a campus site for Gilani's International Quranic Open University.

MOA's blatant lies and absurdly ridiculous propaganda are reminiscent of a very colorful figure once known in the West as Baghdad Bob who, even while U.S. tanks were rolling into central Baghdad directly behind him, was standing on a rooftop declaring, "Be assured, Baghdad is safe, secure and great."

Deny. Deny. Deny. And, of course, when all else fails, accuse the accusers.

Hurt said the legal action Fresno was taking against GateWay and its leaders was similar to the unfair, prejudiced and vindictive prosecution that took place against Synanon and their leaders, whose only goal was to heal drug addicts.

Referencing the Baladullah camp, Hurt said, "This is a poor group of folks in the mountains escaping the inner-city problems of drugs and violence." For all his efforts to deny any association with Sheikh Gilani, Hurt's statement read as if it came straight from MOA's propaganda handbook.

"They are very nice, peaceful, law-abiding citizens," he said. "I have taken my wife and kids up there for picnics and we have always had fun there."[10]

But there was more than "picnics" and "fun" going on at the Baladullah camp. There was even more than fraud, misappropriation of funds and falsifying records surrounding their GateWay charter-school scam.

Baladullah played the host to at least three other criminals.

Tabari Shabir, a resident of the Baldullah compound, would be arrested in November 2003 by federal authorities for shipping 52 kilos of cocaine from Oakland to Atlanta and Philadelphia.

James Hobson, who was a fugitive after being arrested in 1999 on charges of conspiracy to sell illegal guns to felons, was not only found inside the Baladullah compound in March, 2001, but was also an employee of GateWay Charter Academy. He was arrested after returning from lunch.

Shootout

The most infamous criminal, however, was a young man named Ramadan Abdullah—the same Abdullah who engaged in a gun battle with police and ultimately shot to death a young deputy sheriff.

Abdullah came to Baladullah by way of MOA's headquarters in Hancock, New York. He was just 20 years old when he arrived. He was obviously well-trained in guerilla warfare at the Hancock camp, but also reportedly suffered from mental illness.

Because Gilani offers courses in psychiatric healing through his International Quranic Open University, it's not surprising that his camps attract Muslims with mental disorders. This is also beneficial to the Gilani terrorist structure because it can blame crimes committed by its members on these mental disorders, whether true or not.

Regardless of the actual merits of his mental condition, police believe on Aug. 21, 2001, Ramadan Abdullah left the camp on a mission to steal weapons for the Baladullah compound. Ultimately, he ended up in the tree house of Robert Champlin, who called the Sheriff's Department, and the gun battle ensued on a neighbor's property.

The Sheriff's Department would later say "the number of rounds fired and the way Abdullah lay flat on the ground awaiting Deputy Erik Telen to round the corner may indicate firearms training." And these words were expressed by the Sheriff's Department before they knew Abdullah had spent time in Gilani's Hancock, New York, compound, known for its guerilla-training exercises.

"They went back in, knowing they were facing gunfire. It was a firefight," said Capt. Carlos Mestas of the Fresno Sheriff's Department.

At 12:31 a.m. Abdullah finally surrendered to police. Refusing to take any blame for Deputy Telen's death, Abdullah perversely stated that the police officer basically killed himself.

"I didn't kill him," Abdullah said. "He killed himself by walking into the living room when he heard the 'chung-chung' of me locking and loading the gun and he kept coming."

Abdullah, the Muslim soldier that he was (or the Soldier of Allah he was trained to be) also said, "I pulled the trigger while I was in prayer."[11]

Abdullah and his attorney immediately began an insanity defense, and his trial was delayed for years as psychologists argued if he was competent to stand trial. He was facing the death penalty, and some argued that his claims of insanity were faked to both delay the trial and avoid execution. Three psychologists examining Abdullah would diagnose him as suffering from schizophrenia. Three other psychologists argued that Abdullah was faking his condition.

In a June, 2002, interview with one psychologist, Abdullah was asked if he was simply "playing games" and pretending to be incompetent. According to the psychologist's report, Abdullah "smiled, leaned forward and whispered, 'I am playing games.' "[12]

Seven years after Telen's murder, Abdullah finally dropped his insanity defense to avoid a trial that could result in the death penalty. Judge Ralph Nunez then convicted Abdullah of the murder of Deputy Sheriff Telen and sentenced him to life in prison.

Such was the backdrop of the Baladullah compound before and during its embezzlement of $1.3 million in a fake charter-school scam. The drama included murder, connections to former terrorists and direct knowledge of acts of terrorism, hiding fugitives, sounds of gunfire inside the camp, housing individuals who either sold large quantities of illegal drugs or sold illegal weapons to felons, employing one of those felons at the school and having armed guards at the entrance gates.

"Nothing here to see" was the constant refrain of the Baladullah camp residents, despite evidence to the contrary which could easily be found simply by scratching the surface. But any surface-scratching was immediately met with accusations of racist and religious discrimination.

"It is racism and anti-Muslim hysteria," said Khadijah Ghafur, leader of the Baladullah camp, regarding the investigation into the charter-school program. "These are the real reasons for the revocation."

Khadijah's second husband, Salih Ghafur, had the audacity to blame the city's investigation of the charter-school program on the 9-11 attacks. "When the World Trade Center fell, I was engulfed in shock and grief. That was soon followed by worry for our people at Baladullah," said Ghafur.

How could Salih Ghafur be in shock and in grief over the World Trade Center attack when one of the organization's own members, Rodney Hampton-El, helped participate in the bombing of the World Trade Center during its first attack in 1993? Such deception and victim-playing is standard fare for Muslims of the Americas. Perhaps the loudest voice in the wounded "woe is me" plaint—almost Rodney Dangerfield in its comical "please pity me" attitude—was the female leader of the Baladullah camp, Khadijah Ghafur.

Born as Deanna Moton in Selma, Alabama, Khadijah Ghafur was the daughter of a Christian minister. She grew up as a civil rights activist and did not convert to Islam until her college years.

Drinking the Toilet Water

When she was just 14 years old, Khadijah said she was arrested in Selma during one particular civil rights demonstration and thrown into jail along with 28 other teenage girls. She was placed in a small holding cell, according to her version of the event, and forced to drink toilet water. Many years later, faced with accusations of stealing 1.3 million city dollars in the fake charter-school program, she used her "toilet drinking" story to once again play the victim.

"I know we are going to stay open one way or another," she predicted, wrongly it turns out. "I did not drink that toilet water in Selma to come to Fresno and be abused."

Doubting her whole "toilet drinking" experience is not hard to do, considering the habitual, even laughable, lies she has told in the past. In 1995, as president of the Fresno-based Women's International Network, she was suspected of fraudulently promoting Mike Tyson, the controversial boxer, as a guest speaker at its Mother's Day benefit dinner. Tyson said he had never been contacted by the women's forum or Ghafur.

"I have not personally been contacted by anyone associated with this organization," Tyson would say. He accused Ghafur of "playing games."[13]

Ghafur also told reporters that the Baladullah camp had no connection to Sheikh Gilani, a lie that even the most careless of reporters could expose, considering that the camp featured an entrance sign boasting of Gilani's International Open Quranic University. Ghafur then went on to deny any connection to Muslims of the Americas. But when this became another apparent lie, she explained that her only affiliation with MOA was that she completed some paperwork to join a group delivering medicine to Africa in 2000.[14] In reality, Ghafur's first husband was the West Coast leader of Muslims of the Americas, Abdullah Baqi.

The lies, of course, did not stop when Khadijah Ghafur began operating state-sponsored chartered schools. Ghafur lied about the numbers of teachers, administrators and maintenance people she employed, claiming 162 employees when she could only produce fingerprints for 88. Two of those fingerprints belonged to convicted felons, whom Ghafur refused to fire even when she was told she had no choice but to terminate their employment.

She lied about the number of students she had, claiming 500 students when city officials could only identify a small number of children who actually attended the schools. Students would be recorded as having been at two different schools on the same day. One school was found to have no students at all. In another instance, Ghafur claimed that one of her schools had a 100 percent attendance on a day when a Fresno County school official visited and found the school closed.

In perhaps her boldest lie, Ghafur claimed certain schools were a part of GateWay Charter Academy without those schools having any knowledge that such claims were being made about them.

Ghafur claimed, for instance, the Blackhouse Institute of Education was part of the GateWay Academy. This came as a surprise to the principal of Blackhouse, who was shocked to learn Ghafur added his 11 students to her charter schools.

"This is a dishonorable thing what they did to us," Ta Biti Akmoa, the school's principal, said. "I don't know what they were doing."[15]

By the end of the city's investigation, officials cited the GateWay Charter Academy with building safety violations, hiring teachers without credentials, hiring employees without criminal background checks, charging tuition illegally, failing to provide salary information and citing illegal attendance records.

Most importantly, Ghafur was charged with failure to account for $1.3 million. The assignment of the criminal investigation went to Special Agent Thomas Win, a white-collar crime investigator in Fresno. Win had no doubt where the money went.

"She used GateWay as a storefront to funnel money to a cause. And there is no doubt in my mind her cause was Gilani," Win concluded.[16]

Even though Ghafur had denied any association with Sheikh Mubarik Gilani or his Muslims of the Americas, the city concluded this is exactly the person, and the reason, for her fraud upon the city.

Authorities even found a letter inside Ghafur's apartment in Fresno, inside a briefcase, that was addressed to Sheikh Gilani.

"My dearest Abu," Ghafur wrote, meaning "My dearest teacher." She promised Gilani "a steady cash flow to you," but added this caution: "I can't afford a verified paper trail against me that would stop my service and dedication to you."

In August, 2006, Khadijah Ghafur was convicted of grand theft and sentenced to 14 years in jail. She remained defiant even after her conviction, determined to rely on the only strategy Muslims of the Americas understands when confronted with the truth about their criminal acts: "This is what Muslims have to deal with," she said from her prison cell.

☪

Call it what you want—fear, pacification, laziness, political correctness, ignorance or just plain incompetence—Muslims of the Americas took advantage of Fresno's inability and refusal to see the Baladullah camp for what it was: a branch of an Islamic terrorist group which had a history rich in criminal activity.

They allowed Muslims of the Americas to throw dust in their eyes, first to blind them ... and then rob them.

Before handing over a single dime to the Baladullah camp, and with a little investigative work, Fresno authorities could have known that Khadijah Ghafur had been married to the West Coast leader of Jamaat Al Fuqra and that this leader was a friend of Stephen Paster, who bombed an Oregon hotel. And both Ghafur and her husband left a former camp that had typewritten notes detailing the murder of an imam in Michigan and photos of a Detroit mosque bombed by the group in 1983.

These details, which were uncovered by a variety of reporters, could easily have been discovered by government authorities, who exercise much more investigative powers than newspaper journalists.

Fresno authorities could also have easily learned that Jamaat Al Fuqra was listed by the U.S. State Department as a group that "seeks to purify Islam through violence" and that it had a criminal past of committing fraud, such as the $335,000 workers' compensation scam discovered in Buena Vista, Colorado.

And without much digging, Fresno authorities could have learned that the group was suspected of committing fire-bombings, murder, assassinations, gun-running, drug-running and even kidnapping. Even the most cursory of searches would have led Fresno authorities to discover that several members of Jamaat Al Fuqra were convicted of conspiracy to commit murder in the death of a Tucson, Arizona, imam who was stabbed dozens of times in what he thought was the safety of his own home mosque.

Even after giving Baladullah $1.3 million, the evidence that this was a terrorist-connected group was flashed in front of their eyes several times. Two of their members were arrested as fugitives on the compound; one of them was even employed at the charter school. Another member left the compound in search of weapons and killed a deputy sheriff.

There were rapid gunfire and armed guards at the compound. The attorney for the group and a board member of the charter school was a former member of Synanon, whose founder once claimed, "I am quite willing to break some lawyer's legs, and next break his wife's legs, and threaten to cut their child's arm off."

But still, the dust remained in the eyes of many officials, and even the local Sheriff's Department.

It was after all these crimes had been discovered, and the community started to become alarmed, that Lt. Greg Langford of the Tulare County Sheriff's Department said he was "more afraid for the people of Baladullah than of them."

Suddenly, it was the community members who were the potential terrorists. But when the dust finally settled, and when authorities finally wiped the dust out of their eyes, it was clear that this compound was nothing more than an Islamic group with terrorist intentions.

As Special Agent Thomas Win said of Khadijah Ghafur, "She used GateWay as a storefront to funnel money to a cause. And there is no doubt in my mind her cause was Gilani."

And there is not doubt that Gilani's cause is Islamic terrorism. As Ali Aziz, who spent eight years as an undercover agent inside Gilani's American-based compounds on behalf of the New York Police Department, stated:

"It's very simple. MOA is asleep. They are asleep. They are a bomb."

APPENDIX A
AL FUQRA COLORADO CHARGES
Information taken from 2005 Department of Justice report, "Identifying the Links Between White-Collar Crime and Terrorism," summarizing charges stemming from the Colorado Al Fuqra case.

Fuqra Case: Charges under Colorado Organized Crime Control Act (COCCA)

Count One (see Table 10)	Conducting an enterprise through a pattern of racketeering activity	1) false worker's compensation claims 2) failure to file income tax returns 3) theft of rental property
Count Two	Investing proceeds of racketeering activity in real estate	1) false worker's compensation claim payments funneled to real estate escrow account 2) money in escrow account used for land payments 3) land titled in name of James D. Williams
Count Three	Conspiracy to violate COCCA	1) agreement to engage in criminal enterprise a) agreement to file false worker's compensation claims b) agreement not to file tax returns c) agreement to steal rental property 2) agreement to use racketeering proceeds to purchase real estate
Counts Five, Ten, and Thirteen	Theft	1) forgery 2) theft of rental property

Fuqra Case: Patterns of Racketeering

False worker's compensation claims	1) Upshur/Williams claims 2) Johnson/Green claims 3) Woods/Pierre claims 4) Williams/McClane claims
Failure to file tax returns	1) Edward I. McGhee 2) James L. Upshur 3) Chris Childs 4) James D. Williams
Theft of rental property	1) Center Rental theft 2) Wagner Rental theft 3) Action Rental thefts 4) AAA Rental thefts

APPENDIX B
SUSPECTED FUQRA ACTIVITIES

This appendix contains information taken from 2005 Department of Justice report, "Identifying the Links Between White-Collar Crime and Terrorism."

Suspected Fuqra Activities: Training Compounds and Activities, by State

State	City/County	Description	State	City/County	Description
AL	Marion	Training compound	MO	Kansas City	Activity, bombing
AZ	Tempe	Activity, bombing	NJ	Jersey City	Activity
	Tucson	Activity, murder	NY	Binghamton	Activity
CA	Badger	Activity, murder		Buffalo	Activity
	Baladulla	Training compound		Deposit	Training compound
	Barstow	Activity		Hancock	Training compound – U.S. Headquarters
	Fresno	Activity	NC	N/A	Activity
	Los Angeles	Activity, murder	OH	Akron	Activity, bombing, murder
	Oak Hill	Training compound	OK	Talihina	Training compound
	San Diego	Activity, bombing	OR	Portland	Activity, bombing
CO	Buena Vista	Training compound	PA	Philadelphia	Activity, bombing, murder
	Colorado Springs	Activity	SC	York County	Training compound
	Denver	Activity, bombing	TN	Dover	Training compound
	Englewood	Activity	TX	N/A	Training compound
DC		Activity		Houston	Activity, bombing
FL	N/A	Activity	VA	Falls Church	Training compound
GA	Augusta	Activity, murder		Red House	Training compound
	Commerce	Training compound		Roanoke	Activity
	Macon	Training compound	WA	Onalaska	Training compound
IL	Rockford	Activity, bombing		Seattle	Activity, bombing, murder
KS	Overland Park	Activity, kidnapping		Tacoma	Activity, murder
MA	Quincy	Activity, bombing	WV	Bethany	Activity, bombing, murder
MD	Baltimore	Activity	WI	N/A	Activity
	Hyattsville	Training compound			
MI	Canton	Activity, murder			
	Clinton township	Activity, bombing, murder			
	Coldwater	Training compound			
	Dearborn Heights	Activity			
	Detroit	Activity, bombing, murder			

APPENDIX C
MAP OF SELECTED FUQRA COMPOUNDS
AND ACTIVITIES

The information in this appendix was compiled by Christian Action Network.

Jamaat al-Fuqra in the United States

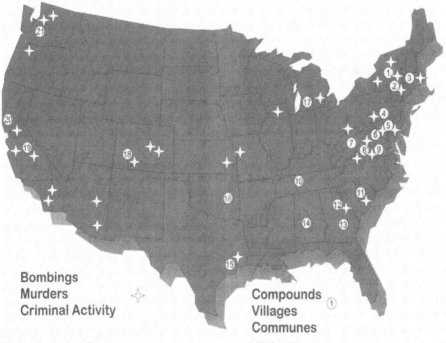

Bombings
Murders ✦
Criminal Activity

Compounds ①
Villages
Communes

Known Jamaat ul-Fuqra camps

1. Deposit, NY
2. Hancock, NY (National Headquarters)
3. Springfield, MA
4. Philadelphia, PA
5. Hyattsville, MD
6. Fairfax, VA
7. Bethany, WV
8. Red House, VA
9. Meherrin, VA
10. Dover, TN
11. York, SC
12. Commerce, GA

14. Marion, AL
15. Houston, TX
16. Talhina, OK
17. Coldwater, MI
18. Buena Vista, CO
    (Raided and shut down by Colorado authorities in 1992)
19. Baladulla, CA
    (Leader convicted of scamming state out of $1.3 million in 2006. Compound now abandoned)
20. Oak Hill, CA
21. Onalaska, WA

Note: This map represents only a partial listing of 35 Jamaat ul-Fuqra camps in the U.S. Other camps remain undisclosed by law enforcement or Jamaat ul-Fuqra.

APPENDIX D
ACTUAL AND SUSPECTED CRIMINAL ACTIVITY
OF JAMAAT AL FUQRA

The information in this appendix was compiled by Christian Action Network.

- Bombing and attack on the Hare Krishna Temple of San Diego, CA. (8/31/79)
- Attack on an Iranian mosque, Queens, N.Y. (11/21/79)
- Attack on the Islamic Cultural Center, Tempe, AZ. (9/1/82)
- Fuqra west coast leader James Jennings arrested while concealing rifle and silencer in trunk of car, 1983.
- The bombing of the Hotel Rajineesh, Portland, OR. (7/29/83)
- Dr. Mozaffar Ahmed shot dead after Fuqra member dined with him, seeking to learn more about the Ahmadiyya sect, Canton, MI. (8/8/83)
- Bombing of the Ahmadi headquarters three times in 1983 and once in 1985, Baltimore, MD.
- Firebombing of a Hare Krishna temple, Philadelphia, PA. (6/16/84)
- Bombing of the Integral Yoga Society and the Vedanta Society, Seattle, WA. (6/17/84)
- Defective bomb found at the Vedanta Society, Kansas City, MO. (7-8/1/84)
- John Liczwinko, member of Seattle Vedanta Society, attacked, Seattle, WA. (8/1/84)
- Firebombing of International Society for Krishna Consciousness, Denver, CO. (8/1/84)
- Hindu physician Srinivasu Dasari kidnapped, Overland Park, KS. (8/1/84)
- Triple homicide bludgeoning deaths of Tariq Rafay, wife and daughter, Seattle, WA. (8/1/84)
- Fire breaks out a power station, Leesdale, CO. (2/1/85)
- Attack on local mosque, Houston, TX. (6/22/85)
- Attack on Vat Thothikalam Lao, Rockford, IL. (8/5/85)
- Attack on a Laotian temple, Rockford, IL. (12/1/85)

- Attack on Hare Krishna member Randal Gorby, Bethany, WV. (5/28/86)
- Doctor Vousseph Mouna assassinated outside Humana Hospital, Augusta, GA. (9/17/88)
- Large cache of terrorist weapons and material discovered in storage locker rented by Al Fuqra, Colorado Springs, CO. (9/16/89)
- Imam Rashad Khalifa assassinated, Tucson, AZ. (1/31/90)
- Attack on the Islamic Center of Quincy, MA. (3/30/90)
- Attack on the Islamic Culture Center of San Diego, CA. (1/11/91)
- Five Al Fuqra members arrested at Niagara Falls border crossing and charged in a plot to bomb a Hindu temple and Indian theater near Toronto, Canada. Five members were successfully convicted; all of them served their time and were released. (10/3/91)
- Fuqra member Earl Grant indicted on charges of transporting explosives. (7/1/93)
- Al Fuqra compound raided in Buena Vista, CO. (10/8/92)
- Nine Al Fuqra members convicted in "Day of Terror" plot to bomb New York landmarks, Lincoln and Holland tunnels, FBI building and United Nations. (1/17/96)
- Federal Emergency Management Agency links Jamaat Al Fuqra to 1993 World Trade Center bombing. (8/18/97).
- Fuqra member James Hobson arrested for smuggling and selling illegal firearms. (3/01)
- Ben Benu, Vincent Pierre and his wife are arrested for illegally buying guns, Red House, VA. (9/20/01)
- Fuqra member Abdur-Rauf Abdullah shoots and kills Fresno Deputy Sheriff Eric Talen, Dunlap, CA. (8/21/01).
- The Boston Globe reports that shoe bomber Richard Reid is suspected of having ties to Jamaat Al Fuqra and is a follower of Sheikh Mubarik Gilani. (1/6/02)
- Wall Street Journal reporter Daniel Pearl is kidnapped and later beheaded while attempting to attend an interview with Jamaat Al Fuqra leader Sheikh Gilani, Karachi, Pakistan. (1/23/02)

- Jamaat Al Fuqra leader Khadijah Ghafur is sentenced to 14 years in jail for bilking California out of $1.3 million in a charter school scam, Dunlap, CA. (8/24/06)
- Fuqra and Al Qaeda member Lyman Faris pleads guilty in federal court in a plot to blow up the Brooklyn Bridge. (5/1/03)
- Fuqra member Tabari Malik Shabir arrested and charged with possession and attempted possession to distribute 57 kilograms of cocaine. (11/14/04)
- Muslims of the Americas compounds in California, Virginia and Georgia suspected of burglarizing 11 cell phone stores throughout the San Francisco Bay area, stealing more than 800 phones. (12/27/04)
- Fuqra member Lindsey Germaine dies while carrying out the London subway bombing attack. (7/7/05)
- Six Fuqra members from West Virginia, Virginia and Delaware arrested and charged with conspiracy to traffic counterfeit goods in a criminal operation totaling $19 million. (3/7/07)
- Three Muslims of the Americas members arrested in Baltimore, MD, while transporting 400 units of heroin from Philadelphia to Lynchburg, VA. (8/25/07)
- The Jawa Report reveals that members of Muslims of the Americas are accused of tax fraud in the New York City area involving the filing of false tax returns and collecting 24-hour rapid returns. (1/4/10)

APPENDIX E
FAKE COMPANIES ASSOCIATED WITH AL FUQRA

This appendix contains information taken from 2005 Department of Justice report, "Identifying the Links Between White-Collar Crime and Terrorism," summarizing fraudulent companies set up by Al Fuqra, and research conducted by Christian Action Network.

Organization	Description
Professional Security International (PSI)	Headquartered in Colorado and headed by Fuqra member James D. Williams
786 Security Firm, aka 786 Security Co.	Headquartered in New York and operated by Fuqra member Husain M. Abdallah, aka Eugene Clarence Spencer
Dagger Investigative Services	Associated with 786 Security Firm and located in New York
Watchdog Securities	Associated with 786 Security Firm and located in New York
Mills Security	Associated with 786 Security Firm and located in New York
CCC Carpentry	Operated by Fuqra member Chris Childs
RDW Construction	Operated by Fuqra member James Upshur
Ray and Ken, subcontracting company	Associated with various Fuqra members
McClane's Carpenter & Home Builders	Operated by Fuqra member James D. Williams
CML Construction	Associated with various Fuqra members
R&D Carpenters	Associated with various Fuqra members
Muslims of America (the Americas)	Founded by Sheikh Gilani
Quaranic Open University	Founded by Sheikh Gilani
White Hawk Security Intl.	Associated with Muslims of the Americas compound in Meherrin, VA

APPENDIX F
AL FUQRA ORGANIZATIONAL STRUCTURE

This appendix contains information taken from 2005 Department of Justice report, "Identifying the Links Between White-Collar Crime and Terrorism," summarizing the organizational structure and flow of income.

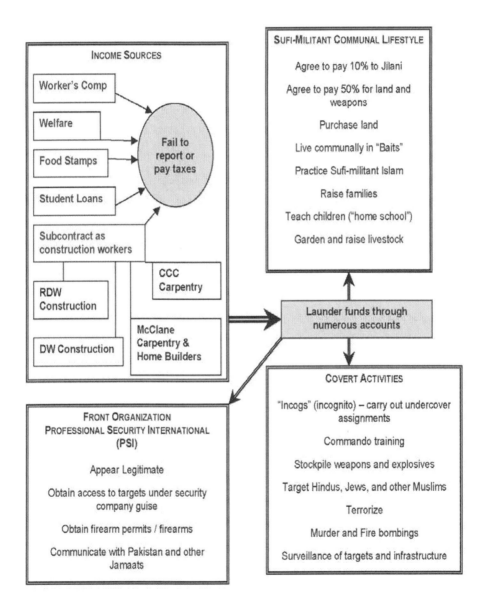

APPENDIX G
BELTWAY SNIPER'S TIMELINE, 2002

Wednesday, Oct. 2

- James D. Martin was killed by a sniper outside a Shopper's Food Warehouse in Silver Spring, MD.

Thursday, Oct. 3

- Four more people are killed at various locations during a two-hour shooting spree in Montgomery County, MD.
- Pascal Charlot is killed at 9:15 p.m. while standing on a street in Washington., D.C.
- Police announce they are investigating the shootings as the work of a serial sniper, and describe the gunman as a "skilled shooter."

Friday, Oct. 4

- A 43-year-old woman is shot and wounded outside a Michael's craft store in Fredericksburg, VA.
- Police set up a tip hotline and offer a reward of $50,000. The reward eventually grows to $500,000.
- Authorities say the same high-powered weapon was used to kill at least three of five Maryland residents.
- Spotsylvania County, VA, police said witnesses to the Fredericksburg shooting described a possible suspect vehicle in that case as a mid-sized, newer model car.

Saturday, Oct. 5

- Police link the Fredericksburg shooting with the sniper.

Sunday, Oct. 6

- Investigators complete geographic profile of the killer. FBI works on a psychological profile.

Monday, Oct. 7

- A 13-year-old boy in Bowie, MD., is shot outside his school in Bowie, MD., but survives. Investigators quickly link that shooting to the sniper.

Wednesday, Oct. 9

- Dean Harold Meyers, 53, is shot dead at a gas station near

Manassas, VA.

- The Washington Post and WUSA-TV report a tarot "death" card was found near the Bowie crime scene. The card read, "Dear policeman, I am God." Montgomery County Police Chief Charles Moose, who is heading the task force hunting down the sniper, blasts media and others for information leaks.

- A woman is questioned by Prince George's County, MD., police. Law enforcement say she may have dropped off a man seen walking into a wooded area near a local high school. Officials search for but cannot find the man.

Thursday, Oct. 10

- Virginia police report two males were seen driving away in a white vehicle after the Oct. 9 shooting of Meyers.

- Maryland police detain a Kensington, MD., man "of previous interest" to investigators after being called to his home and finding a cache of weapons. The man was not arrested.

- Prince William County, VA, police link the Meyers murder to the sniper shootings.

Friday, Oct. 11

- 53-year-old Kenneth Bridges is shot dead while pumping gas at an Exxon station in Massaponax, VA. A white van was spotted leaving the area. Virginia police caution public not to focus just on white vans.

Saturday, Oct. 12

- Police release composites images of a white box truck similar to the one witnesses said they saw near some of the shootings.

- Spotsylvania County, VA, police link Bridges' death to the other shootings.

Monday, Oct. 14

- Baltimore, MD., police seize a white van in Baltimore and find an assault rifle, sniper manual and ammunition similar to the .223 bullets used in sniper attacks. The van's owner, an ex-Marine, is questioned and released.

- Linda Franklin, 47, is shot dead as she and her husband load packages into their car outside a Home Depot store in Falls Church, VA. Witnesses give information about license plates on vehicles seen fleeing the scene, including a light-colored Chevrolet Astro van with a burned-out taillight. Another witness describes the possible shooter as a dark-skinned man, possibly Hispanic or Middle Eastern, in a white van.

Tuesday, Oct. 15

- Ballistics evidence connects Franklin's death to the sniper.
- Defense Department announces it will provide military surveillance aircraft in the hunt. Army begins searching its records for people with sniper training.

Wednesday, Oct. 16

- Witness to Franklin's shooting tells police the shooter used an AK-74 rifle and was of a certain ethnic descent.
- Police issue a "how-to" list of tips for potential witnesses.

Thursday, Oct. 17

- Police announce evidence from Home Depot witness is "not credible."

Friday, Oct. 18

- Police arrested Matthew Dowdy, 37, of Falls Church, VA for providing false information to authorities. He is arraigned Monday, Oct. 21.

Saturday, Oct. 19

- A 37-year-old man is shot and critically wounded while leaving a Ponderosa steakhouse with his wife in Ashland, VA. Witnesses say they heard the shot coming from a nearby wooded area. Roadblocks are set up along I-95 in Maryland and Virginia and police search for a white 2000 Chevrolet van with Maryland plates and a ladder rack.

Sunday, Oct. 20

- Surgeons remove the bullet from the man shot in Ashland and give it to authorities for testing. Sniper task force heads to the scene.
- Police believe the Beltway Sniper left a note with a telephone number at the Ponderosa scene. Police ask the person who left the message to contact them.

Monday, Oct. 21

- Police in Virginia surround a white Plymouth Voyager minivan with a roof rack and a phone booth adjoining a gas station in Hanover County, VA. Two men are taken into custody, but later turned over to the Immigration and Naturalization Service after it is determined they had no role in the shootings.
- Moose holds news conference and delivers a message: "The message that needs to be delivered is that we are going to respond to a message that we have received... We are preparing a response at this time."
- Police connect Saturday's Ponderosa shooting to the sniper.
- Moose sends another message: "The person you called could not hear everything that you said ...The audio was unclear and we want to get everything right. Call us back so that we can clearly understand."

Tuesday, Oct. 22

- Conrad Johnson, a 35-year-old bus driver, is shot in the chest and wounded while on a parked commuter bus in Montgomery County. He dies at the hospital.
- Reports say a note found at the Ponderosa scene demanded $10 million and warned the killings would continue unless cash was paid by a stated deadline. It also threatened children.

Wednesday Night, Oct. 23

- Around 7 p.m.: New reports say police are searching the yard of a Tacoma, Wash., home, for ammunition evidence.
- Investigators comb through John Lee Malvo's student records at Bellingham High School in Bellingham, Wash.
- Around 7:30 p.m.: Federal law enforcement officials confirm the raid in Tacoma is related to the sniper case.
- 8:30 p.m.: Seattle police say they are conducting a consentual search that they cannot confirm is part of the sniper case.
- 11:45 p.m.: Montgomery County Police Chief Charles Moose holds a press conference and announces an arrest warrant for John Allen Muhammad, also known as John Allen Williams, described as "armed and dangerous." Moose says the man may he be traveling with Malvo.
- Police issue an alert for a blue 1990 Chevrolet Caprice with New Jersey plates NDA-21Z Caprice and a white 1989 Chevrolet Celebrity with Maryland plates ZWE-517. Police caution Muhammad is not necessarily the Beltway Sniper.
- Moose issues his final statement to the sniper, saying, among other things: "You've asked us to say, quote, We have caught the sniper like a duck in a noose, end quote. We understand that hearing us say this is important to you."

Thursday, Oct. 24

- 3:19 a.m.: The sniper task force arrests Muhammad, 42, and Malvo, while they sleep in a car off I-70 in Frederick County, MD. A motorist and an attendant at the rest stop call police at 1 a.m. after they spot the pair sleeping inside one of the cars sought in the sniper investigation. Their car was a blue 1990 Chevrolet Caprice with New Jersey plates NDA-21Z.
- Around 5:30 a.m.: Police confirm arrests and say a warrant

is being sought to search the vehicle. Reports say a search warrant has been issued in Alabama.

- 9 a.m.: Montgomery, Ala., police confirm that sniper task force called them on Sunday to see whether a September shooting at a liquor store there is related to the sniper shootings. A caller to the sniper investigation tip line claimed responsibility for both the sniper shootings and the Sept. 21 shooting outside ABC Beverage. Malvo's fingerprint was reportedly found on a gun magazine found at the Alabama crime scene.
- 9:30 a.m.: Reports say a gun was found in the car in custody and that Muhammad is being charged on a federal gun violation and Malvo as a material witness.
- 10:30 a.m.: Bellingham, Wash., officials say suspects in custody are working alone and not with an organized group. The officials add that authorities first had contact with Malvo Dec. 18 after noticing "suspicious activity." Malvo said he came to the area to finish high school.
- Around 11 a.m.: The blue Caprice is towed to Gaithersburg, MD, and described as a "wealth of evidence." Reports say a rifle found in the car shoots .223 caliber bullets.
- 11:55 a.m.: Reports say police found a gun, a scope and a tripod in the car as well as a hole in the trunk of the car police suspect was used to point the gun.
- Authorities confirm that a Bushmaster XM-15 rifle found in Muhammad's car has been linked by ballistics to 11 of the 14 shootings, including one in which no one was injured.

Friday, Oct. 25

- 10:30 a.m.: Montgomery, Ala., police say they will charge Malvo and Muhammad with capital murder. They say a positive ID was made placing Muhammad at the scene of the Sept. 21 shooting there and will charge Malvo as an adult.
- A federal search warrant for the Caprice says that Muhammad also went by the names Wayne Weeks and Wayne Weekley. The warrant says that "numerous personal belongings" were found in the car when authorities arrested the men and that belongings indicated the car was being used as a residence.
- Investigators ask residents of south Camden, N.J., what they know about the two sniper suspects. Authorities are also looking for Nathaniel Osbourne, who co-owns the car in which the suspects were found.

FOOTNOTES

INTRODUCTION

1   "What to make of the Islamic compounds across America affiliated with the Pakistani radical group Jamaat al-Fuqra?" by Mira L. Boland, Wall Street Journal, March 18, 2002.
2   "Pillar of Lies," Sheikh Mubarik Ali Gilani (www.iqou-moa.org/sheikh_jilani/pillar_of_lies1.htm)
3   "What to make of the Islamic compounds across America affiliated with the Pakistani radical group Jamaat al-Fuqra?" by Mira L. Boland, Wall Street Journal, March 18, 2002.

CHAPTER 1

1   "Historic House: The story behind that building with the words 'Happiness Is Submission to God,' " by Emily Bowen, Tucson weekly, Feb. 25, 2010.
2   Wikipedia (http://en.wikipedia.org/wiki/Rashad_Khalifa).
3   Ibid.
4   "Identifying the Links between White-Collar Crime and Terrorism," by John Kane & April Wall, p. 29, U.S. Department of Justice report, Document No.: 209520, 2005.
5   "Al Fuqra: Holy Wars of Terrorism," p. 5, Anti-Defamation League report, 2005.
6   "Identifying the Links between White-Collar Crime and Terrorism," by John Kane & April Wall, p. 29, U.S. Department of Justice report, Document No.: 209520, 2005.
7   Ibid, p. v.
8   Ibid, p. 25.
9   "Sheikh Gilani's American Disciples," by Mira L. Boland, The Weekly Standard, March 11, 2002.
10   "Patterns of Global Terrorism," U.S. Department of State Report, 2005.
11   Justice Department document, marked "Dissemination Restricted to Law Enforcement," 2006.
12   "Identifying the Links between White-Collar Crime and Terrorism," by John Kane & April Wall, p. 22, U.S. Department of Justice report, Document No.: 209520, 2005.

13   Ibid, p. 26-29.
14   "Al Fuqra: Holy Wars of Terrorism," p. 6, Anti-Defamation League, 1993.
15   Interview with Susan Fenger conducted by Christian Action Network, 2006.

CHAPTER 2

1   From a poem by Sheikh Mubarik Gilani, published by the International
      Quranic Open University, seized by federal investigators in 1991, published
      March 18, 2002, "The Weekly Standard."
2   Names changed for their protection.
3   Bob Smietana, "Islamville Community Weathers Suspicions," the Tennessean,
      March 28, 2010.
4   Sheikh Mubarik Ali Gilani, "Pillar of Lies, An Excerpt from the Forthcoming
      Book: "Life, Mission and Miracle of Abu—The Father of The Muslims of The
      Americas," posted online at http://www.iqou-moa.org/sheikh_jilani/pillar_of_
      lies1.htm.
5   Ibid.
6   Zachary Crowley, "Jamaat al-Fuqra Dossier," Center for Policing Terrorism,
      March 16, 2005.
7   Mira L. Boland, "What to Make of the Islamic Compounds Across America
      Affiliated with the Pakistani Radical Group Jamaat al-Fuqra?" Wall Street Jour-
      nal, March 18, 2002.
8   Foundation for Defense of Democracies, http://islamizationwatch.blogspot.
      com/2009/11/darul-islam-movement-in-united-states.html.
9   Ibid.
10   Ibid.
11   Sheikh Mubarik Ali Gilani, "Pillar of Lies, An Excerpt from the Forthcoming
      Book: "Life, Mission and Miracle of Abu—The Father of The Muslims of The
      Americas," posted online at http://www.iqou-moa.org/sheikh_jilani/pillar_of_
      lies1.htm.
12   Zachary Crowley, "Jamaat al-Fuqra Dossier," Center for Policing Terrorism,
      March 16, 2005.
13   Ibid.
14   Douglas J. Hagmann, founder & director of the Northeast Intelligence Net-
      work, May 29, 2006.
15   Mira L. Boland, "What to Make of the Islamic Compounds Across America
      Affiliated with the Pakistani Radical Group Jamaat al-Fuqra?" Wall Street Jour-
      nal, March 18, 2002.
16   Zachary Crowley, "Jamaat al-Fuqra Dossier," Center for Policing Terrorism,
      March 16, 2005.
17   Ibid.
18   See Chapter 13, interview with undercover agent Ali Aziz.
19   Zachary Crowley, "Jamaat al-Fuqra Dossier," Center for Policing Terrorism,
      March 16, 2005.
20   Douglas J. Hagmann, founder & director of the Northeast Intelligence Net-
      work, May 29, 2006.

21   Sheikh Mubarik Ali Gilani, "An editorial by His Eminence, El-Sheikh Syed Mubarik Ali Shah Gilani," MOA web site (http://www.iqou-moa.org/news/articles/roots_of_terrorism.php).

22   Ibid.

23   Zachary Crowley, "Jamaat al-Fuqra Dossier," Center for Policing Terrorism, March 16, 2005.

24   Sheikh Mubarik Ali Gilani, "Pillar of Lies, A Excerpt from the Forthcoming Book: "Life, Mission and Miracle of Abu—The Father of The Muslims of The Americas," posted online at www.iqou-moa.org/sheikh_jilani/pillar_of_lies1.htm.

25   MOA web site (www.iqou-moa.org)

26   http://umarlee.com/2010/07/27/after-salafeeyah-dreams-of-sheikh-gilani-and-the-path-to-sufism/#comment-34482

27   Sheikh Giliani, "Qu'ranic Psychiatry," MOA web site (www.iqou-moa.org).

28   Uri Geller is a Jewish "paranormalist" and psychic popular in the 1970s, who most believe performs easily replicated magic tricks.

29   Sheikh Giliani, "Qu'ranic Psychiatry," MOA web site (www.iqou-moa.org).

30   Sheikh Mubarik Ali Gilani, "Pillar of Lies, A Excerpt from the Forthcoming Book: "Life, Mission and Miracle of Abu—The Father of The Muslims of The Americas," posted online at www.iqou-moa.org/sheikh_jilani/pillar_of_lies1.htm.

31   Ibid.

32   Mira L. Boland, "What to Make of the Islamic Compounds Across America Affiliated with the Pakistani Radical Group Jamaat al-Fuqra?" Wall Street Journal, March 18, 2002.

33   Ibid.

34   Ibid.

35   Zachary Crowley, "Jamaat al-Fuqra Dossier," Center for Policing Terrorism, March 16, 2005.

36   Ibid.

37   Ibid.

38   Muslims of the Americas web site: http://www.iqou-moa.org/newsflashes/newsflash/final-confirmation-of-hazrat-imam-mahdi.html/

39   "Patterns of Global Terrorism," U.S. Department of State Report, 2005.

CHAPTER 3

1   Farah Stockman, "Bomb Probe Eyes Pakistan Links Extremist May Have Influenced Reid," The Boston Globe, Jan. 6, 2002.

2   Robert Sam Anson, "The Journalist and The Terrorist," Vanity Fair, August 2002.

3   Ibid.

4   Ibid.

5   Farah Stockman, "Bomb Probe Eyes Pakistan Links Extremist May Have Influenced Reid," The Boston Globe, Jan. 6, 2002.

6   Michael Elliott, "The Shoe Bomber's World," Time Magazine, Feb. 16, 2002.

7   Farah Stockman, "Bomb Probe Eyes Pakistan Links Extremist May Have Influenced Reid," The Boston Globe, Jan. 6, 2002.

8   Michael Elliott, "The Shoe Bomber's World," Time Magazine, Feb. 16, 2002.

9   David Kohn, "CBS' Man In Pakistan Tracks Him Down," CBS News, March 13, 2002.

10   Mariane Pearl, "A Mighty Heart," Scribner, 2003, p.11.

11   Robert Sam Anson, "The Journalist and The Terrorist," Vanity Fair, August 2002.

12   Mubasher Bukhari, "Gilani was in the Jihadi Business for Money," Pakistani Newspaper Friday Times, date unknown.

13   From a Soldiers of Allah training video, seized by federal authorities.

14   Robert Sam Anson, "The Journalist and The Terrorist," Vanity Fair, August 2002.

15   Mariane Pearl, "A Mighty Heart," Scribner, 2003.

16   John Kane & April Wall, "Identifying the Links between White-Collar Crime and Terrorism," U.S. Department of Justice report, Document No.: 209520, 2005.

17   Wajid Ali Syed, "Sheikh Gilani has roots in the US?" Asian Tribune, June 16, 2009.

18   Anti-Defamation League, http://www.adl.org/terrorism/symbols/Jaish-e-Mohammed.asp

19   Mubasher Bukhari, "Gilani was in the Jihadi Business for Money," Pakistani Newspaper Friday Times, date unknown.

20   Anti-Defamation League, http://www.adl.org/terrorism/symbols/Jaish-e-Mohammed.asp.

21   Mariane Pearl, "A Mighty Heart," Scribner, 2003.

22   Ibid.

23   Saeed Shah, "Terror Group Builds Big Base Under Pakistani Officials' Noses," McClatchy Newspapers, September 13, 2009.

24   Sheikh Mubarik Ali Gilani, "Exposing Roots of Terrorism in USA," http://www.iqou-moa.org/editorial/terror_roots.htm)

25   Ibid.

26   Mariane Pearl, "A Mighty Heart," Scribner, 2003, p.94.

27   Daniel Pearl, "Pakistan Has Ties to Group it Vowed to Curb," Wall Street Journal, Dec. 24, 2001.

28   Robert Sam Anson, "The Journalist and The Terrorist," Vanity Fair, August 2002.

29   Michel Chossudovsky, "The Role of Pakistan's Military Intelligence (ISI) in the September 11 Attack," Professor of Economics, University of Ottawa, Nov. 2, 2001.

30   Mubasher Bukhari, "Gilani was in the Jihadi Business for Money," Pakistani Newspaper Friday Times, date unknown.

<u>CHAPTER 4</u>

1   Kashmir Information Network.

2   http://www.kashmiri-pandit.org/old/index-old2.html.

3   Ajit Doval, "Islamic Terrorism in South Asia and India's Strategic Response," 2007, Oxford University Press.

4   Wikipedia.

5   Steven Coll, "Ghost Wars: The Secret History of the CIA, Afghanistan, and Bin Laden, from the Soviet Invasion to September 10, 2001," 2004, Penguin Press, 2004.

6   Sheikh Mubarik Ali Gilani, "Soldiers of Allah" combat training video.

7   Sheikh Mubarik Ali Gilani, "Pillar of Lies, A Excerpt from the Forthcoming Book: "Life, Mission and Miracle of Abu—The Father of The Muslims of The Americas," posted online at http://www.iqou-moa.org/sheikh_jilani/pillar_of_lies1.htm.

8   Ibid.

9   Sheikh Mubarik Ali Gilani, "Soldiers of Allah" combat training video.

10   Ibid.

11   Ibid.

12   Quran V.2:216.

13   Sheikh Mubarik Ali Gilani, "Soldiers of Allah" combat training video.

14   Wikipedia.

15   "Law enforcement source: Jamaat al-Fuqra/Muslims of America involved in tax return fraud plot," The Jawa Report, Jan. 4, 2010, http://mypetjawa.mu.nu/archives/200254.php.

CHAPTER 5

1   John Kane & April Wall, U.S. Department of Justice report, Document No.: 209520, "Identifying the Links between White-Collar Crime and Terrorism," p. 30, 2005.

2   John Kane & April Wall, U.S. Department of Justice report, Document No.: 209520, "Identifying the Links between White-Collar Crime and Terrorism," p. 26, 2005.

3   Interview With Susan Fenger by Christian Action Network, 2006-2007.

4   John Kane & April Wall, U.S. Department of Justice report, Document No.: 209520, "Identifying the Links between White-Collar Crime and Terrorism," p. 29, 2005.

5   Interview With Susan Fenger by Christian Action Network, 2006-2007.

6   Ibid.

7   John Kane & April Wall, U.S. Department of Justice report, Document No.: 209520, "Identifying the Links between White-Collar Crime and Terrorism," p. 60, 2005.

8   Interview With Susan Fenger by Christian Action Network, 2006-2007.

9   Ibid.

10   Ibid.

11   Ibid.

12   Ibid.

13   Ibid.

14   Colorado Attorney General's Office (http://www.ago.state.co.us/Reports/fuqra.stm).

15   Interview With Susan Fenger by Christian Action Network, 2006-2007.

16   Northeast Intelligence Network (http://homelandsecurityus.com/archives/1613), February 2007.

17   Interview With Susan Fenger by Christian Action Network, 2006-2007.

18   John Kane & April Wall, U.S. Department of Justice report, Document No.: 209520, "Identifying the Links between White-Collar Crime and Terrorism," p. 53, 2005.

19   Interview With Susan Fenger by Christian Action Network, 2006-2007.

20   John Kane & April Wall, U.S. Department of Justice report, Document No.: 209520, "Identifying the Links between White-Collar Crime and Terrorism," p. 53, 2005.

CHAPTER 6

1   Alex Tizon, "Sniper Suspect John Allen Muhammad's Meltdown," The Seattle Times, Nov. 10, 2002.

2   Christian M. Weber, "Soldiers for the Truth," as reported by WorldNetDaily. com, November 11, 2002.

3   "Sniper's Siblings Describe Violent Upbringing," CNN online (http://articles. cnn.com/2004-02-10/justice/sprj.dcsp.sniper.beaten_1_dean-harold-meyers-sniper-spree-lee-boyd-malvo?_s=PM:LAW).

4   Ibid.

5   Alex Tizon, "Sniper Suspect John Allen Muhammad's Meltdown," The Seattle Times, Nov. 10, 2002.

6   Michelle Malkin, The Jihadi Snipers Revisited," May 25, 2006 (http://michellemalkin.com/2006/05/25/the-jihadi-snipers-revisited/).

7   Alex Tizon, "Sniper Suspect John Allen Muhammad's Meltdown," The Seattle Times, Nov. 10, 2002.

8   "Snipers Were Terrorists and Illegal Aliens" (http://www.warriorsfortruth. com/beltway-sniper-news.html).

9   Alex Tizon, "Sniper Suspect John Allen Muhammad's Meltdown," The Seattle Times, Nov. 10, 2002.

10   Ibid.

11   Ibid.

12   Ibid

13   "Snipers: Their Secret Gay Life," November 2002 (http://www.freerepublic. com/focus/news/780767/posts).

14   "Sniper Killings, Hideout, Clustered Near Old Al-Fuqra Terror Target," November 4, 2002 (http://www.freerepublic.com/focus/news/782390/posts).

15   Alex Tizon, "Sniper Suspect John Allen Muhammad's Meltdown," The Seattle Times, Nov. 10, 2002.

16   Dr. Paul Williams, "Deadly Muslim Deobandi Movement Now Omnipresent Throughout America," May 12, 2010 (www.thelastcrusade.com).

17   www.wikipedia.com.

18   "Snipers Were Terrorists and Illegal Aliens" (http://www.warriorsfortruth.
      com/beltway-sniper-news.html).

19   Alex Tizon, "Sniper Suspect John Allen Muhammad's Meltdown," The Seattle
      Times, Nov. 10, 2002.

20   Christian M. Weber, "Soldiers for the Truth," as reported by WorldNetDaily.
      com, November 11, 2002.

21   Tom Jackman, "For TV, Malvo Boosts Sniper Rampage's Victim Count," The
      Washington Post, July 30, 2010.

22   Dr. Paul Williams, "Deadly Muslim Deobandi Movement Now Omnipresent
      Throughout America," May 12, 2010 (www.thelastcrusade.com).

23   Mira L. Boland, "Sheikh Gilani's American Disciples," The Weekly Standard,
      March 11, 2002.

CHAPTER 7

1   www.thereligionofpeace.com.

2   Mary Tabor, "A Trial in Canada Is Watched in U.S.," Oct. 16, 1993.

3   "Three Fuqra Bombers Deported From Canada," The politics of CP (http://
      politicsofcp.blogspot.com/2006/04/three-fuqra-bombers-deported-from.
      html), April 07, 2006.

4   Lee Berthiaume, The untold story of Hasanville's shadowy past," The Ottawa
      Citizen, May 4, 2002.

5   Air & Space Power Journal, July 1, 2008.

6   "The Frankenstein the CIA created," The Guardian (http://www.guardian.
      co.uk/world/1999/jan/17/yemen.islam/print), Jan. 17, 1999.

7   Ibid.

8   Ibid.

9   Ibid.

10   J.M. Berger, "Al Qaeda Recruited U.S. Servicemen: Testimony Links Plot To
      Saudi Government," www.intelwire.com, July 1, 2004.

11   Ibid.

12   "Dr. Rashid: aka Clement Rodney Hampton-El" (www.rotten.com%252Fli
      brary%252Fbio%252Fcrime%252Fterrorists%252Fdr-rashid%252F/doctor-
      id/840289.html).

13   "The Frankenstein the CIA created," The Guardian (http://www.guardian.
      co.uk/world/1999/jan/17/yemen.islam/print), Jan. 17, 1999.

14   Ibid.

15   "Dr. Rashid: aka Clement Rodney Hampton-El" (www.rotten.com%252Fli
      brary%252Fbio%252Fcrime%252Fterrorists%252Fdr-rashid%252F/doctor-
      id/840289.html).

16   Ibid.

17   "1993 World Trade Center bombing, Wikipedia (http://en.wikipedia.org/
      wiki/1993_World_Trade_Center_bombing).

18   Tom Morganthau, "The New Terrorism," Newsweek, July 5, 1993.

CHAPTER 8

1   John Kane & April Wall, "Identifying the Links between White-Collar Crime and Terrorism," U.S. Department of Justice report, April 2005.

2   "MOA Members Busted in Counterfeit Goods Scam," Gates of Vienna, March 13, 2007 (http://gatesofvienna.blogspot.com/2007/03/moa-members-busted-in-counterfeit-goods.html).

CHAPTER 9

1   John Kane & April Wall, "Identifying the Links between White-Collar Crime and Terrorism," U.S. Department of Justice report, April 2005.

2   Art Moore, "Should Muslim Quran be USA's top authority?" *WordNetDaily*, May 1, 2003 (http://www.wnd.com/?pageId=18561#ixzz1HQtXDJc7).

3   An example of this type of lawsuit is the one brought against the state of Oklahoma after its citizens had enacted a ban against Sharia Law being considered in court cases. In November 2010, CAIR won an injunction against the state, allowing the Oklahoma courts to consider Sharia in its decisions.

4   "MPAC Pursues Islamist Ideology in Guise of Civil Rights Defender," February 9, 2010 (http://www.investigativeproject.org/1785/mpac-pursues-islamist-ideology-in-guise-of-civil).

5   John Guandolo, "The Muslim Brotherhood in America," www.bigpeace.com.

6   Ibid.

7   Ibid.

8   Ibid.

9   Ibid.

10   Bridgette Gabriel, "U.S. Treasury Department to Host Shariah Compliant Financing Forum." Nov.3, 2008.

11   "An Explanatory Memorandum: On the General Strategic Goal for the Group in North America," May 22, 1991, posted online (http://www.investigativeproject.org/documents/case_docs/445.pdf).

12   www.Wikipedia.com

13   Ibid.

14   Walid Phares, director of the Future Terrorism Project at the Foundation for Defense of Democracies, as quoted in "Napolitano and Muslim Brotherhood Affiliates Met Secretly," Feb. 4, 2010, (www.familysecuritymatters.org).

CHAPTER 10

1   Dervishes are Sufi-style mystics known for their extreme aestheticism and poverty. The whirling Dervish is a Muslim of the Mevlevi Order in Turkey; the whirling is part of a formal ceremony known as the Sema, performed to try to reach religious ecstasy. The practice today has become a tourist attraction in Turkey.

2   Winston Churchill, "The River War: An Historical Account of the Reconquest of the Soudan," originally published in 1899 by Longmans, Green & Co.

3   Ibid.

4   Ibid.

5   www.wikipedia.com

6   Ibid.

7   It was rumored that the Mahid (Muhammad Ahmad) was already dead at this point of typhus.

8   www.wikipedia.com.

9   Ibid.

10   Ibid.

11   "Imamat vs. Prophethood," undated, http://www.al-islam.org/encyclopedia/chapter6b/8.html

12   "Oceans of Light," part of the Islamic Hadith.

13   In-person interview with Christian Action Network, fall 2010.

14   Christian Action Network founder and President, Martin Mawyer – the author of this book – has been targeted numerous times by Sheikh Gilani and other MOA members in the press and online blogs.

15   "Imam El Sheikh Syed Mubarik Ali Gilani Qadri's Rebuttal to the False Accusations by Zionist Action Group aka Christian Action Network," Islamic Post, Nov. 23, 2009

16   An honorific Islamic title, showing deference to a person.

17   Gilani's comments were also posted online at http://www.yanabi.com/forum/Topic347511-35-2.aspx.

18   The meeting between Gilani and the Mahdi is assumed to have occurred sometime in 2009.

19   Islamic Post.

20   http://welc0m2myworld.blogspot.com/2010/01/hazrat-sultan-bahu-allah-bless-his-soul.html

21   This building, also known as the House of Allah, is located in Mecca in Saudi Arabia. The statement that the Mahdi will appear there contradicts Gilani's earlier statement that the Mahdi will appear at the Dome of the Rock in Jerusalem.

22   In-person interview with Christian Action Network, fall 2010.

23   New Year's Message by Sheikh Mubarik Ali Gilani, posted online January 2011 at http://www.holyislamvillesc.org/sheikh/publications/new-years-message.html

24   Ibid.

CHAPTER 11

1   Jonathan Curiel, "7 Arrested In Raids After Editor's Slaying," San Francisco Chronicle, Aug. 9, 2011.

2   Thomas Peele, "Reporter Gets New Death Threat," The Chauncey Bailey Project, April 9, 2011.

3   Chris Thompson, "The Sinister Side of Yusuf Bey's Empire," East Bay Express, Nov. 12, 2002.

4   Chris Thompson, "How Official Oakland Kept the Bey Empire Going," East Bay Express, Nov. 20, 2002.

5   Ibid.

6   Ibid.

7   Ibid.

8   Chris Thompson, "The Sinister Side of Yusuf Bey's Empire," East Bay Express, Nov. 12, 2002.

9   Ibid.

10   Chris Thompson, "How Official Oakland Kept the Bey Empire Going," East Bay Express, Nov. 20, 2002.

11   Matthai Kuruvila, "Bey Used 100 'Wives' To Bilk Welfare," San Francisco Chronicle, Nov. 18, 2007.

12   Dan Noyes, "Unsolved 1986 Murder Linked to Bakery," KGO-TV, April 8, 2008.

13   Chris Thompson, "How Official Oakland Kept the Bey Empire Going," East Bay Express, Nov. 20, 2002.

14   Ibid.

15   Chris Thompson, "The Sinister Side of Yusuf Bey's Empire," East Bay Express, Nov. 12, 2002.

16   Chris Thompson, "How Official Oakland Kept the Bey Empire Going," East Bay Express, Nov. 20, 2002.

17   Bob Butler, Word Press, "Chauncey Bailey Murder Trial Jury Asks To Hear More Testimony," May 26, 2011.

18   CBS/AP. "Confessed Killer Resumes Testimony In Oakland Journalist Murder Case," March 28, 2011.

19   Angela Hill and Harry Harris, "Bailey's Confessed Killer: 'I'm a Good Soldier,'" Inside Bay Area, Sept. 18, 2007.

20 "   Jurors Hear Police Recording Saying Bey IV Bragged About Journalist's Death," The Chauncey Bailey Project, April 27, 2011.

21 "   Yusuf Bey IV: 'Not a Normal Person,' Prosecutor Says," The Chauncey Bailey Project, May 18, 2011.

22   Yusuf Bey, "True Solutions," October 2002.

23 "   Yusuf Bey IV Discusses Religious Beliefs in Jail Calls," The Chauncey Bailey Project, April 29, 2009.

24 "   Yusuf Bey IV: 'Not a Normal Person,' Prosecutor Says," The Chauncey Bailey Project, May 18, 2011.

25 "   Witness: Bey IV Had Bailey Killed, Whites Are Devils, Bakery a Beautiful Place," The Chauncey Bailey Project, April 13, 2011.

26   Chris Thompson, "How Official Oakland Kept the Bey Empire Going," East Bay Express, Nov. 20, 2002.

27   Dan Noyes, "Unsolved 1986 Murder Linked to Bakery," KGO-TV, April 8, 2008.

CHAPTER 12

1   " 'Jackal' book praises Bin Laden," BBC News, June 26, 2003.

2   "Carlos the Jackal faces new trial," BBC News, May 4, 2007.

3   "Carlos the Jackal Calls Bin Laden a Martyr," Associated Press, May 19, 2011.

4   Lee Berthiaume, "The Untold Story of Hasanville's Shadowy Past," Ottawa Citizen, May 4, 2002.

5   Ibid.

6   "Bomb Probe Eyes Pakistan Links Extremist May Have Influenced Reid," The Boston Globe, Jan. 6, 2002.

7   Dan Dickerson, "Journal of Counterterrorism and Homeland Security International," fall 2010 issue.

CHAPTER 13

1   See Chapter 5, "The Gang That Couldn't Shoot Straight," for a detailed description of this case.

2   In an August 2011, the NYPD's role as one of the nation's most active anti-terrorism intelligence agencies is confirmed. The article states that the NYPD is able to conduct surveillance in ways which the FBI and CIA are unable to because of legal constraints. The NYPD operates not just in New York City, but throughout the nation and in foreign countries, as well. This confirms Ali's statements that the NYPD helped him travel to the other countries to continue his undercover work. (Matt Apuzzo and Adam Goldman, The Arab American News, "With CIA help, NYPD moves covertly in Muslim areas," August 2011.)

3   Scribd. (http://www.scribd.com/doc/25324369/Surah-Maidah-Translation-Sheikh-Syed-Mubarik-Ali-Shah-Gilani).

4   "Final Confirmation of Hazrat Imam Mahdi," Islamic Post, Oct. 15, 2009.

5   Scribd. (http://webcache.googleusercontent.com/search?q=cache:O9DxG9QgkG0J:www.scribd.com/doc/36541670/Shaykh-%E2%80%98Abdul-Qadir-Jilani+Gilani+slaughter+a+chicken&cd=4&hl=en&ct=clnk&gl=us&source=www.google.com).

6   See Chapter 9, "The Coming of the Mahdi," for a detailed description of the topic.

CHAPTER 14

1   K. Alan Kronstadt, "Pakistan-U.S. Relations," Congressional Research Service, Feb. 6, 2009.

2   See Chapter 4, "Solders of Allah," for more information on this video.

3   WikiLeaks, as reported by Dipanjan Roy Chaudhury, "U.S. ignored Bhutto's plea for evaluation of security," India Today, May 23, 2011 (http://news.oneindia.in/2011/05/22/usignored-bhuttos-plea-for-evaluation-of-securitywikileaid0126.html) .

4   Ibid.

5   "Pakistani spies spent millions lobbying U.S.," www.foxnews.com, July 19, 2011.

6   Hawala is a form of Islamic money lending with exorbitant interest, and also includes illegal money laundering.

7   Peter Chamberlin, "Daniel Pearl and the Mumbai Attackers" (http://therearenosunglasses.wordpress.com/links-to-peter%E2%80%99s-articles/daniel-pearl-and-the-mumbai-attackers/).

8   2006-2007, Interview With Susan Fenger by CAN/PRB.

9   Dan Dickerson, "Iran Would Strike First," Journal of Counterterrorism and Homeland Security International, published by the International Association for Counterterrorism and Security Professionals, fall 2010 issue.

10   2006-2007, Interview With Susan Fenger by CAN/PRB.

11   Ibid.

12   Ibid.

13   "Final Report of an Investigation of Mismanagement and Misconduct by the Bureau of Water Supply Police," New York Department of Investigation report, issued March 1992 (http://www.scribd.com/doc/65734/NYC-Department-of-Investigation-Report)

14   Ibid.

15   Interview with WLTX-TV, posted online at http://www.youtube.com/watch?v=_bMgkJya5DQ&feature=player_embedded#at=48.

<u>CHAPTER 15</u>

1   William Overend, "Muslim Hamlet Blames Sept. 11 for New Scrutiny," Los Angeles Times, Feb. 21, 2002.

2   "Fresno, Calif., Charter School at Center of Three Inquires," Fresno Bee, Jan. 2, 2002.

3   "Charter School Founder Sentenced," ABC 7 KGO-TV, Aug. 25, 2006.

4   Diana Marcum, "Muslims in the hills," Fresno Bee, Jan. 6, 2002.

5   William Overend, "Muslim Hamlet Blames Sept. 11 for New Scrutiny," Los Angeles Times, Feb. 21, 2002.

6   Sean Webby and Brandon Baily, "Cleric's followers have hopscotched around California," San Jose Mercury News, Feb. 3, 2002.

7   Ibid.

8   Cindy C. Combs and Martin Slann, "Encyclopedia of Terrorism," Checkmark Books, 2003.

9   Dave Mitchell, "Light to celebrate 25th anniversary of its Pulitzer," The Point Reyes Light, April 15, 2004.

10   William Overend, "Muslim Hamlet Blames Sept. 11 for New Scrutiny," Los Angeles Times, Feb. 21, 2002.

11   Diana Marcum, Marc Benjamin and Louis Galvan, "Ambush killed Fresno deputy," Fresno Bee, Aug. 23, 2001.

12   Chris Collins, "Seven Years To Trial," Fresno Bee, March 26, 2008.

13   "Fax Says Tyson Will Not Attend Fund-Raiser in Fresno" Fresno Bee, May 11, 1995.

14   Diana Marcum, "Muslims in the hills," Fresno Bee, Jan. 6, 2002.

15   Brandon Bailey and Sean Webby, "State officials raid Gateway charter school," San Jose Mercury News, Jan. 25, 2002.

16   Sean Webby and Brandon Bailey, "The mysterious saga of Sister Khadijah," San Jose Mercury News, Feb. 11, 2007.

Index

Symbols

A

B

C

D

N

Naimah 194

Nation of Islam 84, 85, 86, 87, 90, 94, 167, 177

Niagara Falls 10, 264

North American Islamic Trust 139

NYPD 182, 184, 185, 186, 187, 188, 189, 191, 192, 193, 194, 195, 196, 197, 198, 199, 203, 204, 205, 206, 207, 212, 213, 214, 215, 216, 217, 218, 285

O

Oakland, California 165, 180

Oakland Post 166

Organization of the Islamic Conference 138

Ottawa 103, 278, 281, 285

P

Pakistan 7, 8, 9, 11, 12, 6, 10, 14, 15, 17, 19, 21, 22, 25, 26, 27, 33, 35, 36, 37, 38, 41, 43, 44, 45, 46, 47, 49, 50, 51, 54, 55, 56, 57, 61, 62, 66, 72, 76, 78, 103, 104, 156, 161, 164, 194, 202, 203, 206, 210, 211, 214, 215, 217, 220, 222, 223, 225, 226, 227, 228, 229, 232, 235, 248, 264, 277, 278, 285

Paster, Stephen Paul 5, 248

Pearl, Daniel 33, 33–51, 226, 229, 232, 264

Pearl, Mariane 39

Pierre, Vicente Rafael 73, 77

Pillar of Lies 10, 13, 15, 16, 18, 23, 26, 27, 57, 275, 276, 277, 279

Professional Security International (PSI) 8, 9, 76, 266

Prophet Mohammed 2, 15, 18, 22, 83, 106, 115, 129, 142, 151, 152, 153, 157, 158, 159, 209

Q

Qadri 156, 157, 208, 209, 283

Quran 1, 2, 3, 22, 24, 25, 40, 61, 95, 139, 151, 159, 167, 178, 190, 197, 208, 242, 279, 282

Quranic Open University 15, 17, 23, 24, 57, 242, 245, 247, 250, 251, 276

R

S

T

About the Authors

Martin Mawyer is the Founder and President of Christian Action Network, a non-profit public advocacy and education group based in Lynchburg, Virginia. Mawyer began his career as a freelance journalist, and has authored several books, including *Silent Shame, The Pro-Family Contract With America* and *Pathways to Success*. He has produced a number of documentary films, including *Homegrown Jihad, Islam Rising, Sacrificed Survivors* and *America's Islamic Threat*. He has appeared on *The O'Reilly Factor, Hannity, Larry King Live, Pat Robertson's 700 Club, NBC's Today Show* and *Entertainment Tonight*.

Patti A. Pierucci is an award-winning writer who spent nearly two decades as a journalist. She is also a documentary scriptwriter, and has worked as a ghostwriter for a number of prominent public figures, including members of Congress.

Made in the USA
San Bernardino, CA
25 February 2013